CHARMING
SMALL HOTEL
GUIDES

FRANCE

& CORSICA

CHARMING SMALL HOTEL GUIDES

FRANCE

& CORSICA

Edited by Chris Gill

GUILD PUBLISHING

LONDON · NEW YORK · SYDNEY · TORONTO

This edition published 1990 by Guild Publishing
by arrangement with Duncan Petersen Publishing Ltd,
5 Botts Mews, London W2 5AG

Conceived, designed and produced by Duncan Petersen
Edited by Fox & Partners, The Old Forge,
Norton St Philip, Bath BA3 6LW

A CIP catalogue record for this book is available from the British Library

CN 4371

Typeset by Lineage Ltd, Watford, Herts
Originated by Regent Publishing Services, Hong Kong
Printed by G. Canale & C. SpA, Turin

Contents

Introduction

Here is a new accommodation guide series with a singular focus on places which are both charming and small: in France, for example, the recommendations have usually fewer than 20 rooms, rarely more than 30 (except in Paris, where we aimed to find hotels with fewer than 40 rooms).

The *Charming Small Hotel Guides* look different from others on the market; their descriptive style is different; and they are compiled differently. They are, in fact, designed to satisfy what we believe to be the real needs of today's traveller; needs which have been served at best haphazardly by existing guides.

Our entries employ, above all, words: they contain not one symbol. They are written by people with something to say, not a bureaucracy which has long since lost the ability to distinguish the praiseworthy from the mediocre. The editorial team is small and highly experienced at assessing and writing about hotels; at noticing all-important details. Every entry, however brief, aims to give a coherent and definite feel of what it is actually like to stay in that place.

Although we have made use of reports from members of the public, and would welcome more of them (see box), we have placed great emphasis on consistency.

These are features which will only reveal their worth as you use your *Charming Small Hotel Guide*. Its other advantages are more obvious: the use of colour photographs to depict 100 or so of the entries, which, from the outside at least, are particularly appealing or interesting; the ease of reference, with clear geographical designations for all entries.

Small French hotels

Small hotels have always had the appeal that they can offer the traveller a personal welcome and personal attention, whereas larger places are necessarily more institutional. But small hotels in France have a special place in the hearts of travellers. Almost without exception, they are family-run, and have often been in the same family for generations. Many serve exceptionally good food. And despite general inflation in France, their rooms remain generally affordable.

The establishments described in this guide are simply the 300 or so small hotels, *auberges* and bed-and-breakfast places that we believe most discriminating travellers would prefer to stay in, given the choice. Even so, some undeniably pricey places are included. But there are plenty of places in this guide costing less than 400F a night for two.

Our ideal hotel has a peaceful, pretty setting; the building itself is either handsome, appealing, historic, or has a distinct character. The rooms are spacious, but on a human scale not grand or intimidating. The decorations and furnishings are harmonious, comfortable and impeccably maintained, and include antique pieces meant to be used, not revered. The proprietors and staff are dedicated, thoughtful and sensitive in their pursuit of their guests' happiness – friendly and welcoming without being intrusive. Last but not least, the food, whether simple or ambitious, is fresh, interesting and carefully prepared. Elaborate facilities such as saunas or trouser-presses count for little in these guides, though we do generally list them.

Of course, not every hotel scores top marks on each of these counts. But it is surprising how many do respectably well on most fronts.

How to find an entry
In this guide, the entries are arranged in a sequence starting in the north and working southwards, in sweeps from west to east. Corsica comes last in the sequence.

To find a hotel, simply browse through headings at the top of the pages until you find the area you want to visit. Or, to locate a specific place, use the indexes which list the entries alphabetically by name and by location.

On pages 10 to 17 there are, in addition, maps showing the locations of all the entries.

Reporting to the guides
When we come to prepare revised editions, we hope to be able to reflect the experiences of people who have stayed in the hotels recommended here, or who have found other places which seem to deserve an entry. On page 9 is further information on reporting to the guides.

How to read an entry
At the top of each entry is a coloured bar highlighting the name of the town or village where the establishment is located, along with a categorization which gives some clue to its character. These categories are as far as possible self-explanatory.

The factbox given for each hotel follows a standard pattern which requires little explanation; but:

Under **Tel** we give the telephone number starting with (1) if the hotel is in the Paris area; if dialling such a number within Paris, you should omit the (1). When dialling from Paris to the provinces, or vice-versa, you must preface the complete number with 16. When dialling a provincial number in the provinces, the eight digits we give are all you need to dial.

Introduction

Under **Location** we give information on the setting of the hotel and on its parking arrangements.

Under **Meals** we list what is available.

The basic **Prices** are given, as is normal in France, per room and not per person. They include tax and service and as far as possible are valid for 1989. Breakfast is extra: allow 20F to 50F, according to the style of the place.

Normally, a range is given, representing the smallest and largest amounts you might pay in different circumstances – typically, the minimum is the cost of the cheapest room in low season, (which may be a single) while the maximum is the price of the costliest room in high season (though seasonal variations are not widely applied in France). Thus, with an appropriate allowance for inflation, you can usefully estimate the cost of rooms in years following publication.

If a price for dinner, bed and breakfast (DB&B) or full board (FB) is given, this is because the hotel does not in practice offer room-only terms. These prices are given *per person*. After the room price, we give an indication of the cost of individual meals.

Our lists of facilities in bedrooms cover only mechanical gadgets and not ornaments such as flowers or consumables such as toiletries or free drinks.

Under **Facilities** we list public rooms and then outdoor and sporting facilities which are either part of the hotel or immediately on hand; facilities in the vicinity are not listed, though they sometimes feature at the end of the main description in the **Nearby** section, which is necessarily selective.

We use the following abbreviations for **Credit cards:**
AE American Express
DC Diners Club
MC MasterCard (Access/Eurocard)
V Visa (Barclaycard/Bank Americard/Carte Bleue etc)

The final entry in a factbox is normally the name of the proprietor(s); but where the hotel is run by a manager we give his or her name instead.

Reporting to the guides

Please write and tell us about your experiences of small hotels and *auberges* whether good or bad, whether listed in this edition or not. As well as hotels in France, we are interested in hotels in Britain, Spain, Portugal, Austria, Switzerland, Germany and other European countries, and those in the eastern United States.

The address to write to is:
Chris Gill,
Editor,
Charming Small Hotel Guides,
The Old Forge,
Norton St Philip,
Bath, BA3 6LW,
England.

Checklist
Please use a separate sheet of paper for each report; include your name, address and telephone number on each report.

Your reports will be received with particular pleasure if they are typed; and if they are organized under the following headings:
Name of establishment
Town or village it is in, or nearest
Full address, including post code
Telephone number
Time and duration of visit
The building and setting
The public rooms
The bedrooms and bathrooms
Physical comfort
   (chairs, beds, heat, light, hot water)
Standards of maintenance and housekeeping
Atmosphere, welcome and service
Food
Value for money

We assume that in writing you have no objections to your views being published unpaid, either verbatim, or in an edited version. Names of outside contributors are acknowledged, at the editor's discretion, on the final page of each guide.

If you would be interested in looking at hotels on a professional basis on behalf of the guides, please include on a separate sheet a summary of your travel experience and hotel-going.

Master location map

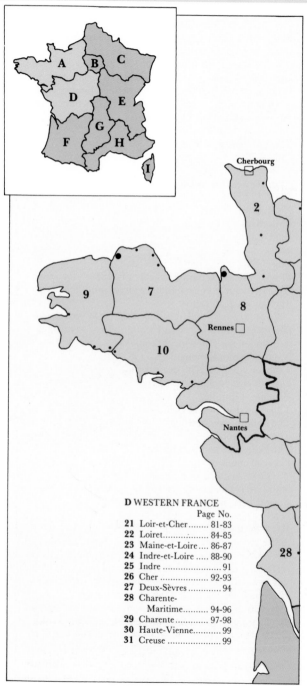

Cherbourg

2

9 7

8

Rennes

10

Nantes

28

(Continued on following two pages)

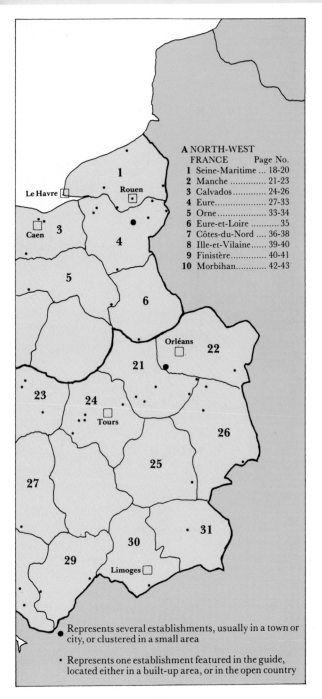

A NORTH-WEST FRANCE Page No.

● Represents several establishments, usually in a town or city, or clustered in a small area

• Represents one establishment featured in the guide, located either in a built-up area, or in the open country

Master location map

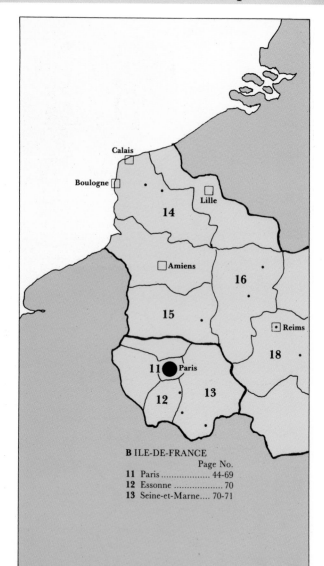

Calais

Boulogne

Lille

14

Amiens

16

15

Reims

11 Paris

18

12

13

● Represents several establishments, usually in a town or
city, or clustered in a small area

. Represents one establishment featured in the guide,
located either in a built-up area, or in the open country

(Continued on following two pages)

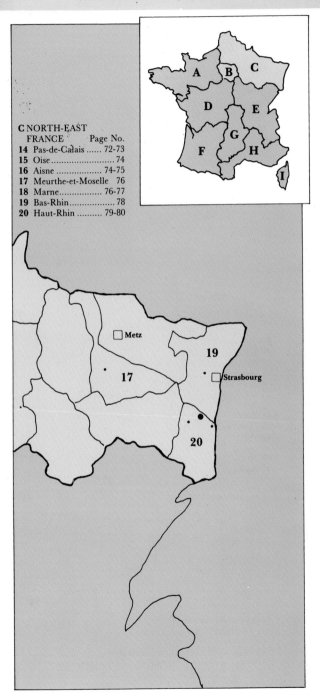

☐ Metz

19

· **17**   ☐ Strasbourg

20

Master location map

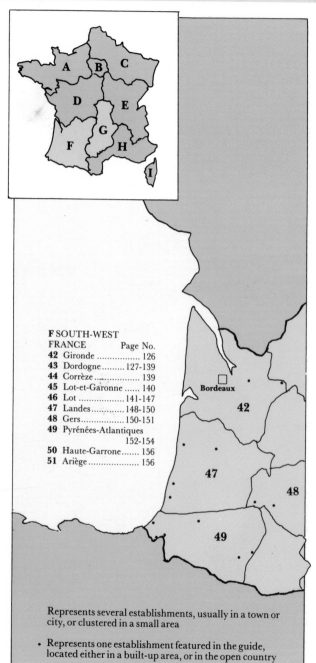

□ Represents several establishments, usually in a town or city, or clustered in a small area

• Represents one establishment featured in the guide, located either in a built-up area, or in the open country

(Continued on following two pages)

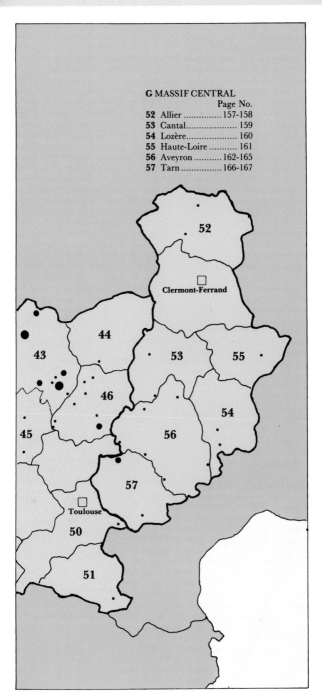

Master location map

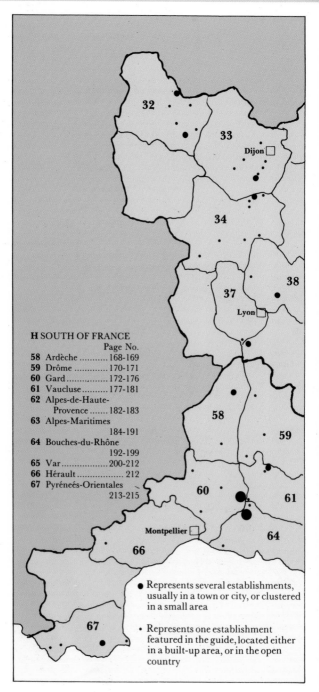

● Represents several establishments, usually in a town or city, or clustered in a small area

• Represents one establishment featured in the guide, located either in a built-up area, or in the open country

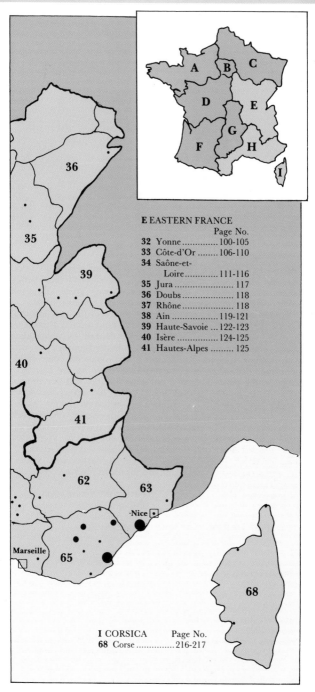

Seine-Maritime

Château hotel, Bézancourt

Château du Landel

Discovery of this family-run château made our inspector's week. M. and Mme Cardon have gradually transformed their family home into a friendly, relaxed hotel offering grace and good living – without any trace of ostentation – and remarkable value.

Tucked away in a remote, grassy corner of the vast forest of Lyons, the wide, shuttered 18thC house (built around a medieval core) is reached by a sweeping drive flanked by immaculate lawns. The main public rooms are beautifully furnished – mostly with family heirlooms – and many of the rooms have fine 18thC panelling. Bedrooms vary considerably: those on the first floor verge on the palatial, decked out with antiques and fine drapes, while those on the second floor, under the eaves, are much simpler, decorated in a carefully co-ordinated Laura Ashley style. But all enjoy pleasant views over the estate, and absolute peace and quiet. The restaurant now seems to come second to the hotel – there are no set menus, and the *carte* is fairly short. But, apart from mediocre coffee, our inspector's meal was satisfactory.

Nearby beech forest; Gisors (25 km) – castle; Les Andelys (30 km) – ruins of Château Gaillard; Beauvais (40 km).

Bézancourt 76220 Gournay-en-Bray
Tel 35.90.16.01
Location on edge of Fôret de Lyons, 12 km SW of Gournay; in large estate with ample private car parking
Meals breakfast, lunch, dinner
Prices rooms 260F-380F, DB&B 380F (for one); extra bed 90F (for child); meals about 200F
Rooms 17 double, 15 with bath, 2 with shower; one single; all rooms have central heating, phone

Facilities 2 dining-rooms, sitting-room, conference room; tennis
Credit cards MC, V
Children welcome; cot available
Disabled single room on ground floor
Pets dogs accepted by arrangement, at extra charge
Closed mid-Nov to mid-Mar; restaurant only Sun dinner and Mon
Proprietors M. and Mme Cardon

Seine-Maritime

Le Normandie

Caudebec was almost entirely rebuilt after the war, in a safe but uninspiring style – but it enjoys a fine setting on the Seine. The same is true of the Normandie, standing on the river promenade, looking across the road to a small garden. Its decoration and furnishing lack style, but the atmosphere is friendly, and everything is clean and well cared for. The bedrooms are simple, but reasonably spacious and comfortable, many with river views. Food, professionally served in a bright, airy restaurant, is carefully prepared and sound value.

Nearby Church of Notre Dame; Jumièges (15 km) – abbey ruins.

19 Quai Guilbaud 76490 Caudebec-en-Caux
Tel 35.96.25.11
Location in middle of town beside river, 36 km NW of Rouen; with garden and private car parking
Meals breakfast, lunch, dinner
Prices rooms 140F-275F; meals 55F-155F
Rooms 15 double, 3 with bath, 12 with shower (one twin), one single with shower; all rooms have central heating, TV, phone
Facilities dining-room, sitting-room
Credit cards MC, V
Children accepted **Disabled** no special facilities **Pets** accepted
Closed Feb
Proprietors families Gremoud and Philippe

Auberge du Clos Normand

This simple old *auberge* epitomises the rustic appeal of Normandy. It is set in countryside, close to a forest, and built of patterned brick and timber with a shady, flowery garden and stream behind. Inside, ceilings are criss-crossed with ancient beams adorned with plates and ornaments; brass pots gleam on the walls and farm noises drift through the windows; and, last but not least, M. Hauchecorne's cooking is classically Norman, involving much cholesterol and alcohol. The bedrooms (in a converted outbuilding) have recently been renovated.

Nearby Dieppe – château/museum; beaches along coast.

22 Rue Henri IV, Martin-Eglise 76370 Neuville-les-Dieppe
Tel 35.82.71.01
Location in countryside on D1, 5 km SE of Dieppe; with garden, ample car parking
Meals breakfast, lunch, dinner
Prices rooms 200F-310F; meals à la carte
Rooms 8 double, 3 with bath, 5 with shower (2 twin); one family room with bath; all rooms have central heating, phone
Facilities dining-room, sitting-room
Credit cards AE, MC, V
Children welcome
Disabled no special facilities
Pets welcome if well behaved
Closed mid-Dec to mid-Jan; Mon evening, Tue
Proprietor M. Regis Hauchecorne

Seine-Maritime

Hôtel de la Cathédrale

This ancient hotel is a matter of yards from the cathedral, tucked away down a narrow pedestrian street. Behind its half-timbered façade, the building rambles around a pretty informal court-yard, with staircases and corridors wandering off in all directions. Some parts of the building are, in fact, much less ancient than the exterior suggests, and you might find yourself staying in a room built in the 1930s rather than the 1390s. Some of the chintzy, traditional-style bedrooms are somewhat faded, too, though they are clean and comfortable enough. There is no restaurant, but a wide choice of places to eat within walking distance.

Nearby Cathedral, churches of St-Maclou and St-Ouen, Palais de Justice, Place du Vieux Marchè.

12 Rue St-Romain 76000 Rouen	have central heating, phone
Tel 35.71.57.95	**Facilities** breakfast room, sitting-area
Location in middle of old city, next to cathedral; public car parking nearby	**Credit cards** not accepted
	Children accepted
	Disabled access difficult
Meals breakfast	**Pets** accepted
Prices rooms 130F-250F	**Closed** never
Rooms 23 double and one family room, all with bath or shower (3 twin); all rooms	**Proprietor** M. Olivier-Perrot

Le St-Pierre

Patrice Kukurudz and Bernard Huet have created a thriving business at this smart, pink-washed restaurant-with-rooms by the Seine. Showy modern decoration dominates, especially in the airy pink-and-purple riverside restaurant. The cooking is pro-fessional and inventive, with some interesting *bonnes bouches* offered at various stages of the meal. The cheapest menu is not available at weekends or late in the evening; the alternatives are all fairly pricey, although the quality is undeniable. There are seven bedrooms, most looking over the river; and for summer drinks and meals, a pleasant waterside terrace.

Nearby Rouen – cathedral, old town, museums.

La Bouille 76530 Grand Couronne	rooms have central heating, phone
Tel 35.23.80.10	**Facilities** bar, sitting-room
Location on banks of the Seine, 20 km SW of Rouen; public car parking; garden	**Credit cards** V
	Children accepted if well behaved
Meals breakfast, lunch, dinner	**Disabled** no special facilities
	Pets not accepted
Prices rooms 280F-350F; menus 120F-220F	**Closed** Tue evening and Wed out of season
Rooms 7 double rooms, 4 with bath, 3 with shower; all	**Proprietors** Bernard Huet and Patrice Kukurudz

Manche

Auberge de la Sélune

Book well in advance if you wish to experience the pleasures of this splendid small hotel. As most guidebooks have discovered, it offers outstanding value for money – and although Ducey does not have much appeal, it makes a perfectly satisfactory base for touring Normandy and making excursions into Brittany. As a result, the *auberge* is nearly always full.

It is difficult to decide whether the housekeeping or the food earns the prize, as both are first-class. The whole place is freshly decorated – mainly in bright floral prints, but with more panache than that usually implies in France – and spotlessly kept; there are fluffy towels and endless hot water, crisp linen and sound beds. Jean-Pierre Girres's cooking is excellent; his fish, seafood and *pâtisserie* are particularly well regarded; crab pie is one of his noted specialities. The pretty and spacious dining-room is popular with locals, and dinner can take some time to serve – but there is not much else to occupy your time in the evening here. Breakfast is above average, too.

Josette Girres is not a chatty hostess, but her welcome is genuinely warm. If the hotel has a drawback it is its position: fronting directly on to the street, parking is awkward.

Nearby Salmon fishing (River Sélune); Avranches (10 km) – museum; Le Mont-St-Michel (15 km) – fortified abbey on island.

2 Rue St-Germain 50220 Ducey
Tel 33.48.53.62
Location by river in village, on N176 11 km SE of Avranches; with small garden and some car parking
Meals breakfast, lunch, dinner
Prices rooms 170F-190F; menus 55F-130F
Rooms 18 double, all with bath (5 twin); one single; one family room with bath; all rooms have central heating, phone
Facilities sitting-room, bar, conference room; salmon fishing
Credit cards DC, MC, V
Children accepted
Disabled no special facilities
Pets not accepted
Closed mid-Jan to mid-Feb
Proprietor Jean-Pierre Girres

Le St-Pierre (see opposite)

Manche

Château de la Salle

If you arrive at Cherbourg from the UK towards the evening, the long and rather dull stretch of the Cotentin peninsula offers few interesting or notably comfortable hotels within reasonable driving distance. This small château is an exception – and it is much in demand as a consequence. Spacious and well-decorated bedrooms (some with four-poster beds) look out over the large park; the dining-room, with its huge fireplace (and log fire) is baronial. The young Basque chef is making a mark with his cooking, and Cécile Lemesle is a welcoming hostess. If you can get a room, you should be content here.

Nearby Coutances – 13thC Gothic cathedral; Hambye (15 km).

Montpinchon 50210 Cerisy-la-Salle
Tel 33.46.95.19
Location in countryside 12 km SE of Coutances; in large grounds with car parking
Meals breakfast, lunch, dinner
Prices rooms 290F-350F, suites 490F-590F; menu 95F
Rooms 10 double, 9 with bath, one with shower (5 twin); all rooms have central heating, TV, phone
Facilities sitting-room, 2 dining-rooms
Credit cards AE, DC, V
Children accepted
Disabled no special facilities
Pets accepted in bedrooms only
Closed 2 Nov to 20 Mar
Proprietors Michel and Cécile Lemesle

Manche

Château de Quinéville

The Cherbourg peninsula is not an exciting introduction to France, and there is little in Cherbourg itself to detain the tourist. But if you want a stopover not too far from the port, in a rural, peaceful setting, close to the sea, the Château de Quinéville measures up well. It stands in a park, together with the ruins of an earlier château and a moat – complete with Muscovy ducks. The classic façade gives the impression of formality, but inside the atmosphere is pleasantly relaxed and friendly, the decoration not too *soigné* and the rooms reasonably priced. There are lovely views over the park and across to the coast.

Nearby Valognes (15 km); Ste-Mère-Eglise–paratroop museum.

Quinéville 50310
Montebourg
Tel 33.21.42.67
Location 300 m from the sea, 8 km E of Montebourg; in park, with ample parking
Meals breakfast, lunch, dinner
Prices rooms 220F-250F; DB&B (for one) 275F-335F; menus 70F-150F
Rooms 12 double, 7 with bath, 5 with shower (no twin); all rooms have phone
Facilities dining-room, sitting-room, bar
Credit cards V
Children accepted
Disabled no special facilities
Pets accepted
Closed 1 Jan to 31 Mar
Manager Mme Monette Regnault

Verte Campagne

Verte Campagne certainly lives up to its name. It lies deep in the countryside and is all you might expect from an 18thC Norman farmhouse. The building is covered in creepers, the garden bursting with flowers and the interior, full of old ceramics and copper pots, is cosy and inviting. The main dining-room is charming and intimate – pride of place going to a large stone fireplace, where log fires blaze in winter. The eight bedrooms vary in size – the smallest is prettily decorated in pink, but barely big enough to swing a cat.

Nearby Coutances (10 km); Hambye (15 km); Mont-St-Michel.

Hameau Chevallier 50660
Trelly
Tel 33.47.65.33
Location in countryside 1.5 km outside village, 12 km S of Coutances; with garden and ample car parking
Meals breakfast, lunch, dinner
Prices rooms 150F-280F, single room 80F; menu 105F-125F
Rooms 7 double, 5 with bath (3 twin); one single; one family room with shower; all rooms have central heating, phone
Facilities 3 dining-rooms, 2 sitting-rooms
Credit cards AE, MC, V
Children welcome; special meals available **Disabled** one suitable bedroom in annexe
Pets accepted **Closed** 15-30 Nov, 14-28 Feb
Proprietor Mme Meredith

Calvados

Moulin du Pré

The Moulin du Pré lacks the appeal of the classical French *moulin* hotel – although it stands in open country, it is sandwiched between a car park and a private house (so does not feel as rural as it might) and its decoration and furnishing are in the main dreary. But the key exception is the large beamed, flower bedecked restaurant. It is this and the delicious local dishes served that make the place worth the short detour from the main Cabourg-Caen road. Bedrooms (no twins) are not stylish, but they are inexpensive, and have some antiques.

Nearby Ranville (5 km); Caen (15 km); Bayeux (40 km).

Rte-de-Gonneville-en-Auge, Bavent 14860 Ranville
Tel 31.78.83.68
Location in countryside off D513 8 km SW of Cabourg; in garden with car parking
Meals breakfast, lunch, dinner
Prices rooms 115F-210F; menus 185F-230F
Rooms 10 double, 8 with bath; all rooms have phone
Facilities dining-room, sitting-room
Credit cards AE, DC, MC, V
Children accepted
Disabled access difficult
Pets accepted in dining-room only
Closed Oct, first two weeks Mar; restaurant only Sun dinner and Mon out of season
Proprietors M. Hamchin and M. Holtz

Hôtel d'Argouges

Even without the famous 'tapestry', the pretty and historic town of Bayeux would be worth a visit, and it has recently acquired an additional attraction in this small town hotel. This intimate, friendly and perfectly placed 18thC house makes an ideal base for exploring the coast, the sights of Caen and – as the hotel has no dining-room – the restaurants of Bayeux. The elegant, well restored public rooms contain many original features, and there is a secluded garden and terrace. Bedrooms, furnished in a simple modern style, are all comfortable.

Nearby Cathedral, Bayeux Tapestry; Caen (28 km).

21 Rue St-Patrice 14400 Bayeux
Tel 31.92.88.86
Location off busy square in middle of town; with garden and private car parking (some garages)
Meals breakfast
Prices rooms 210F-390F
Rooms 22 double, 17 with bath, 5 with shower (13 twin); one single and 2 family rooms, all with bath; all rooms have central heating, phone, minibar
Facilities lobby, sitting-room, breakfast room, small meeting-room
Credit cards AE, DC, MC, V
Children welcome; baby-sitting available
Disabled access difficult
Pets accepted in bedrooms
Closed never
Proprietors M. and Mme Daniel Auregan

Calvados

La Pommeraie

'L'odeur de mon pays était dans une pomme' reads the motto you will find by your bedside (accompanied by a marzipan apple) as you slide between your crisp, neatly turned sheets at La Pommeraie, emphasising the attention to detail and respect for Norman traditions that underlie this polished operation – an ideal choice if you feel in need of pampering on your first or last night in France.

The Scaviner family make no bones about their priorities: it is the restaurant (Le Manoir d'Hastings) which takes pride of place, and they have earned the reputation of having one of the finest tables in Normandy, using traditional local ingredients – fresh fish, seafood, cheeses, calvados – to stunning and original effect. The generosity of the cheapest menu is particularly impressive. Service is immaculate but friendly, the surroundings smartly furnished in a restrained country style, presided over by a huge stone fireplace and fine antiques.

The bedrooms are in a long, low and relatively modern block (the main buildings were originally a 17thC priory) which is rather bland in style, but no effort is spared to make guests comfortable; a complimentary basket of exotic fruit is placed in each room. None of this comes cheaply, but prices include an excellent breakfast complete with home-made brioches.

Nearby Pegasus bridge, Paratroop Museum; Ranville (2 km) – cemetery; Riva-Bella (5 km); Caen (10 km); Bayeux (40 km).

18 Ave de la Côte de Nacre
14970 Bénouville
Tel 31.44.62.43
Location on edge of village, 3 km from Ouistreham ferry port, 15 km SW of Cabourg; with garden and ample car parking
Meals breakfast, lunch, dinner
Prices rooms 570F-800F; menus 160F-370F
Rooms 11 double, all with bath and shower (3 twin); all rooms have phone, TV, minibar
Facilities dining-room, sitting-room, bar
Credit cards AE, DC, V
Children welcome; baby-sitting available
Disabled access easy; some ground-floor bedrooms
Pets accepted
Closed first 2 weeks in Feb
Proprietors Scaviner family

Calvados

Converted mill, Clécy

Hostellerie du Moulin du Vey

This old, creeper-clad water-mill stands right at the heart of some of the best scenery in the region, where the River Orne has carved a majestic valley between green, rolling hills. It is within easy driving distance of the ferry port at Caen, and makes an attractive first- or last-night stop.

Both the buildings and the park-like surroundings of the mill are beautifully kept, and there is a pleasant waterside terrace for eating and drinking, with a garden beyond. Food in the half-timbered, rather barn-like restaurant, just across the courtyard from the main building, is unremarkable by exacting Norman standards but it is carefully prepared and served, and the less expensive menues are sound value. Bedrooms are comfortable, furnished simply but with touches of style, and reasonably priced by Norman standards. Some rooms are in the annexe, the Relais de Surosne, 3 km away on the other side of the village, but this too is peaceful, and the small Gothic-style house and its lush garden have considerable charm.

Nearby Suisse Normande region; Thury-Harcourt (10 km) – ruined château, park and garden; Falaise (30 km) – castle, William the Conqueror's birthplace; Caen (35 km) – Normandy Museum.

Le Vey 14570 Clécy
Tel 31.69.71.08
Location 2 km E of Clécy and 35 kms S of Caen; with river terrace and car parking
Meals breakfast, lunch, dinner
Prices rooms 270F-460F; menus 105F-290F
Rooms 17 double (7 twin) all with bath; 2 family rooms, one with bath, 1 with shower; all rooms have central heating, phone
Facilities dining-room, TV room, banqueting-room, conference room
Credit cards AE, DC, MC, V
Children accepted
Disabled no special facilities
Pets accepted but not in dining-room
Closed Dec
Proprietor Denise Leduc

Eure

Riverside hotel, Les Andelys

Hôtel de la Chaîne d'Or

This solid 18thC coaching inn has a splendid position on the banks of the Seine, beneath the hilltop ruins of Richard the Lionheart's castle – and that, it must be admitted, is a large part of its appeal. Our most recent reporter was greatly impressed by the food served in the beamed and flower-decked riverside restaurant, but others have been disappointed. The cheapest bedrooms are distinctly basic – though the best ones are huge, and elegantly furnished with antiques; don't be surprised if there is noise from river barges. Service is generally efficient, but inconsistent – and uncomfortably formal at times.

Nearby Church of Notre-Dame, ruins of Château Gaillard.

27 Rue Grande 27700 Les Andelys
Tel 32.54.00.31
Location in riverside town 40 km SE of Rouen; with car parking and courtyard
Meals breakfast, lunch, dinner
Prices rooms 120F-320F; menus 115F-230F
Rooms 11 double (4 twin), 3 family rooms, most with bath or shower; all rooms have central heating; most rooms have phone
Facilities sitting-room, dining-room, bar
Credit cards AE, DC, MC, V
Children welcome
Disabled no special facilities
Pets tolerated
Closed Jan; Mon
Proprietor Jean-Claude Foucault

Village inn, Le Bec-Hellouin

Auberge de l'Abbaye

Le Bec-Hellouin is a great medieval Benedictine monastery, much ruined and partially restored, and one of Normandy's major sights. Despite this, the village which has grown up around the church remains small and peaceful, and the timbered *auberge* with a terrace of sun-shaded tables overlooking the village green seems almost too good to be true – the archetypal atmospheric Norman inn, simple and welcoming. The tiled floors, rough stone walls and gleaming furniture set the scene for typical regional meals – dishes with apples and cider, of course, as well as quantities of cream. The rustic-style bedrooms are small, simple and cheerful. There is no sitting-room.

Nearby Abbey; Pont-Audemer (25 km) – church of St-Ouen.

Le Bec-Hellouin 27800 Brionne
Tel 32.44.86.02
Location in middle of village, 3 km N of Brionne; with ample car parking
Meals breakfast, lunch, dinner
Prices rooms 250F-280F; meals 120F-220F
Rooms 6 double, all with bath (3 twin); one family room; central heating, phone
Facilities bar, dining-room
Credit cards DC, V
Children accepted
Disabled no special facilities
Pets accepted
Closed early Jan to mid-Feb; also Mon evening and Tue out of season
Proprietor M. Sergent

Eure

Le Petit Coq aux Champs

A thatched house with its own heliport – it sounds unlikely, but convention counts for little at this secluded retreat amid rolling meadows. Le Petit Coq offers an intriguing mixture of the rustic, the sophisticated and the plain idiosyncratic.

The Pommiers have put huge efforts into upgrading and extending the 19thC building, which has two main wings – one mainly for eating, one mainly for sleeping – with a large, airy, modern extension between. The style varies considerably – modern cane furniture in the large sitting-room, while antiques predominate in the traditional-style restaurant, which has a huge open fireplace at one end. A small, intimate piano bar has been squeezed into the back of the new part of the building. The bedrooms are all furnished and arranged differently, some brightly coloured, others more restrained. Some are quite small.

While Mado Pommier busies herself at the front of the house, her husband Francis and son Patrick run the kitchen, with a serious attention to detail and local traditions. Apart from a hastily concocted dessert (the advertised menu item had run out) our inspector's meal was faultless, and beautifully served.

Nearby Pont-Audemer – half-timbered houses, church of St-Ouen; Honfleur (30 km) – old port, 15thC wooden church.

Champigny 27500 Pont-Audemer
Tel 32.41.04.19
Location in countryside, 6 km S of Pont-Audemer; in gardens with ample car parking
Meals breakfast, lunch, dinner
Prices rooms 450F-850F, family rooms 1,200F; menus 200F-240F
Rooms 12 double, with bath and shower (4 twin); one single with shower; 2 family rooms, with bath and shower; all rooms have central heating, phone; TV on request
Facilities sitting-room, 4 dining-rooms, piano bar, TV room; swimming-pool, mini-golf, heliport
Credit cards AE, DC, MC, V
Children very welcome; special meals available in separate dining-room
Disabled dining-rooms and 8 bedrooms are on ground floor
Pets welcome
Closed never
Proprietors Pommier family

Eure

Hôtel du Grand Cerf

This hotel's neat half-timbered façade overlooks the ancient covered market and main square of the pretty small town of Lyons-La-Forêt. The building is narrow – either side of the tiny hallway there is just room for a cosy salon-cum-bar full of antiques, and a long, thin restaurant in a timeless, rustic style, with abundant hunting mementoes. Game figures on the menu, but there is a wide selection of fish and seafood dishes to choose from, too. The bedrooms are modest, simply decorated and in some cases rather dark, but with beams and antique furniture. There is a pleasant small garden and parking area at the back.

Nearby Beech forest; Les Andelys (20 km) – ruined château.

Place Benserade 27480 Lyons-la-Forêt
Tel 32.49.60.44
Location on market place in small town 36 km SE of Rouen; with garden and car parking
Meals breakfast, lunch, dinner
Prices rooms 200F-250F; menu 200F
Rooms 8 double (2 twin), 4 with bath, 4 with shower; all rooms have central heating, phone
Facilities dining-room, sitting-room/bar
Credit cards AE, DC, MC, V
Children accepted
Disabled access very difficult
Pets accepted if well behaved
Closed mid-Jan to mid-Feb
Proprietor M. Colignon

Château de la Râpée

At the end of a long rutted track through dense forest from Bazincourt lies this 19thC Gothic mansion: grandly conceived but executed on a modest scale.

Inside, M. and Mme Bergeron have carefully preserved all the original features. The larger of the two dining-rooms (not always in use) is bright and airy, with windows on three sides, the smaller one modest and intimate. The food is excellent – generous portions of traditional regional cooking.

Nearby Gisors – castle; Jouy-sous-Thelle (25 km) – church; Beauvais (30 km) – cathedral; Giverny (45 km) – Monet.

Bazincourt-sur-Epte 27140 Gisors
Tel 32.55.11.61
Location in countryside 4 km NW of Gisors; in small park with ample car parking
Meals breakfast, lunch, dinner
Prices rooms 250F-350F; menus 115F-155F
Rooms 10 double, 7 with bath, 2 with shower (5 twin); 3 rooms can accommodate families; all rooms have central heating, phone
Facilities sitting-room, 2 dining-rooms, bar, banqueting-room; riding stables next door
Credit cards AE, DC, V
Children by arrangement
Disabled no special facilities
Pets small ones accepted
Closed mid-Jan to end Feb, mid- to end Aug; Wed
Proprietors M. and Mme Bergeron

Eure

Auberge du Vieux Puits

Although war-damaged Pont-Audemer still has a charming historic centre, with timbered houses and canalised streams, it is rather dwarfed by the nondescript suburbs which have grown up around it. The Vieux Puits shines out like a beacon – a wonderful, half-timbered, 17thC building (once a tannery), all crooked beams and leaded windows. The inside is a medievalist's dream, with its twisting wooden staircases and dark beams hung with shining copper and ancient pewter.

Jaques Foltz and his charming wife bring out the best in the building, by keeping the style simple and restrained. The small, intimate salon and dining-rooms are carefully furnished with antiques, and are decorated with fresh flowers; and they have avoided the temptation to upgrade or modernise the bedrooms in the old building, some of which are quite small and verge on the basic. But across the peaceful, informal courtyard (decked out with flowers in summer, and presided over by a magnificent weeping willow) a wing has been added to provide six new bedrooms – smarter and well equipped, but in keeping.

M. Foltz sees the *auberge* very much as a restaurant with rooms, and those who want to stay are encouraged to have dinner. To do so is hardly a penance, with a wide range of indulgent Norman dishes on offer.

Nearby Half-timbered houses, church of St-Ouen; Honfleur (25 km).

6 Rue Notre-Dame-du-Pré
27500 Pont-Audemer
Tel 32.41.01.48
Location near middle of town; with small garden and car parking
Meals breakfast, lunch, dinner
Prices rooms 100F-330F; menus 150F-240F
Rooms 12 double (4 twin), 6 with bath, 5 with shower; 11 have phone

Facilities dining-room with bar/sitting-area
Credit cards MC, V
Children welcome
Disabled 2 ground-floor rooms, specially equipped
Pets accepted in dining-room
Closed mid-Dec to mid-Jan, last week Jun to first week Jul; Mon evening, Tue
Proprietors Jacques and Hélène Foltz

Eure

Riverside hotel, St-Pierre-du-Vauvray

Hostellerie St-Pierre

A bizarre concoction: a modern building, triangular in plan with a turret on one corner, dressed up with fake timbers to look like a traditional Norman manor-house – and located only a short drive from the Paris-Rouen motorway. But don't dismiss it. The St-Pierre is set on the banks of the Seine, far enough from the traffic noise to justify *Relais du Silence* status, and it has other attractions too.

Not the least of these is the cuisine – classical in style but inventive in approach, and of outstanding quality, with the emphasis on fish and seafood – witness the enormous tank of langoustes and other consumables dominating the heavily decorated dining-room (which has big picture windows looking on to the river). The hotel's other public areas are limited, and solid rather than elegant, but the bedrooms are thoroughly comfortable and well-equipped, and many have balconies overlooking the river. (For the full flavour of this eccentric establishment, opt for the top room in the turret, with exposed beams and token four-poster.) The garden, which stretches down to the water's edge, is a relaxing place to sit. The hotel is family-run, and service is friendly and efficient.

Nearby Louviers – church of Notre-Dame; Acquigny (10 km) – château; Gaillon (15 km) – château; Giverny (30 km) – Monet's house and garden; Rouen (35 km).

Chemin des Amoureux
27430 St-Pierre-du-Vauvray
Tel 32.59.93.29
Location on edge of village 8 km E of Louviers, beside Seine; with gardens and car parking
Meals breakfast, lunch, dinner
Prices rooms 330F-440F, suite 560F; menus 145F-315F
Rooms 14 double (4 twin), all with bath; all rooms have central heating, phone, TV
Facilities dining-room, sitting-room
Credit cards V
Children accepted
Disabled lift/elevator
Pets accepted at extra charge
Closed Jan and Feb
Proprietor Alain Potier

Eure

Le Clos

Our inspectors could hardly lavish enough praise on the Clos, which seems to embody all that is best in French château-style hotels without the all-too-common pretension and vulgarity.

The Clos is on the edge of the pleasant but unremarkable town, in a quiet back street – though with a busy bypass visible (and just audible) in the background. It is a rather comical turn-of-the-century building of highly patterned brickwork, with a mock-medieval tower, set in well-kept leafy grounds with lawns and creeping willows that are overlooked by a large terrace. Inside, everything is of the highest quality: smart, antique-style cane chairs, heavy linen tablecloths and huge bunches of flowers in the dining-room, neat reproduction armchairs in the salon, chintzy drapes in the bedrooms, deep pile carpets everywhere – even in the luxurious bathrooms. There is plenty of space too – although the building is not large, there are only nine bedrooms, all of them light and airy, and furnished in individual style. Patrick Simon masterminds the kitchen, where he produces a range of classical dishes with absolute professionalism and finesse. But the *pièce de résistance* is the wickedly tempting dessert trolley.

All this comes at a price – but is well worth it if you feel like pampering yourself for a night or two.

Nearby Church of la Madeleine (flamboyant tower); Haras du Pin (40 km) – stud farm; Chartres – cathedral.

98 Rue de la Ferté-Vidame
27130 Verneuil-sur-Avre
Tel 32.32.21.81
Location on edge of town,
56 km NW of Chartres and
39 km SW of Evreux; with
gardens and car parking
Meals breakfast, lunch,
dinner
Prices rooms 380F-520F,
suites 680F; menus 160F-
260F, children's 80F
Rooms 9 double (2 twin), 2
suites, all with bath; all

rooms have central heating,
phone, TV
Facilities 2 dining-rooms,
sitting-room, bar; tennis
court, jacuzzi
Credit cards AE, DC, MC, V
Children welcome
Disabled 3 rooms in garden
on ground floor
Pets accepted
Closed Dec and Jan; Mon
out of season
Proprietors Patrick and
Colette Simon

Bois Joli (see opposite)

Orne/Eure

Les Saisons

A group of cottages – some old, some modern – clustered around a shady garden make up this unusual hotel, close to the Seine and to the Seine motorway (though happily out of earshot of the latter). The cottage rooms are fresh and attractive, some with working fireplaces, and the dining-rooms (in the main hotel building and a separate outbuilding) are calm and elegant. Like his predecessors, the Bouchinets, Jean Yves Guillet (who took over in late 1987) is sticking to conservative cuisine, not dominated by Norman cream and butter.

Nearby Giverny (30 km); Rouen (35 km) – cathedral, museums.

Vironvay 27400 Louviers
Tel 32.40.02.56
Location in open countryside off N155, 3 km SE of Louviers; in garden with ample car parking
Meals breakfast, lunch, dinner
Prices rooms 290F–350F, suites 490F–590F
Rooms 18 double (7 twin), 4 suites, all with bath and shower; all rooms have central heating, phone, TV, minibar
Facilities 3 dining-rooms, piano bar; tennis
Credit cards AE, MC, V
Children welcome; special meals, baby-sitting by arrangement
Disabled ground-floor bedrooms
Pets accepted
Closed early to late Feb, mid- to late Aug
Proprietor Jean Yves Guillet

Bois Joli

The Bois Joli looks something like an escapee from the Black Forest – a dignified, 19thC building on three floors, partly timbered, surrounded by its own terraces and leafy gardens. Unlike some other spa buildings, the hotel is immaculately kept, and Joël and Chantal Gabriot have made great efforts to create an intimate, friendly welcome. The centrepiece is the simply decorated, panelled restaurant, which serves a range of traditional, well-prepared regional dishes. The bedrooms are notably airy and spacious, with floral wallpapers and fabrics.

Nearby Andaines Forest – walking, riding, cycling.

12 Ave P du Rozier 61140 Bagnoles-de-l'Orne
Tel 33.37.92.77
Location close to middle of resort, facing the racecourse; in gardens, with private car parking
Meals breakfast, lunch, dinner
Prices rooms 170F–350F; meals from 140F
Rooms 18 double (7 twin), 2 family rooms; all with bath; all rooms have central heating, phone; TV on request
Facilities dining-room, sitting-room, lift/elevator
Credit cards AE, DC, MC, V
Children welcome
Disabled no special facilities
Pets accepted, but not in dining-room
Closed mid-Nov to late Mar
Proprietors Joël and Chantal Gabriot

Orne

Converted mill, Villeray

Moulin de Villeray

Over the years, Roland Coldeboeuf has turned this previously derelict mill building into one of the foremost hotels and restaurants of southern Normandy. It is hardly what you would call a simple rustic retreat – take a look at the prices – but the rushing stream and the mill-wheel are still there. And the setting is delectable as ever.

Much of the *moulin* has been rebuilt rather than restored, but its main focus, the restaurant, retains old beams and a huge fireplace – plus a view of the mill-wheel. Comfortable and spacious, with food more than matching up to the surroundings, the dining-room is proof that 'serious eating' can be enjoyable too. Served with confidence and flair, specialities include smoked scallops with sherry, braised turbot with oysters, rack of lamb with pink garlic and basil – and even more impressive desserts. The eccentricities in the dining-room – such as the cheese being served from a goat's skin and the huge, over-the-top coffee trolley, laden with bags of beans and a sugar loaf – are easily forgiven.

The rest of the building is less enticing – there is a rather dreary salon where guests gather for drinks, and the bedrooms are slightly fussy, although extremely comfortable. Outside there is a pleasant terrace, and beyond that a large, relaxing and informal garden.

Nearby Nogent – Gothic and Renaissance buildings; Chartres (55 km) – cathedral; Alençon (55 km) – lace-making.

Villeray 61110 Condeau
Tel 33.73.30.22
Location at foot of village, 10 km NW of Nogent; with garden and car parking
Meals breakfast, lunch, dinner
Prices DB&B (for one) 720F
Rooms 10 double, all with bath and shower (3 twin); all rooms have phone
Facilities sitting-room, dining-room, bar
Credit cards AE, DC, V
Children accepted
Disabled access to restaurant
Pets accepted (must be kept on lead)
Closed Tue lunch and dinner, Wed lunch
Proprietors Roland Coldeboeuf

Eure-et-Loir

Country inn, Cloyes-sur-le-Loir

Hostellerie St-Jacques

An old coaching inn dating from the 16thC, the Hostellerie St-Jacques has lately enjoyed a new lease of life as an *étape gastronomique*. We understand that a new hand is at the helm, so the culinary attractions of the hotel may or may not be sustained. But the Hostellerie seems sure to remain a pleasant place to pause on the way through the Loire.

The dining-room, looking out over the garden, is intimate and elegant – furnished in Louis XIII style with a huge fireplace, ancient tapestries and antiques. But in good weather meals are served in the shade of the trees in the garden, which is a lush expanse leading down to the banks of the little Loir. The bedrooms (which are not large) are furnished in original or reproduction antiques, and are mostly comfortable and well looked after. They are at the back of the house, looking over the garden and thus avoiding any traffic noise.

Nearby Châteaudun (10 km) – feudal château; Vendôme – la Trinité, Porte St Georges; Beaugency (45 km) – bridge, keep.

35 Rue Nationale 28220 Cloyes-sur-le-Loir
Tel 37.98.50.08
Location in village on N10, 28 km NE of Vendôme; with garden and car parking
Meals breakfast, lunch, dinner
Prices rooms 280F-390F; menus 170F-295F
Rooms 22 double, 19 with bath, 3 with shower (5 twin); one family room; all rooms have central heating, phone, TV
Facilities dining-room, sitting-room, bar
Credit cards MC, V
Children welcome **Disabled** lift/elevator **Pets** accepted but not in dining-room
Closed Jan to 5 Feb
Proprietor Eric Thureau

Côtes-du-Nord

Repaire de Kerroch

This beautiful 18thC house has an enviable position right on the quay of the fishing port of Paimpol and has been beautifully restored by previous owners. M Escallet carries on his predecessor's tradition of excellent breakfasts; there are with good-value fixed-price menus of classic dishes, competently cooked; and the bedrooms (generally rather small) are well-furnished and equipped with minibar and double-glazing (the views over the port are attractive, but it can get a little noisy in the morning). Bathrooms are luxurious and spacious. There is a small dining-room, and an attractive little bar with 1930s decoration. Outside are a couple of tables for drinks or lunches.
Nearby Arcouest Point (5 km); Tréguier (15 km).

29 Quai Morand, Port de Plaisance 22500 Paimpol
Tel 96.20.50.13
Location on quayside in middle of town; with car parking on street
Meals breakfast, lunch, dinner
Prices rooms 300F; menus 90F-190F
Rooms 6 double, all with bath (2 twin); one family room with bath; all rooms have phone, minibar
Facilities bar/salon, dining-room, lift/elevator
Credit cards AE, V
Children welcome
Disabled no special facilities
Pets accepted (at a charge)
Closed Tue, Wed
Proprietor M. Escallet

Château de Coatguélen

This fine 19thC château, set in a large park, has a relaxed and friendly atmosphere. Families are well catered for: there is a playroom and good sports facilities, including riding. Bedrooms are large and elegantly decorated, with excellent bathrooms; the attractive, formal restaurant (light, innovative cooking, notably good value at lunch) opens on to a terrace. Throughout, antiques and flowers contribute to a cared-for ambience.
Nearby Coast (5 km); Arcouest (20 km) – boats to Ile de Bréhat; La Roche-Jagu (25 km) – château; Tréguier (30 km) – cathedral.

Pléhédel 22290 Lanvollon
Tel 96.22.31.24
Location 26 km NW of St-Brieuc; in own park with ample car parking
Meals breakfast, lunch, dinner
Prices rooms 670F-860F; meals 180F-320F, children's menu 80F
Rooms 16 double, all with bath (6 twin); 2 single, both with bath; all rooms have central heating, TV
Facilities dining-room, sitting-room, 2 meeting-rooms; golf (9-hole), swimming-pool, riding, tennis
Credit cards AE, DC, V
Children welcome
Disabled access difficult
Pets accepted
Closed mid-Nov to mid-Mar; restaurant only Tue and Wed lunch out of season
Managers Josette and Louis Le Roy

Côtes-du-Nord

Ti Al-Lannec

Trébeurden is an attractive little town spreading down to splendid family beaches on the beautiful 'pink granite' coast of Brittany. Ti Al-Lannec is a handsome family house, completely renovated and opened as a hotel in 1978 by Gérard and Danielle Jouanny, and run by them with a convincing blend of charm, taste and efficiency.

Secluded in wooded grounds, the house stands high up above the sea with a path leading down to the beach; its south-facing terrace has a splendid view looking over the bay of Lannion. It is a supremely comfortable hotel, with that elusive private-house feel. Bedrooms are thoughtfully decorated to feel light and airy but cosy, with fresh flowers and books, small tables and table lamps liberally used. Some have terraces or verandas, a couple have their own small sitting-room. The dining-room has the sea view, and is crisp and fresh with its white linen, rich drapes and old stone walls. Antique and modern furnishings mix well in the comfortable sitting-room. The food – Danielle's province – is excellent, and the arrangements for children are impressive.

Nearby Perros-Guirec (15 km) – large resort; Tréguier (30 km).

Allée de Mezo-Guen, BP 3 22560 Trébeurden
Tel 96.23.57.26
Location in wooded grounds above resort, 10 km NW of Lannion; with ample car parking
Meals breakfast, lunch, dinner
Prices rooms 360F-490F; weekday lunch 100F, dinner menus 145F-250F, children's 65F
Rooms 16 double (8 twin), 2 single, 4 family rooms, all with bath; all rooms have TV, phone
Facilities dining-room, 2 sitting-rooms, bar, billiards room, play room
Credit cards AE, MC, V
Children welcome; early meals, baby-sitting available
Disabled no special facilities
Pets accepted in bedrooms at extra charge
Closed 15 Nov to 15 Mar
Proprietors Danielle and Gérard Jouanny

Côtes-du-Nord

Manoir de Lan-Kerellec

Trébeurden is one of the most attractive beach resorts along Brittany's north coast, though that probably matters little to visitors to what is hardly a bucket-and-spade hotel. The charming young Daubés have turned this handsome and unusual old family house into an elegant and welcoming hotel – a member of the Relais & Châteaux group, but one of the most captivating. It stands in trees high above the rocky shore, with splendid views from tall windows – stretch the budget if you can and opt for one of the larger rooms which have the views.

Nearby Perros-Guirec (15 km); Tréguier (30 km).

22560 Trébeurden
Tel 96.23.50.09
Location in residential area overlooking the sea, 9 km NW of Lannion; with small garden and private car parking
Meals breakfast, lunch, dinner
Prices rooms 610F–1380F; meals 125F–300F
Rooms 12 double, (6 twin), all with bath; 3 rooms can have extra bed; all rooms have central heating, phone, TV
Facilities dining-room, sitting-room, bar
Credit cards AE, DC, MC, V
Children welcome; special menu available
Disabled no special facilities
Pets accepted
Closed Nov to Mar
Proprietor M. Daubé

Kastell Dinec'h

Honeysuckle sprawls over the grey stone walls of this handsome old farmhouse, tucked away down a leafy lane. There is a warm welcome for overseas visitors from Mme Pauwels and her friendly, English-speaking staff. The decoration is *style anglais* too – Laura Ashley wallpapers and a happily informal mix of antique and modern furniture. Bedrooms, some in a converted stable block, are simple, fresh and pretty. Delicious meals – a red R from Michelin for notable value – are served in the elegantly rustic dining-room overlooking a lush courtyard garden.

Nearby Tréguier – cathedral; Château de la Roche-Jagu

Rte de Lannion 22220 Tréguier
Tel 96.92.49.39
Location 1.5 km outside town, off D786 to Lannion; with garden and ample car parking
Meals breakfast, dinner
Prices rooms 210F–340F; menus 85F–230F
Rooms 13 double (7 twin), 2 family rooms, all with bath; all rooms have central heating; 10 rooms have phone
Facilities dining-room, sitting-room, TV room; swimming-pool
Credit cards MC, V
Children accepted
Disabled 2 rooms with access
Pets not accepted in public rooms
Closed Jan to mid-Mar, 2 weeks end of Oct
Proprietor Bernard Pauwels

Ille-et-Vilaine

Town mansion, St-Malo

La Korrigane

This handsome, turn-of-the-century mansion near the centre of St-Servan, just south of St-Malo harbour, has been beautifully restored and is furnished throughout with antiques. The elegant bedrooms are spacious and individually decorated, and have comfortable armchairs, beautiful lamps and mirrors, paintings, and countless other touches. Bathrooms are luxurious. There are two sitting-rooms, all perfectly in style with the atmosphere of a fine private home. On summery days, you can have your breakfast in the small, pretty garden – there is no restaurant. This is an excellent place for a romantic short break without the children; if you feel so inclined, you can even watch English television.

Nearby Emerald Coast; Château du Bosq (10 km); Dinan (35 km).

39 Rue Le Pomellec 35403
St-Malo
Tel 99.81.65.85
Location in S part of town, near harbour; with gardens and ample car parking
Meals breakfast
Prices rooms 300F-450F
Rooms 10 double, all with bath or shower; all rooms

have TV, phone, central heating
Facilities 2 sitting-rooms
Credit cards AE, V
Children accepted
Disabled no special facilities
Pets accepted
Closed Nov to Mar
Proprietor Mme Le Bourhis

Ille-et-Vilaine/Finistère

Hôtel Elizabeth

Inside the old city walls, behind a harmonious 17thC facade, the Elizabeth is an entirely modern construction, and offers well planned accommodation and a high degree of comfort. The bedrooms in the main building are in various styles of Louis (XIII, XIV and XV), while those in an annexe are modern; each has a small sitting area for breakfast (which is reputed to be good). Public rooms consist only of a small, cosy bar/sitting area in the rough-stone-walled cellars. There is no restaurant, but that is no hardship – there are several close by in the walled town, notably the Duchesse Anne, an attractive *brasserie*.

Nearby Emerald Coast; Château du Bosq (10 km); Dinan (35 km) – Rue du Jerzual, castle; Mont-St-Michel (55 km).

2 Rue de Cordiers 35400 St-Malo	bath; all rooms have central heating, TV, phone
Tel 99.56.24.98	**Facilities** bar
Location within the old fortress walls of the town; street car parking nearby	**Credit cards** AE, DC, MC, V
	Children accepted
	Disabled lift/elevator available
Meals breakfast	
Prices rooms 280F-386F	**Pets** dogs accepted
Rooms 15 double, 11 with bath, 4 with shower (5 twin); 2 family rooms, both with	**Closed** never
	Proprietor Mme Raverat

Les Moulins du Duc

This unusual hotel is many people's idea of heaven: utterly secluded in its wooded grounds, with a large and photogenic pond complete with fat, contented ducks. The main building is a former mill, rustic and attractive, with windows overlooking the little river; there is a relaxing modern sitting-room and bar, candlelit dining-rooms (one non-smoking) and an excellent indoor swimming-pool. The accommodation is in two-storey cottages scattered around the grounds; the bedrooms are spacious and well-equipped. Breakfast can be had on the lawn by the pond.

Nearby Concarneau (25 km) – Ville Close (walled town).

29116 Moëlan-sur-Mer	shower; all rooms have phone, TV, minibar
Tel 98.39.60.73	
Location beside river 2 km N of village, 10 km SW of Quimperlé; in large grounds with ample private parking	**Facilities** dining-rooms, sitting-room, bar; swimming-pool
	Credit cards AE, DC, MC, V
Meals breakfast, lunch, dinner	**Children** welcome
Prices rooms 440F-1,040F; menus 165F-355F; children's 60F	**Disabled** ground-floor rooms
	Pets accepted
	Closed mid-Jan to end-Feb
Rooms 22 double (11 twin), 5 suites; 22 with bath, 5 with	**Proprietors** Quistrebert family

Finistère

Seaside hotel, Raguenès-Plage

Chez Pierre

A favourite with British visitors, Chez Pierre has a charming lack of pretension and is particularly popular with families – games and television rooms, children's meals, bicycles and sailboards – and is close to a sandy beach. Adult needs are met, too: a terrace for drinks, copious sitting areas, and surprisingly good cooking for this sort of seaside hotel.

Nearby Quimperle (30 km) – church; Quimper (35 km) – fine arts and Brittany museums, cathedral, boat trips on Odet estuary.

Raguenès-Plage 29139 Nevez
Tel 98.06.81.06
Location in countryside 15 km SE of Concarneau; with terrace, gardens and car parking
Meals breakfast, lunch, dinner
Prices rooms 100F-300F; DB&B (for one) 161F-259F; full board 190F-295F; menus 95F-115F
Rooms 22 double, 12 with bath, 10 with shower (6 twin); 2 single; 6 family rooms, 4 with bath, 2 with shower; all rooms have phone
Facilities dining-room, sitting-room, bar, TV room, playroom
Credit cards MC, V
Children welcome; special meals available
Disabled no special facilities
Pets dogs accepted, but not in dining-room
Closed 28 Sep to 30 Mar
Proprietor Xavier Guillou

Seaside hotel, Ste-Anne-la-Palud

Hôtel de la Plage

Strictly, the Plage is rather large for our purposes, and rather smartly impersonal (it is a Relais & Château member). But it combines a splendid seaside setting – the immaculate white building stands in manicured gardens above a vast beach – with one of the best kitchens in Brittany (specialising, of course, in seafood). Mme Lecoz and her staff generate a welcoming atmosphere; service is sometimes a little slow but always friendly, and details are not overlooked. Bedrooms are comfortable, and some have stunning views (worth booking ahead).

Nearby Beach; Locronan (10 km) – town square; Quimper.

Ste-Anne-la-Palud 29127 Plonévez-Porzay
Tel 98.92.50.12
Location in countryside 4 km W of Plonévez and 25 km NW of Quimper; with garden and ample car parking
Meals breakfast, lunch, dinner
Prices rooms 350F-700F; menus 160F-300F
Rooms 20 double (10 twin), 2 single, 4 family rooms, 4 suites, all with bath; all rooms have central heating, TV, phone
Facilities sitting-room, dining-room, bar, conference room
Credit cards AE, DC, MC, V
Children welcome **Disabled** lift/elevator **Pets** accepted but not in dining-room
Closed mid-Oct to Apr
Proprietor M. Lecoz

Morbihan

Auberge Bretonne

This small, welcoming *auberge* is perched on a headland overlooking the waters of the River Vilaine. There are only five bedrooms: cooking takes pride of place here. Jacques Thorel, owner and chef, is an exponent of light, natural dishes, using the best of the local ingredients. Bretons come from far afield for the six-course *menu dégustation*, and seafood specialities, such as stuffed sea urchins, lobster with *cèpes* and turbot with spices. Bedrooms are prettily furnished in rural Breton style. The public rooms – a large dining-room and two small salons – are friendly rather than elegant.

Nearby Parc de Brière (15 km) – salt marshes; Guérande (25 km) – moated town; Vannes (40 km) – cathedral.

2 Place du Guesclin 56130 La Roche-Bernard **Tel** 99.90.60.28 **Location** overlooking River Vilaine, 30km SE of Vannes; with car parking in front **Meals** breakfast, lunch, dinner **Prices** rooms 180F-280F; meals 130F-250F **Rooms** 5 double, all with	bath and shower (one twin); all rooms have central heating; 3 rooms have TV **Facilities** dining-room, 2 small sitting-rooms **Credit cards** MC, V **Children** accepted **Disabled** no special facilities **Pets** accepted **Closed** 15 Nov to 15 Dec **Proprietor** Jacques Thorel

Auberge des Deux Magots

There is a prim look to this 17thC stone house in the middle of La Roche-Bernard, but a warm welcome within. Joël Morice, chef here since 1965 and proprietor since 1981, sets the same high standards in the running of the hotel that he does in the kitchen – the furniture in the elegant dining-rooms and bedrooms may be reproduction, but it is all part of a careful, fresh decorative scheme. (The TV room is, as TV rooms will be, rather a let down.) M. Morice's good-value menus concentrate on traditional regional dishes (which of course include seafood).

Nearby Parc Régional de Brière (15 km); Guérande (25 km).

1 Place du Bouffay 56130 La Roche-Bernard **Tel** 99.90.60.75 **Location** in the middle of town, with public parking in front **Meals** breakfast, lunch, dinner **Prices** rooms 200F-250F, suites/family rooms 320F-400F; menus 50F-180F **Rooms** 12 double, 9 with bath, 3 with shower (4 twin);	2 family rooms with bath; all rooms have phone **Facilities** 2 dining-rooms, TV room, bar **Credit cards** MC, V **Children** tolerated **Disabled** no special facilities **Pets** not accepted **Closed** restaurant only Mon; Sun eve and Mon out of season **Proprietors** M. and Mme Joël Morice

Morbihan

Seaside hotel, Vannes

Le Roof

This white-painted modern hotel, right on the Gulf of Morbihan, is quiet at night but bustling at noon, when families return from the beach or the nearby swimming-pool, and yachtsmen come to eat a seafood platter. It is a jolly place, with a dining-room designed to resemble the inside of a boat and a terrace with sunshades for outdoor eating. Bedrooms are simple, but comfortable enough. The Mollé family make adults and children equally welcome. As we go to press, we understand that Le Roof is undergoing modernization and enlargement.

Nearby Château du Plessis-Josso (15 km); Carnac (30 km).

Presqu'ile de Conleau 56000 Vannes
Tel 97.63.47.47
Location on seashore, 4 km S of middle of town; with terrace and ample car parking
Meals breakfast, lunch, dinner
Prices rooms 180F-260F; menus 70F-280F
Rooms 9 double, 8 with bath, one with shower (2 twin); 4 family rooms, 3 with

bath, one with shower; all rooms have phone, central heating
Facilities 2 dining-rooms, bar
Credit cards AE, DC, V
Children welcome
Disabled no special facilities
Pets accepted if well behaved
Closed mid-Jan to mid-Feb
Proprietor Mme Mollé

Paris

Town guest-house, Paris

Esmeralda

A small hotel of great charm and character, the Esmeralda occupies a building dating from the 16thC in the oldest quarter of the city, close to Notre-Dame. Michèle Bruel is an ex-sculptress who has made the place distinctly arty and individual: a fascinating collection of *objets d'art* are scattered through the hotel, mixing well with the old beams, stone walls and quarry-tiled floors. A slightly eccentric 1920s style prevails in the bedrooms; most of them are small, dark and cosy, but no two are alike. There was only one bathroom when Michèle Bruel moved in many years ago; now most of the rooms have their own.

Nearby St Julien-de-Pauvre – oldest complete church in Paris; Ile de la Cité – Notre Dame; Beaubourg (across the river).

4 Rue St-Julien-le-Pauvre
75005 Paris
Tel (1) 43.54.19.20
Location left bank, near
Notre Dame; public car
parking close by
Meals breakfast
Prices rooms 85F-370F
Rooms 12 double, all with
bath (2 twin); 7 single, 4 with
shower; one family room

with bath; all rooms have
central heating, phone
Facilities breakfast room
Credit cards not accepted
Children welcome
Disabled no special facilities
Pets accepted
Closed never
Proprietor Michèle Bruel

Town hotel, Paris

Hôtel des Tuileries

The situation of this small hotel – an attractive 18thC mansion – is hard to beat: close to the beautiful Place Vendôme and the exclusive shops of the Rue du Faubourg St-Honoré, yet at the same time in a small quiet street – so quiet in fact that the hotel has managed to become a *Relais du Silence* (one of only two in the whole of Paris). The two small salons double up as the breakfast room and bar, and are furnished with velvet seats, floral walls, paintings and patterned carpets. Bedrooms are prettily furnished in a similar style, with reproduction antiques – front ones are the most elegant and spacious.

Nearby Tuileries, Louvre, Opéra, Rue de Rivoli.

10 Rue St-Hyacinthe 75001
Paris
Tel (1) 42.61.04.17
Location in middle of city, N
of Tuileries; with public car
parking nearby
Meals breakfast
Prices rooms 270F-700F
Rooms 26 double (12 twin),
2 suites, all with bath; all
rooms have central heating,
phone, minibar, hairdrier,

safe
Facilities breakfast room,
bar
Credit cards AE, DC, V
Children accepted
Disabled no special facilities
Pets accepted
Closed never
Proprietors Monique Poulle
Vidal and Marie Madeleine
Le Hérisse

Paris

L'Hôtel Guy Louis Duboucheron

The Rue des Beaux-Arts, a side street in the heart of St-Germain-des-Prés, has been the home of many artists and writers. L'Hotel's particular claim to fame is that it was the last abode of Oscar Wilde; as the plaque on the door will tell you, he 'died here beyond his means'. Then a local hotel of no real distinction, it is now the most lavish establishment on the Left Bank, and in terms of glamour, ranks alongside the five-star hotels across the Seine. Film and pop stars and politicians figure on the guest list, along with the merely super-rich.

Bedrooms are sumptuous. All thick-pile carpets, Venetian marble bathrooms and antiques, they are the ultimate in luxury – although only the Penthouse (which takes up to five) could be described as spacious. Nostalgia value is high: you might sleep in the very bed where Oscar Wilde died, or enjoy the art deco furniture in the Mistinguett room.

Public rooms are equally extravagant. The winter garden has been converted into a glamorous piano bar/restaurant with fountain, goldfish, flowers and exotic plants. Both bar and restaurant are open until the early hours of the morning, and are popular haunts for Parisian high society.

Nearby Palais du Louvre (over the Pont des Arts); church of Saint Germain-des-Prés; Delacroix museum; Rue de Buci and Rue de Seine – one of the best food-markets in Paris.

13 Rue des Beaux Arts
75006 Paris
Tel (1) 43.25.27.22
Location in Saint-Germain-des-Prés
Meals breakfast, lunch, dinner
Prices rooms 850F-1,700F, suites 2,300F-3,000F; lunch menu 150F; dinner menu 160F
Rooms 23 double, 13 with bath, 10 with shower (15 twin); 3 suites; one single, with bath; all rooms have central heating, minibar, phone, radio, TV, video
Facilities 2 restaurants (winter garden, cellar bar)
Credit cards AE, DC, MC, V
Children accepted
Disabled no special facilities
Pets accepted
Closed never
Manager Alain Philippe Feutre

Hôtel des Tuileries (see opposite)

Paris

Le Pavillon

This 18thC former convent, off a long, narrow shopping street leading from Les Invalides to the Eiffel Tower, is a pleasure to come home to – set back beyond a little courtyard behind wrought-iron gates, looking cheerfully provincial and a little secretive. Inside, there are no public rooms save the smart little reception area, so breakfasts are served (promptly, at any hour) in the bedrooms. (Many of these are shoe-box-sized, so guests must scrabble to find a space for the groaning tray held aloft by a patient maid.) The rooms are prettily decorated and well kept, bathrooms are neat and functional. Prices are commendably low.

Nearby Hôtel des Invalides, Eiffel Tower, Rond Point de Champs Elysées, Modern Art and Rodin Museums.

54 Rue St-Dominique 75007 Paris
Tel (1) 45.51.42.87
Location set back off a shopping street, close to Eiffel Tower; with car parking nearby
Meals breakfast, snacks
Prices rooms 295F; family room 400F
Rooms 16 double, with shower (4 twin); 1 single, with shower; 1 family room with bath; all rooms have central heating, phone
Facilities reception area only
Credit cards MC, V
Children accepted
Disabled access difficult
Pets accepted
Closed never
Proprietor Mme Paoli

Hôtel Monceau Lenox

This turn-of-the-century house is in a quiet residential area of Paris (not far from the Champs Elysées), but is well served by the metro and bus networks. It was thoroughly refurbished a couple of years ago, and is now prettily furnished and decorated, and feels cared for. Breakfast is served (7 sorts of *confiture*, 3 sorts of tea) in a small courtyard – some of the bedrooms lead on to it – or in the rooms. There is no dining-room, but light meals can be served in the bedrooms – cheese, charcuterie, foie gras and so on. The small sitting-room also serves as a bar. The house rule is to 'make yourself at home' – after a hard day's sightseeing, an inviting prospect.

Nearby Parc de Monceau, Arc du Triomphe, Champs Elysées.

18 Rue Léon Jost 75017 Paris
Tel (1) 46.22.60.70
Location in residential area, close to Champs Elysées; with public car parking nearby
Meals breakfast
Prices rooms 450F-490F, suites 950F-1,200F
Rooms 18 double (3 twin), all with bath; all rooms have central heating, colour TV, phone, minibar
Facilities some rooms have private sitting-area
Credit cards AE, DC, MC, V
Children accepted **Disabled** no special facilities **Pets** small dogs tolerated
Closed never
Proprietor Jean Marc Eber

Paris

Hôtel St-Germain-des-Prés

This small Left Bank hotel in a characteristic street of St-Germain-des-Prés stands out for charm and individuality, although perhaps not for notably good taste and certainly not for coherence of interior design. Its bedrooms are all furnished in different styles and colours – one with a huge canopied four-poster bed, another with exposed 18thC beams, another with pretty modern floral fabrics. Downstairs there is one large salon-cum-breakfast-room with leather armchairs, flowery carpet and a mass of plants. The Rue Bonaparte is not one of the quietest.

Nearby Louvre, Conciergerie, Delacroix Museum, Café Procope (haunt of literati – Molière, Voltaire, Balzac); church of St-Germain-des-Prés.

36 Rue Bonaparte 75006 Paris
Tel (1) 43.26.00.19
Location close to church of St-Germain-des-Prés; public car parking only
Meals breakfast
Prices rooms 480F-550F
Rooms 29 double (6 twin), one single; all with bath or shower; all rooms have central heating, phone, TV, radio, minibar
Facilities breakfast/sitting-room
Credit cards V
Children accepted
Disabled access possible; lift/elevator
Pets not accepted
Closed never
Proprietor M. Le Boudec

Hôtel St-Louis

Of the three sister hotels on this busy street on the Ile-St-Louis, this is the simplest and cheapest. It is converted from a 17thC townhouse, and M. and Mme Record look on it more as a large family-run house than a formal hotel. The welcoming atmosphere, combined with the ideal location for sightseeing and the modest prices, more than make up for any lack of facilities (the only public room is the stone-vaulted basement salon, used for breakfast) and the small size of the bedrooms, which are all decorated in simple and largely modern fashion with the addition of rustic-style furniture.

Nearby Church of Saint Louis-en-L'Ile; Ile de la Cité – Notre Dame; Boulevard Saint Germain (just over the river).

75 Rue St-Louis-en-l'Île 75004 Paris
Tel (1) 46.34.04.80.08
Location on island in the Seine; public car parking nearby
Meals breakfast
Prices rooms 380F-490F
Rooms 12 double, 15 with bath, 6 with shower (9 twin); all rooms have phone
Facilities breakfast room
Credit cards not accepted
Children welcome if well behaved
Disabled 2 ground-floor bedrooms
Pets accepted if small and well behaved
Closed never
Proprietors M. and Mme Record

Paris

Town hotel, Paris

Hôtel Perreyve

A plain hotel, lacking character but marked out by a pleasant, provincial air. The bedrooms, small and functional with muted decoration and few frills (but sparkling-clean tiled bathrooms), echo the prim sobriety of the ground-floor salon, with its carefully arranged upright chairs, central dining-table and potted plants. One could well imagine an old widow, dressed in black, knitting in a corner. The Perreyve, owned and personally run by M. Doumergue, is situated in a quiet, unremarkable stretch of the Rue Madame, just a few paces from the Jardin du Luxembourg, and tolerably well placed for exploration of the Left Bank as a whole.

Nearby Luxembourg gardens and Palace, church of St-Germain-des-Prés, Delacroix Museum, Café des Deux Magots.

63 Rue Madame 75006 Paris
Tel (1).45.48.35.01
Location in Jardin du Luxembourg district; car parking nearby
Meals breakfast
Prices rooms 275F-350F
Rooms 28 double, 12 with bath, 16 with shower (10 twin); 2 single, with shower; all rooms have central heating, TV, phone
Facilities sitting-room/breakfast room
Credit cards AE, DC, MC, V
Children welcome
Disabled no special facilities
Pets not accepted
Closed never
Proprietor René Doumergue

Town hotel, Paris

Hôtel de la Place des Vosges

The Place des Vosges, now restored to its former glory as part of the general revitalization of the formerly run-down Marais area (between Beaubourg and the Bastille), is one of the loveliest squares in Paris. The Hôtel de la Place des Vosges is an attractive 17thC house, entirely in harmony with the style of the area, in a quiet street only 25 metres from the square. The salon Louis XIII is suitably traditional and rustic in style: exposed beams, roughcast stone walls, tapestry-covered chairs and curtains. Bedrooms are more modern in style, with less character, but they are well kept – and reasonably priced.

Nearby Place des Vosges (oldest square in Paris), Bastille, Victor Hugo museum, Hôtel de Ville, Carnavalet museum.

12 Rue de Birague 75004 Paris
Tel (1) 42.72.60.46
Location off Place des Vosges, in Marais district; with private garages 300 m away
Meals breakfast
Prices rooms 300F-350F; children under 2 free
Rooms 15 double, 10 with bath, 5 with shower (4 twin); one family room with bath; all rooms have central heating, phone
Facilities sitting-area
Credit cards AE, DC, MC, V
Children welcome
Disabled no special facilities
Pets accepted if well behaved
Closed never
Proprietor M. Cros

Paris

Town hotel, Paris

Hôtel le Ste-Beuve

There can be few bed-and-breakfast establishments more stylish than this turn-of-the-century hotel, in Paris or anywhere else. All is discretion and understatement: light, plain decoration; restrained patterns in the rich fabrics; beds draped in white; sparse furnishing, employing well-placed antiques mixed with modern designs; fresh flowers strategically placed. A log fire burns in the little classically-styled salon – not a place to while away evenings, but a civilized meeting-place. Cold meals are served in the bedrooms (there is no dining-room) at any time; breakfast – the best available croissants and *confitures* – arrives on a tray beautifully laid with English porcelain.

Bobette Compagnon, the arbiter of all this exquisite taste, is obviously intent on making the most of her hotel, organizing 'theme' weekends – perhaps including visits to the opera – and putting on exhibitions of contemporary artists' work in the sitting-room.

Nearby Montparnasse tower; Postal Museum; Jardin du Luxembourg; Blvd St-Germain within easy walking distance.

9 Rue Ste-Beuve 75006 Paris
Tel (1) 45.48.20.07
Location between Blvd Montparnasse and Jardin du Luxembourg; car parking in Blvd Montparnasse
Meals breakfast; cold dishes available at all times
Prices rooms 550F-880F
Rooms 22 double (9 twin), all with bath; all rooms have phone, TV, minibar, safe
Facilities sitting-room
Credit cards AE, DC, MC, V
Children accepted
Disabled no special facilities
Pets small dogs accepted
Closed never
Proprietor Bobette Compagnon

Paris

Récamier

A cheap and cheerful hotel overlooking the shady backwater of Place St-Sulpice and the church of the same name. It is one of the quieter hotels of central Paris and, although somewhat austere from the outside, it is welcoming within. One of the two small sitting-rooms doubles up as a breakfast room, and anyone worried about the absence of a bar can rest assured that there are plenty of watering-holes nearby – this is, after all, St-Germain-des-Prés. Bedrooms are small and modern, and all have been recently redecorated. All in all, a sensible choice as a quiet, central and reasonably priced base.

Nearby Luxembourg Palace and gardens; St-Germain-des-Prés – cafés, shops; church of St-Sulpice; Delacroix Museum.

3 bis Place St-Sulpice 75006 Paris
Tel (1) 43.26.04.89
Location near Luxembourg Palace and Blvd St-Germain; public car parking in square
Meals breakfast
Prices rooms 200F-350F
Rooms 30 double (13 twin), 11 with bath, 11 with shower; 1 single; 1 family room with bath; all rooms have central heating, phone
Facilities 2 sitting-rooms
Credit cards not accepted
Children accepted by arrangement
Disabled lift/elevator
Pets not accepted
Closed never
Proprietor G Dauphin

Welcome

What better location for a left-bank hotel (unless peace is your priority) then on the corner of the Boulevard St-Germain and the bustling, colourful Rue de Seine, with its food shops and stalls? The Welcome's first-floor sitting-room, done out in rustic style, looks out on to both streets – as do some of the bedrooms above, which share its triangular shape. The bedrooms are small but prettily decorated, and the even smaller bathrooms do not lack polish or facilities. The top-floor rooms are in the mansard roof space, with attendant shortage of headroom. The welcome is warm.

Nearby Luxembourg Gardens.

66 Rue de Seine 75006 Paris
Tel (1) 46.34.24.80
Location just off Boulevard St-Germain towards Seine; with public car parking nearby
Meals breakfast
Prices rooms 350F-410F
Rooms 26 double, 17 with shower, 9 with bathroom (9 twin); 4 single with shower; all rooms have central heating, phone, TV
Facilities sitting-room
Credit cards not accepted
Children accepted
Disabled access difficult, small lift/elevator
Pets not accepted
Closed never
Proprietor M. Henneveux

Paris

Town hotel, Paris

Hôtel du Vieux Marais

Completely renovated in 1979 (both inside and out) by the friendly Rumiels family, this tall townhouse offers reasonably priced accommodation which is both comfortable and stylish – in an area of the city which remains short of hotels despite its recent transformation from near-slum to fashionable residence. The street in which it lies is not notably attractive, but it is quiet, despite its convenience for right-bank sightseeing. The bedrooms were being refurbished again last year, so by now they (and their light, modern bathrooms) should be as fresh and bright as ever.

Nearby Hôtel de Ville, Beaubourg (Pompidou centre), Les Halles, Rue de Rivoli, Place des Vosges, Ile de la Cité.

8 Rue du Plâtre 75004 Paris
Tel (1) 42.78.47.22
Location close to the Hôtel de Ville and Place des Vosges; with public car parking nearby
Meals breakfast
Prices rooms 225F-500F
Rooms 16 double (4 twin), 6 family rooms, all with bath; 8 single, all with shower; all rooms have central heating, phone
Facilities breakfast room, sitting-room
Credit cards not accepted
Children accepted
Disabled no special facilities
Pets not accepted
Closed never
Proprietor Mme Rumiel

Town hotel, Paris

Hôtel Mayflower

Under the same ownership as the Lord Byron and right next door to it, the Mayflower shares the same refined but relaxed atmosphere and, not surprisingly, is similarly well run. It lacks the Lord Byron's attraction of a courtyard, but to some extent compensates with a sitting-room (doubling as a breakfast room) which is unusually elegant and comfortable for a Paris bed-and-breakfast, with comfy sofas and low tables. Bedrooms, in a mix of styles, are pretty and calm, and mainly spacious – as are the bathrooms.

Nearby Arc de Triomphe, Champs Elysées, Blvd Haussmann (Jacquemart-André Museum, shopping), Ave Foch (Armenian Museum), Bois de Boulogne.

3 Rue de Chateaubriand 75008 Paris
Tel (1) 45.62.57.46
Location close to Arc de Triomphe and Champs Elysées; public car parking nearby
Meals breakfast
Prices rooms 390F-550F
Rooms 18 double (5 twin), 6 single, all with bath; all rooms have central heating, phone, TV, minibar
Facilities sitting-room, breakfast area
Credit cards MC, V
Children accepted
Disabled lift/elevator, but access difficult
Pets accepted
Closed never
Proprietor Mme Coisne

Paris

Thoumieux

Thoumieux lies in the shadow of the Eiffel tower. It is essentially a restaurant-with-rooms, the focal point being the jolly bistro: the house-wine is drinkable, while the the country-style cooking (*andouillettes, boudin, rillettes, cassoulet au confit de canard*) is good and cheap. The fairly spacious bedrooms are modern and comfortable, with attractive fabrics and crisp, Italian-style furniture. There is a pleasant breakfast/sitting-room, decorated in shades of grey. An efficient, friendly place.

Nearby Hôtel des Invalides – military museum; Rodin museum; Palais de Chaillot and gardens.

79 Rue St-Dominique 75007 Paris
Tel (1) 47.05.49.75
Location between Eiffel Tower and Les Invalides; with public car parking nearby
Meals breakfast, lunch, dinner
Prices rooms 450F; meals about 120F
Rooms 4 double, all with bath (all twin); 6 single, all with bath; all rooms have central heating, TV, phone, radio
Facilities 2 sitting-rooms, dining-room
Credit cards AE, V
Children accepted
Disabled no special facilities
Pets accepted
Closed Mon
Proprietor Jean Bassalert

Hôtel Etoile Pereire

The Etoile Pereire is well placed both for motorists (take the Porte de Champerret exit from the Périphérique) and air travellers – the Air France terminal is a short taxi-ride away. The hotel has been smartly done out in a restrained modern style – plain pale walls, glass tables and low armchairs on polished floors in the little sitting-room, a slightly clubby atmosphere (dark velvet armchairs) in the little bar, delicately austere decoration in the immaculate bedrooms. Note the wide range of prices: some of the rooms are split-level, with living as well as sleeping space. Breakfast is an *à la carte* affair – something of a treat, but not cheap.

Nearby Arc de Triomphe, Champs-Elysées, Bois de Boulogne.

146 Blvd Pereire 75017 Paris
Tel (1) 42.67.60.00.
Location on broad boulevard in residential area, close to Périphérique, NW of middle; with garage parking (70F for 24hr)
Meals breakfast
Prices rooms 400F-800F
Rooms 26 double, 23 with bath, 3 with shower (6 twin); all rooms have central heating, phone, TV, minibar
Facilities bar, sitting-room, conference room
Credit cards AE, DC, MC, V
Children accepted; cots available
Disabled no special facilities
Pets not accepted
Closed never
Manager Feruccio Pardi

Paris

Hôtel Verneuil-St-Germain

Long established but completely renovated in 1987, the Verneuil-St-Germain – between the Blvd St-Germain and the river, not far fro– the marvellous new Musée d'Orsay – initially makes a great impression, with its Manhattan-style reception rooms. Classical statues on a polished wooden floor are reflected in a wall of mirrored glass which contrasts with other walls of cream-painted stone and a ceiling of exposed beams. Furnishings are imaginative, with richly striped curtains, and attractive sofas and armchairs in spotted and Paisley prints.

The bedrooms, disappointingly, are something of an anti-climax, lacking the promise of the stylish ground floor; they are smart but unexceptional, uniformly decorated with pastel-coloured wallpapers and stripey curtains and bedspreads. Ask for a good-sized room – some are very small. The marble-tiled bathrooms are well equipped – there seems to be a craze for wall-mounted hairdriers just now. In the basement there is an attractive stone-walled breakfast room, with appropriately traditional-style furniture; breakfast is copious, including fruit juice and croissants.

Nearby Musée d'Orsay, Tuileries, Louvre, Ile de la Cité, Notre Dame, St-Germain-des-Prés.

8 Rue de Verneuil 75007 Paris
Tel (1) 42.60.82.14
Location in middle of St-Germain-des-Prés; in quiet street with public car parking nearby
Meals breakfast
Prices rooms 370F-550F
Rooms 21 double (4 twin), 5 family rooms, all with bath; all rooms have central heating, TV, phone, radio, alarm
Facilities breakfast room, 2 sitting-rooms
Credit cards AE, V
Children welcome; baby-sitting available
Disabled no special facilities
Pets welcome if well behaved
Closed never
Proprietor Mme Chekroun

Hôtel Émile Pereire (see opposite)

Paris

Family

In the same street as the famous house of Chanel, this is a truly bourgeois hotel incongruously placed in Paris's most exclusive *quartier*. In recent years it has all seemed a trifle faded, which has only added to the charm of the place – the huge, well kept bedrooms have accommodated a real hotchpotch of furniture, from good antique bureaux to cheap 1950s armchairs. But we understand that a major renovation will take place for 1989, and the result is not at this stage predictable. As the name implies, this is a good choice for a family, though there is no restaurant. You could couple a stay here with a meal at Le Trumilou (84, Quai de l'Hôtel de Ville, 4ieme), a lovely bistro with much the same old-fashioned appeal – and prices – as the Family Hotel.

Nearby Tuileries; Louvre; Champs Elysées; Place Vendôme; Place Madeleine; Opéra; Faubourg St-Honoré – shopping.

35 Rue Cambon 75001 Paris
Tel (1) 42.61.54.84
Location between Jardin des Tuileries and Blvd des Capucines; public car parking nearby
Meals breakfast
Prices rooms 350F-450F
Rooms 23 double (9 twin), 2

single, 1 suite; all with bath; all rooms have central-heating, phone, TV
Credit cards V
Children accepted
Disabled lift/elevator
Pets not accepted
Closed never
Proprietor Mme Steinbech

Hôtel de Lutèce

Roland Buffat has two success stories on the Ile-St-Louis – the Deux-Isles (*qv*) and the Lutèce. (He was also the owner of the St-Louis until quite recently.) This is the younger of the hotels, and like its sister has been converted from one of the island's original townhouses. The foyer and salon have something of the feel of a Provençal country house, with flagstone floor, beamed ceiling (originally from a Louis XIV château), bouquets of flowers and a stone fireplace where log fires roar in winter. What bedrooms lack in space (most are decidedly small) they make up for in charming decoration and antique furnishings. Prices are relatively high, but for a combination of prime location and country-house charm the Lutèce is a good choice. There is no bar here, but guests can use the one at the Deux-Isles down the road.

Nearby Church of St Louis-en-l'Ile, Notre-Dame, Conciergerie, Bastille, Place des Vosges, Blvd St-Germain, Hôtel de Ville.

65 Rue St-Louis-en-l'Ile 75004 Paris
Tel (1) 43.26.23.52
Location on l'Ile-St-Louis
Meals breakfast
Prices rooms 555F
Rooms 23 double, 13 with bath, 10 with shower (10

twin); all rooms have TV, phone, hairdrier
Facilities sitting-room
Credit cards not accepted
Children accepted
Disabled no special facilities
Pets accepted **Closed** never
Proprietor M. Buffat

Paris

Hôtel Riboutté Lafayette

One of a chain of six, this small cheerfully furnished hotel lies close to the Rue Lafayette – convenient for nightlife and department stores. Public rooms consist of reception and small salon, prettily furnished in rattan and bamboo, floral fabrics, plants and bouquets of flowers. Bedrooms are small, friendly and individual – some with painted-wood furnishings, others with floral fabrics and lithographs. All the rooms are quiet, whether overlooking the courtyard or the street (windows are double-glazed), and the atmosphere is almost provincial. This is not one of the most conspicuous of the city's charming small hotels, but worth considering as a cheap and cheerful base.

Nearby Folies Bergères; a short walk away is the Opéra, Blvd Haussman and church of Sacré-Coeur.

5 Rue Riboutté 75009 Paris
Tel (1) 47.70.62.36
Location NE of middle of city, close to Gare du Nord; with car parking nearby
Meals breakfast
Prices rooms 280F-310F
Rooms 18 double, 5 with bath, 13 with shower (6 twin); one single with shower; 5 family rooms, with shower; all rooms have TV, phone
Facilities 2 sitting-rooms
Credit cards V
Children accepted
Disabled no special facilities
Pets dogs accepted
Closed never
Manager Mme Claudine Gourd

Hotel d'Angleterre

There is a good reason why the Angleterre is so named – the 18thC building was once the British Embassy. And there is still something faintly British about it. It is in a lively area of the Left Bank, but the bedrooms are peaceful, all overlooking a delightful white courtyard with creeping ivy, camelias and a white marble fountain. You can take drinks on pretty ratan chairs in the shade of parasols, or in the bar next door. There are also a civilized, rather formal sitting-room and a charming breakfast room. Many of the bedrooms have recently been refurbished; they are not cheap, but not bad value.

Nearby Delacroix Museum, church of St-Germain-des-Prés, Blvd St-Germain (shops, cafés), Louvre, Ile de la Cité.

44 Rue Jacob 75006 Paris
Tel (1) 42.60.34.72
Location between Seine and Blvd St-Germain, near St-Germain des Prés; with garden
Meals breakfast
Prices rooms 440F-700F, suites 800F-1000F
Rooms 27 double (12 twin), 2 suites, all with bath or shower; all rooms have central heating, phone, TV
Facilities sitting-room
Credit cards AE, DC, MC, V
Children accepted
Disabled 2 ground-floor rooms and lift/elevator
Pets not accepted
Closed never
Proprietor Mme Soumier

Paris

Hôtel Solférino

This is one of the few simple and modestly priced establishments in an area of high-priced hotels. The Left Bank location, on a quiet street close to the Seine and Place de la Concorde, is highly desirable. Built as a private residence 150 years ago, the Solférino today is a small and welcoming family-run hotel with a blend of classical and modern styles in its furnishings. Oil paintings, traditional furniture and carpets are features of the small, high-ceilinged salon; while the breakfast room is light and summery, with plenty of plants. Bedrooms are simple and on the small side, but quiet and prettily furnished.

Nearby Place de la Concorde, Champs E'lysées, Musée d'Orsay, Hôtel des Invalides, Tuileries, Louvre.

91 Rue de Lille 75007 Paris
Tel (1) 47.05.85.54
Location in middle of city, across river from Tuileries; with public car parking nearby
Meals breakfast
Prices rooms 205F-500F
Rooms 27 double, with bath (6 twin); some can take extra bed; 6 single, with shower; all rooms have phone
Facilities sitting-room, breakfast room
Credit cards MC, V
Children accepted
Disabled access difficult
Pets not accepted
Closed never
Proprietor Jean-Paul Cornic

Hôtel de l'Université

Skilfully converted from a town mansion, this popular hotel is in a peaceful and characteristic area of St-Germain-des-Prés. Furnishings throughout are in sober good taste. Authentic exposed beams, wooden doors, antiques and tapestries are features of the foyer, and there are period furnishings in all the rooms. Breakfast is taken at small marble tables overlooking a delightful inner courtyard with flowers and fountain. Bedrooms vary considerably in size and style, ranging from the plainer rooms with shower to luxury apartments with a private terrace; prices vary accordingly. Quietest rooms are at the back and the most luxurious are on the top floor. Book well in advance.

Nearby Louvre, Tuileries, Musée d'Orsay, Ile de la Cité.

22 Rue de l'Université 75007 Paris
Tel (1) 42.61.09.39
Location in St-Germain-des-Prés; public car parking nearby
Meals breakfast, light snacks
Prices rooms 280F-900F
Rooms 21 double, 17 with bath, 4 with shower (12 twin); 7 single, 3 with bath, 4 with shower; all rooms have phone; TV on request
Facilities sitting-room, breakfast room
Credit cards not accepted
Children accepted, but no family-size rooms
Disabled access difficult
Pets not accepted
Closed never
Proprietor Mme Bergmann

Paris

Town hotel, Paris

Hôtel des Deux Iles

The enchanting Ile-St-Louis is one of the most desirable addresses in the city and has long been a popular residential area for wealthy and well-known Parisians (Pompidou among them).

The Deux Iles is one of two hotels in the same street owned and run by Roland Buffat (see also the Lutece). Over a decade ago he converted this 17thC townhouse into what is now one of the most popular small hotels in the city – particularly among those looking for a prime location, combined with charm and individuality. Rooms need to be booked several weeks in advance – and that applies all year round.

It is a far from spacious hotel, but imaginative decoration (M. Buffat is an interior designer by trade) and the private-house atmosphere make up for the smallish size of the rooms. Reception and lounge are particularly attractive: a glassed-in area of plants and flowers gives a tropical feel. The bedrooms (and matching bathrooms) are often decorated in blue and white, and furnished with bamboo and Provençal fabrics. Continuing the theme, the cut-above-average breakfasts are served from blue and white china. The downstairs bar, with its cosy fireplace and relaxing chairs, is a popular haunt for locals.

Nearby Church of St-Louis-en-l'Ile; Boulevard Saint-Germain; l'Ile de la Cité – Notre Dame; Rue de Rivoli.

59 Rue St-Louis-en-l'Ile
75004 Paris
Tel (1) 43.26.13.35
Location on island in the Seine; car parking nearby
Meals breakfast
Prices rooms 455F-555F
Rooms 13 double, 12 with bath, one with shower (4 twin); 4 single, all with shower; all rooms have TV, phone
Facilities bar, sitting-rooms
Credit cards not accepted
Children accepted
Disabled no special facilities
Pets accepted
Closed never
Proprietor Roland Buffat

Paris

Hôtel Agora

This unassuming hotel (without a restaurant) has a range of attractions. Its location in Les Halles – central and full of Parisian life – is good for sightseers and shoppers alike. With its flowery entrance (leading to reception on the first floor) and lacey curtains it is a hotel which contrives to be old-fashioned; yet in other ways it seems modern and even slightly chic. The practical necessities are looked after – all is thoroughly clean, and rooms are well sound-proofed. Furnishings are antique, and the walls are hung with old engravings. Prices are reasonable for Paris and the welcome is friendly. Hard to beat for a simple base in an ideal area.

Nearby Les Halles, Pompidou centre, Ile de la Cité.

7 Rue de la Cossonerie
75001 Paris
Tel (1) 42.33.46.02
Location between Forum des Halles and Blvd Sebastopol; with public car parking nearby
Meals breakfast
Prices rooms 250F-450F
Rooms 27 double, 4 with bath, 23 with shower (12 twin); 2 single, one with bath, one with shower; all rooms have central heating, phone; 5 rooms have TV
Credit cards AE
Children welcome if well behaved **Disabled** access difficult: lift/elevator on first floor **Pets** not accepted
Closed never
Proprietor Claude Fresnel

Hôtel Lenox

Built at the end of the last century, the Lenox started its life as a *pension*, taking in literary figures of the time (James Joyce, for example). Today it is chic and civilized, providing comfortable rooms at reasonable prices. Decoration is in keeping with the style of the building: there are palm trees in the bar, chintz and marble in the salon, English fabrics in the small but elegant bedrooms. The Rue de l'Université is a characteristic street of St-Germain-des-Prés and a particularly good location if you enjoy browsing around book shops and antique galleries.

Nearby Place St Germain-des-Prés – street performers; Rue de Buci and Rue de Seine – food-market; café Procope – haunt of Molière, Racine, Voltaire, Balzac and Anatole France.

9 Rue de l'Université 75007 Paris
Tel (1) 42.96.10.95
Location in St-Germain-des-Prés
Meals breakfast
Prices rooms 380F-530F
Rooms 34 double, 26 with bath, 8 with shower (12 twin); all rooms have TV, phone, central heating
Facilities bar, sitting-room
Credit cards AE, DC, MC, V
Children accepted
Disabled no special facilities
Pets not accepted
Closed never
Proprietor Michel Grenet

Paris

Molière

The Molière may or may not be the oldest hotel in Paris, as it is said to be, but it is certainly among the most charmingly traditional in style and friendly in atmosphere. We must hope that these qualities will not have been sacrificed on the altar of modernity by the time this edition is published – the hotel has recently come under new management, and is about to be thoroughly renovated. Some of the gloomier bedrooms would definitely benefit from brightening up, so there are sure to be gains on that front. The hotel has an excellent right-bank situation, close to sights and shopping.

Nearby Opéra, Louvre, Tuileries, Jardin du Palais Royal, Comedie Français, Place Vendôme, Les Halles, Bourse.

21 Rue Molière 75001 Paris
Tel (1) 42.96.22.01
Location near Palais Royal, on road between Rue de Richelieu and Ave de l'Opéra; with public parking nearby
Meals breakfast
Prices rooms 300F-550F
Rooms 20 double (8 twin), 12 with shower, 8 with bath;

9 family-rooms, 3 single, all with bath; TV, phone
Facilities sitting-room, bar
Credit cards AE, DC, MC, V
Children accepted
Disabled lift/elevator
Pets not accepted
Closed never
Manager Rémy Perraud

Hôtel de Varenne

Situated right beside Les Invalides and close to the Blvd St-Germain, the Hôtel de Varenne is in a near-perfect spot for sightseeing or (more especially) for sitting at pavement cafés watching the world go by. The outside is unassuming and the interior is not the ultimate in style; but it is well cared for, with fresh flowers and pot plants in evidence, and has a friendly, welcoming ambience. There is a small courtyard for summer breakfasts, giving the place a peaceful, countryside appeal. Bedroom furnishings are modern and routine, but the rooms are nicely decorated and fairly spacious.

Nearby Hôtel des Invalides – military museum; Rodin Museum, Musée d'Orsay, Place de la Concorde, Tuileries, Louvre.

44 Rue de Bourgogne 75007 Paris
Tel (1) 45.51.45.55
Location between Hôtel des Invalides and Blvd St-Germain; with public car parking nearby
Meals breakfast
Prices rooms 300F-420F
Rooms 20 double, 11 with bath, 9 with shower (6 twin);

4 single with shower; 3 family rooms; all rooms have central heating, phone, TV
Facilities sitting-room
Credit cards AE, V
Children accepted
Disabled access easy; lift/elevator
Pets accepted at extra charge
Closed never
Proprietor M. Jamim

Paris

Hôtel des Célestins

The heart of the city in the 17thC, the Marais is now a quiet, civilized area of squares and old mansions, many restored to their former glory. The Hotel des Célestins is one of the more modest places in the area – a small, old building standing on a quiet corner close to the Bastille, and not far from the delightful Place des Vosges. Facilities are limited (there is no sitting-room) and bedrooms are far from spacious. But the pretty decoration (antiques, beams and chintzes) and friendly atmosphere make this a sound choice if you are looking for a peaceful, modestly priced base.

Nearby The Bastille; Victor Hugo museum; Picasso museum; Jewish quarter; Carnavalet museum.

1 Rue Charles V 75004 Paris
Tel (1) 48.87.87.04
Location between Place des Vosges and L'Ile Saint Louis; with car parking
Meals breakfast
Prices rooms 280F-450F
Rooms 11 double, 7 with bath, 4 with shower (2 twin); 4 single, all with shower; all rooms have central heating,
phone
Facilities sitting-area in reception
Credit cards V
Children accepted by arrangement
Disabled no special facilities
Pets not accepted
Closed Aug
Proprietor Mme Jacquemin

Hôtel des Grandes Ecoles

A cobbled lane reached through wooden gates leads you into the delightful garden which surrounds the main house and two annexes of this Left Bank hotel, which retains to an incredible degree the ambience of a country house. The name refers to the nearby Sorbonne and Faculté des Sciences; the hotel itself is anything but grand. Bedrooms are pleasantly simple, all over-looking the peaceful garden, and the reception is a cosy, welcoming area. Breakfast, if you want it, is taken in a tiny dining-room. Prices here are hard to beat – very popular with students.

Nearby Boulevard Saint Germain; Ile Saint Louis; Ile de la Cité – Notre Dame; Luxembourg Palace and gardens.

75 Rue de Cardinal Lemoine 75005 Paris
Tel (1) 43.26.79.23
Location in the Latin quarter; with garden and car parking
Meals breakfast
Prices rooms 170F-450F
Rooms 39 double, 24 with bath, 7 with shower (4 twin); one single; 7 family rooms, 6 with bath, one with shower;
all rooms have central heating, phone
Facilities breakfast-room, sitting-room
Credit cards AE, DC, MC, V
Children welcome if well behaved
Disabled no special facilities
Pets welcome if well behaved
Closed never
Proprietor Mme le Floch

Paris

Résidence du Bois

There are few hotels in Paris (or in any other large city) that can boast the tranquil setting and refined atmosphere of the Résidence du Bois. Mme Desponts does her best to ensure that guests feel at home, rather than being lost in the anonymity of a stereo-typed hotel, and she certainly succeeds. Sitting out in the quiet flowery garden or immersed in the opulent surroundings of the salon, you are a world away from the city-hotel norm. What makes the Résidence all the more remarkable is that it is located only a stone's throw from the Etoile – on the opposite side to the Champs E'lysées.

The house was built as a private mansion during the Third Empire, and still has all the charm of an old residence. The setting is exceptionally quiet and serene for a city, and the bed-rooms are large and luxurious with big beds, silk and velvet fabrics, period pieces and excellent bathrooms. There are two salons, with handsome Empire furnishings, tapestries and bouquets of flowers. In winter these rooms can be used for light meals, but in summer you can sit and eat out in the garden – an ideal retreat after a frenetic day in the city.

This is not a place for those on a budget; not only are the rooms expensive, but breakfast adds 135F and Mme Desponts' snacks start at 150F.

Nearby Arc de Triomphe, Champs E'lysées, Bois de Boulogne.

16 Rue Chalgrin 75116 Paris **Tel** (1) 45.00.50.59 **Location** between Ave Foch and Ave de la Grande Armée; with garden; garage parking 10 minutes' walk away **Meals** breakfast, simple meals on request **Prices** rooms 940F-1,640F; meals 150F-700F **Rooms** 18 double, 16 with	bath, 2 with shower (9 twin); one single with shower; all rooms have central heating, phone **Facilities** 2 sitting-rooms, bar **Credit cards** not accepted **Children** welcome **Disabled** access difficult **Pets** welcome **Closed** never **Proprietor** Mme Desponts

Hôtel des Grands Ecoles (see opposite)

Paris

Town hotel, Paris

Hôtel Prince Albert

Reasonably priced rooms of any comfort are hard to come by in the 1st *arrondissement* of Paris (the best-value hotels are nearly all on the Left Bank or in the less desirable quarters of the Right Bank). The Prince Albert, a very small hotel lying roughly halfway between the Louvre and the Opéra, is an exception. As the name suggests, this is a hotel reminiscent of Victorian England and, not surprisingly, it is popular with the British. The sitting-room is welcoming; the corridors upstairs are rather dim, but lead to bedrooms that are well cared for and comfortable – the majority with their own bathrooms.

Nearby L'Orangerie; Tuileries gardens; Place Vendôme.

5 Rue St-Hyacinthe 75001 Paris
Tel (1) 42.61.58.36
Location between Rue de Rivoli and the Opéra; car parking nearby
Meals breakfast
Prices rooms 280F-380F
Rooms 21 double, 20 with bath, one with shower (6 twin); 10 single, all with bath; 2 family rooms with bath; all rooms have central heating, TV, phone, minibar, safe
Facilities sitting-room, breakfast room
Credit cards MC, V
Children accepted
Disabled no special facilities
Pets not accepted
Closed never
Proprietor M. Aubert

Town hotel, Paris

Hôtel Gaillon Opéra

The first reason for the well established popularity of the Gaillon Opéra must be its central location – just a stone's throw from l'Opéra itself, in the heart of the Right Bank shopping district and close to many important sights. But there are other attractions as well. The salon displays the old stone walls and beams of the original 19thC building, and there is a reassuringly rustic feeling about the place as a whole. Bedrooms are neither very light nor spacious – especially at the top of the house, where rooms have been made in the roof-space – but they are warmly and tastefully furnished, many with beams and floral fabrics. Bathrooms are modern and well equipped. Although not expensive for the area, it cannot be called a cheap hotel; but it is a cut above the average in terms of comfort as well as charm.

Nearby Louvre, Opéra, Place Vendôme, Tuileries, Place de la Madeleine, Les Halles.

9 Rue Gaillon 75002 Paris
Tel (1) 47.42.47.74
Location 100 m SE of L'Opéra
Meals breakfast
Prices rooms 460F-590F
Rooms 26 double, all with bath and shower (9 twin); central heating, TV, phone
Facilities sitting-room
Credit cards AE, DC, V
Children accepted
Disabled no special facilities
Pets accepted
Closed never
Managers M. and Mme Wolecki

Paris

St-Dominique

Every year, as in other big cities, various run-down Parisian hotels undergo dramatic face-lifts in the hands of new owners, many aiming more for panache than perfection. The St-Dominique, mercifully, has side-stepped the usual modern glossy design clichés in favour of freshness, simplicity and honest service. No minimalist reception desks or wall-to-wall mirrors here; instead a couple of deep salmon-pink armchairs, a hessian covered floor with a Persian rug, a pine dresser, mirror, fresh flowers. Wooden stairs lead down to a little basement breakfast room with comfy banquette seats and Lloyd loom chairs. The hotel's exterior is eye-catching: a green door flanked by two large paned windows.

Bedrooms are well equipped, with TVs and refrigerators. But in style they echo the simplicity of the public rooms, with sprigged wallpaper and white covers on the comfy beds, and neat white bathrooms. Harmonious pop music plays in the reception area, where staff are young and friendly. Breakfasts are generous and beautifully presented.

Nearby Hôtel des Invalides (military museum), Rodin Museum, Musée d'Orsay, Blvd-St-Germain, church of St-Germain des Prés, Place de la Concorde, Tuileries.

62 Rue St-Dominique 75007 Paris
Tel (1) 47.05.51.44
Location on busy street between Les Invalides and the Eiffel Tower; with patio, and car parking nearby
Meals breakfast
Prices rooms 350F-490F; extra child's bed 60F
Rooms 34 double (10 twin), 14 with bath, 20 with shower; all rooms have central heating, TV, phone, minibar
Facilities sitting-room, breakfast room
Credit cards AE, DC, MC, V
Children accepted
Disabled lift/elevator
Pets accepted
Closed never
Proprietor Alain Michaud

Hôtel Gaillon Opéra (see opposite)

Paris

La Régence-Etoile

The Régence Etoile occupies a 'listed' 1875 house, and is decorated and furnished in suitably traditional style. The bedrooms are mostly spacious and comfortable (those at the front of the house more airy but also more noisy than those at the back – the Ave Carnot is quite a thoroughfare), with smart bathrooms. And there is more space for sitting than is common in Parisian bed-and-breakfast places. The hotel has been family-run since it opened in the 1940s, and Mme Larre's son now assists in the management. The location is convenient for sights west of centre.

Nearby Arc de Triomphe, Champs Elysées, Ave Foch, Bois de Boulogne – Longchamps racecourse and other attractions.

24 Ave Carnot 75017 Paris
Tel (1) 43.80.75.60
Location close to Arc de Triomphe, on one of the roads radiating from it; with public car parking nearby
Meals breakfast
Prices rooms 315F-450F (extra bed 100F)
Rooms 33 double (8 twin), 29 with bath 4 with shower; 5 family rooms with bath; all rooms have central heating, phone, TV
Facilities sitting-room, TV room, bar
Credit cards AE, DC, MC, V
Children accepted
Disabled lift/elevator
Pets not accepted
Closed never
Proprietor Mme J Larre

Hôtel St-Merry

This former presbytery of the Church of St-Merry, next door, was converted to a private residence after the 1789 revolution, and more recently to a highly individual hotel by the charming M. Crabbe. It is not a place for those who put comfort before character: some of the rooms are distinctly small, and in one a flying buttress forms an alarmingly low canopy over the bed. Stone and dark carved wood predominate, with muted and often plain fabrics; the Gothic style is heavy and may not appeal to all tastes. Set in a revitalised area of Paris that is filled with interesting architecture both ancient and modern, the St-Merry fits in well.

Nearby Ile de la Cité – Notre Dame; Pompidou centre.

78 Rue de la Verrerie 75004 Paris
Tel (1) 42.78.14.15
Location in the Marais, close to Rue de Rivoli; with public car parking nearby
Meals breakfast
Prices rooms 320F-580F
Rooms 10 double, one with bath, 5 with shower (4 twin); 2 family rooms, both with shower; all rooms have central heating, phone
Facilities separate bar beneath hotel
Credit cards not accepted
Children accepted **Disabled** no special facilities **Pets** accepted
Closed never
Proprietor Christian Crabbe

Paris

Résidence Lord Byron

In an area dominated by grand and impersonal hotels, the Byron stands out for its personal service and (by local standards) reasonable prices. Bedrooms are modern and rather bland in decoration, with a mixture of old and new furnishings; they tend to be smallish (bigger ones are described as 'small apartments') but they are clean, comfortable and pleasant – many of them overlook the pretty courtyard where breakfast is served on sunny days. A cool and elegant reception area, tastefully furnished with antiques, links this patio with the dignified entrance; there is also a somewhat anonymous sitting-room.

Nearby Arc de Triomphe, Champs Elysées, Blvd Haussmann.

5 Rue de Chateaubriand 75008 Paris **Tel** (1) 43.59.89.98 **Location** between Ave Friedland and Champs Elysées; with garden, and car parking in Champs Elysées **Meals** breakfast **Prices** rooms 420F-720F **Rooms** 23 double (12 twin), 19 with bath, 4 with shower;	2 single with shower; 6 family rooms with bath; all rooms have central heating, phone, TV, minibar **Facilities** breakfast room, sitting-room **Credit cards** MC, V **Children** accepted **Disabled** lift/elevator **Pets** not accepted **Closed** never **Proprietor** Mme Coisne

Hôtel des Marronniers

This tall, gracious hotel, set between a courtyard and a rear garden containing the eponymous horse-chestnut trees, brings the calm of the country into the heart of bustling St-Germain. The inside is country-style too – birds and leaves decorate every available surface, and there are fresh flowers in the spacious stone-vaulted cellars which form the breakfast room and sitting-room that are cosily furnished with rugs and antiques. Bedrooms are similarly furnished, brightly decorated but variable in size. The glazed veranda, overlooking the garden, is the perfect place to laze or read or have breakfast.

Nearby Blvd St-Germain – church of St-Germain-des-Prés; Ile de la Cité – Notre Dame, Conciergerie; Musée d'Orsay.

21 Rue Jacob 75006 Paris **Tel** (1) 43.25.30.60 **Location** between the Seine and Blvd Saint-Germain; with small garden, and public car parking nearby **Meals** breakfast **Prices** rooms 285F-440F, family rooms 455F-675F **Rooms** 30 double (8 twin), 3 single, 3 family rooms; all	with bath or shower; all rooms have central heating, phone **Facilities** breakfast room, sitting-room **Credit cards** not accepted **Children** accepted **Disabled** lift/elevator **Pets** not accepted **Closed** never **Proprietor** M. Henneveux

Paris

Hôtel Prima-Lepic

Set in bustling Montmartre, just 5 minutes walk from Sacré-Coeur, this is a family-run bed and breakfast place. The ground-floor reception and breakfast area is done out as a sort of indoor courtyard, with plenty of green plants, flowers, light walls and ceiling, white garden chairs and tables – giving an airy and peaceful effect even if it doesn't provide the greatest comfort. Bedrooms are individually and well decorated, with a mixture of modern and antique furniture – although they are not over-spacious. Front-facing rooms have recently been double-glazed to cut out street noise. Breakfast is buffet-style, with a choice of breads, croissants and cheeses.

Nearby Sacré-Coeur basilica, Place Pigalle, Moulin Rouge.

29 Rue Lepic 75018 Paris
Tel (1) 46.06.44.64
Location in Montmartre,
with public car parking
nearby
Meals breakfast
Prices rooms 200F-280F
Rooms 33 double (20 twin),
5 family rooms all with bath
or shower; all rooms have
central heating, phone

Facilities sitting-room, bar
Credit cards MC, V
Children accepted
Disabled no special facilities
Pets accepted
Closed never
Proprietors M. and Mme
Mandin

Hôtel de Banville

Finding your way from the Périphérique to the Boulevard Berthier is easy, and parking here does not pose an insoluble problem – so motorists should arrive at the Hôtel de Banville in good humour. Nor will this airy art deco building with flower-filled window boxes dampen your spirits. Inside, all is tastefully decorated and comfortable, bordering on the luxurious. The rooms are not on a grand scale, but light furniture and decorations create a spacious feel; antiques are dotted throughout, and flower arrangements and plants add a reassuring personal touch. Peace is ensured by the efficient sound-proofing.

Nearby Arc de Triomphe, Champs-Elysées, Bois de Boulogne.

166 Blvd Berthier 75017 Paris
Tel (1) 42.67.70.16
Location on service road off
major boulevard, N of Arc
de Triomphe; with garage
and roadside car parking
nearby
Meals breakfast
Prices rooms 450F-480F
Rooms 35 double, 29 with
bath, 6 with shower (13
twin); 4 family rooms, 3 with

bath, one with shower; all
rooms have central heating,
phone, TV, radio
Facilities sitting-room, small
dining-room
Credit cards AE, MC, V
Children welcome; baby-
sitting available
Disabled no special facilities
Pets accepted
Closed never
Proprietor Mme Lambert

Paris

Hôtel Regent's Garden

An elegant 1820s town house, built for Napoléon III's personal physician in what is now (and presumably was then) a chic residential area. The outstanding asset is the shady, peaceful garden, with mature trees, lawn, lavender and tubs of flowers – and tables and chairs for breakfasts on sunny days. But the hotel as a whole is a cut above average in every way – sitting-areas are elegantly decorated in period style, bedrooms are richly furnished (and many of them are enormous), and there is a general air of style and individuality. Not least, there is limited private parking.

Nearby Arc de Triomphe, Champs Elysées, Ave Foch.

6 Rue Pierre-Demours 75017 Paris	shower; 8 suites with bath; all rooms have central
Tel (1) 45.74.07.30	heating, TV, phone, radio,
Location near Place Tristan	minibar, hair-drier
Bernard on Avenue des	**Facilities** 2 breakfast rooms
Ternes, N of Arch de	**Credit cards** AE, DC, MC, V
Triomphe; with garden and	**Children** welcome; under
limited private car parking	12 free
Meals breakfast	**Disabled** lift/elevator
Prices rooms 450F–800F	**Pets** accepted
Rooms 29 double (9 twin),	**Closed** never
all with bath; one single with	**Proprietor** M. Frot

Paris

Town hotel, Paris

Hôtel des Grands Hommes

Since it was built in the 18thC the Grands Hommes has always been a hotel, acquiring its present name because of the surrealist artists and writers who used to stay here (perhaps the best-known among them being André Breton). The building was entirely renovated in 1982, but preserves original features such as exposed beams in the bedrooms, which are individually furnished and thoroughly equipped, with particularly smart bathrooms. Stone-vaulted cellars with a smartly tiled floor now serve as the breakfast room. The lobby is more modern and glossy.

Nearby Panthéon (and its crypt), Luxembourg gardens and palace, Blvd St-Germain; short walk to Notre-Dame.

17 Place du Panthéon 75005 Paris
Tel (1) 46.34.19.60
Location opposite the Panthéon; with public car parking 5 minutes away
Meals breakfast
Prices rooms 400F-650F
Rooms 31 double, all with bath (9 twin); one single with shower; extra beds possible in 10 rooms; all rooms have central heating, TV, radio, minibar, hairdrier
Facilities bar, breakfast room
Credit cards AE, DC, MC, V
Children very welcome; cot and baby-sitting available
Disabled no special facilities
Pets if well behaved
Closed never
Proprietors M. and Mme Brethous

Town hotel, Paris

Hôtel Duc de St-Simon

A stylish hotel on a stylish street, just off the Blvd St-Germain. First glimpsed through two pairs of French windows which open on to a pretty courtyard, the interior looks wonderfully inviting; and so it is – there is a warm, beautifully furnished salon with the distinctly private-house feel that the proprietor seeks to maintain, and elegant yet cosy bedrooms with not a jarring note. Twin bedrooms are more spacious than those with double beds. The white-painted 18thC house backs on to a 19thC building behind, also part of the hotel, with a tiny secret garden wedged in between. Breakfasts are served in your room; service is smiling and courteous.

Nearby Hôtel des Invalides, Musée d'Orsay, church of St-Germain-des-Prés, Rodin Museum.

14 Rue de St-Simon 75007 Paris
Tel (1) 45.48.35.66
Location in St-Germain-des-Prés
Meals breakfast, light meals
Prices rooms 750F-950F; suites 1,000F-1,150F
Rooms 29 double, 28 with bath, one with shower (10 twin); 5 suites, with bath; all rooms have central heating, phone; TV on request
Facilities 2 sitting-rooms, bar
Credit cards not accepted
Children accepted
Disabled no special facilities
Pets not accepted
Closed never
Proprietor M. G Lindqvist

Paris

Hôtel de la Bretonnerie

Paris may have a great many hotels which conform to our requirements but it does not have many small hotels of distinct character. Here is one.

The Bretonnerie is a 17thC townhouse, set in the middle of the picturesque, convenient and (now) fashionable Marais district, and converted with a good deal of sympathy and style. In the public areas and the upper bedrooms there are exposed beams, echoed throughout the house by the sturdy hardwood furniture (some antique, some reproduction). The small basement breakfast and sitting-rooms have a medieval feel, with pale stone vaulted ceilings, iron light fittings, richly coloured fabrics and polished tiled floors. Bedrooms are comfortable and pretty but vary in style; some are arranged with the beds on a mezzanine floor and the 'downstairs' used as a small sitting-area. All have a glossy modern bathroom or shower (most rooms have a bath) and guests will not find any lack of comfort.

Nearby Hôtel de Ville; Pompidou Centre (Beaubourg); Les Halles; Ile de la Cité – Conciergerie, Notre-Dame, Hôtel Dieu.

22 Rue Ste-Croix-de-la-Bretonnerie 75004 Paris
Tel (1) 48.87.77.63
Location in Marais district, off the Rue du Temple, near Hôtel de Ville; with garage car parking nearby
Meals breakfast
Prices rooms 400F-600F
Rooms 28 double (12 twin), 4 single, all with bath or shower; all rooms have central heating, phone, TV
Facilities cellar sitting-room/breakfast room
Credit cards MC, V
Children welcome
Disabled lift/elevator but access difficult
Pets not accepted
Closed never
Proprietor M. P. Sagot

Hôtel des Grands Hommes (see opposite)

Essonne/Seine-et-Marne

Auberge du Moulin de Jarcy

There is nothing very remarkable about this small converted mill. Rooms are simple (no baths or showers) and cooking is modest. The setting, however, *is* exceptional. Only 25 km from Paris, it feels far removed from any city. Built in the 12thC on a secluded island site in the River Yerres, it still retains some of its old beams, fireplaces, and the original mill-wheel. All of the bedrooms overlook the river, and three have private terraces. On warm days, meals can be taken on the riverside terrace; otherwise in the Breton-style dining-room. Run by the same family since 1950, it is a pleasant, friendly inn.

Nearby Châteaux: Vaux-le-Pénil (15 km), Vaux-le-Vicomte.

Rue Boieldieu, Varennes-Jarcy 91480 Quincy-sous-Sénart **Tel** (1) 69.00.89.20 **Location** on an island in the River Yerres, in countryside 3 km W of Brie-Comte-Robert; with garden and private car parking **Meals** breakfast, lunch, dinner **Prices** rooms 150F-180F; menus 80F-120F	**Rooms** 5 double (2 twin); all rooms have central heating **Facilities** 2 dining-rooms **Credit cards** V **Children** accepted **Disabled** access to restaurant only **Pets** accepted in restaurant, but not in bedrooms **Closed** 20 Dec to 15 Jan, 1 Jul to 22 Aug; Mon to Thu **Proprietor** M. Le Moign

Hostellerie de la Clé d'Or

A simple restaurant with rooms: traditional well cooked food, served in ample portions, is the strong point of the Clé d'Or. There is a pretty dining-room with dark-wood furniture and an open fire for winter, and a large shady terrace outside with tables and chairs for summer eating. Bedrooms are mostly in a single-storey annexe and they open out on to the pretty garden – their chief attraction: they are comfortable, with adequate bathrooms, but simple.

Nearby Fontainebleau (10 km) – château and forest.

73 Grande Rue 77630 Barbizon **Tel** (1) 60.66.40.96 **Location** in main street of village, off A6 autoroute; with garden and private car parking **Meals** breakfast, lunch, dinner **Prices** rooms 200F-500F; menus 150F-200F, children's 60F **Rooms** 12 double (3 twin), 8 with bath, 3 with shower; 2	single, 2 family rooms, all with shower; all rooms have central heating, phone, TV; 13 rooms have minibar **Facilities** dining-room, sitting-room, bar, conference room **Credit cards** AE, DC, MC, V **Children** welcome **Disabled** 7 ground-floor bedrooms **Pets** accepted if well behaved **Closed** Sun dinner out of season **Proprietor** Philippe Gayer

Seine-et-Marne

Converted mill, Flagy

Hostellerie du Moulin

In an area short on our kind of hotel, the Moulin stands out as a gem. This imaginatively converted 13thC flour-mill, with gardens and stream, lies in the old farming village of Flagy, about 20 km from Fontainebleau and an hour's drive from Paris. Where possible, features of the old mill (which was grinding corn until the 1950s) have been preserved.

The food is some of the best in the region, drawing plenty of local custom from nearby Montereau (and from farther afield).
Nearby Fontainbleau Château; Sens (40 km) – cathedral.

2 Rue du Moulin, Flagy
77940 Voulx
Tel (1) 60.96.67.89
Location in middle of village, 23 km SE of Fontainebleu; car parking
Meals breakfast, lunch, dinner
Prices rooms 180F-330F (special rates for children); menus from 120F
Rooms 7 double, all with bath (no twins); 3 family rooms, all with bath; all rooms have phone; 3 rooms have TV
Facilities dining-room, bar, sitting-room; fishing
Credit cards AE, DC, V
Children accepted
Disabled access easy to dining-room, but not to bedrooms
Pets accepted
Closed 11 to 23 Sep and 18 Dec to 21 Jan; Sun evening and Mon
Proprietor Claude Scheidecker

Manor-house hotel, Fontenay-Tresigny

Le Manoir

With its half-timbering, steep tiled roof and lush surrounding shrubbery, this mock-Tudor turn-of-the-century mansion could be in the garden of England rather than the Ile de France, at least from the outside. Inside, the impression is emphatically corrected: the decoration and furnishings are distinctively French – rich and ornate, and occasionally gloomy. The bedrooms differ widely in style, so see a selection if the opportunity arises; the best are gloriously spacious and romantic. Fresh pink linen enlivens the grand panelled dining-room, where the increasingly ubiquitous *cuisine classique allègée* is served with due ceremony. Handily placed for both Paris airports.
Nearby Vaux le Vicomte (25 km) – château.

77610 Fontenay-Tresigny
Tel (1) 64.25.91.17
Location in countryside 4 km E of village; ample car parking (and airstrip)
Meals breakfast, lunch, dinner
Prices rooms 400F-800F; menus 200F-350F
Rooms 15 double, 12 with bath, 3 with shower (4 twin); all rooms have phone, TV, minibar
Facilities bar, sitting-room, dining-room, meeting-rooms; heated swimming-pool, tennis
Credit cards AE, DC, MC, V
Children welcome
Disabled access difficult
Pets welcome
Closed mid-Jan to late Mar
Proprietor M. Sourisseau

Pas-de-Calais

Château hotel, Aire-sur-la-Lys

Hostellerie des 3 Mousquetaires

Since it found its way into English guidebooks some years ago, this jolly 19thC château, equidistant from the ferry ports of Boulogne, Calais and Dunkerque, has been unable to meet the demand for its few rooms – bookings have had to be made months ahead. But in 1988 the number of rooms was more than doubled by the conversion of a pavilion in the grounds. With the capacity problem solved, we can only hope that the Venets are able to maintain their exceptional standards.

The hotel is a family-run *logis*, a world away from the classical château pattern. The charming and vigilant Mme Venet is in charge front of house, aided by her daughter-in-law, while husband Marcel and son Philippe prepare regionally based meals offering 'astonishing value' in the spotless open-to-view kitchen. (The cheeseboard is 'magnificent'.) The building is an eccentric mixture of stone-and-brick stripes and pseudo-timbering beneath a steep slate roof, set in a large wooded garden with ponds and streams (ducks and swans) and comfortable chairs dotted about. The interior is traditionally grand in style, the best of the bedrooms (eg 'Milady') huge and elegant; those in the new annexe ones are decorated in a Japanese fashion.

Nearby Aire – Renaissance bailiff's court, collegiate church of St-Pierre; St Omer (20 km) – basilica, fine arts museum.

Château du Fort de la Redoute 62120 Aire-sur-la-Lys
Tel 21.39.01.11
Location in countryside off N43, 2km S of Aire; in parkland, with ample car parking
Meals breakfast, lunch, dinner
Prices rooms 200F-350F; menus 80F-260F
Rooms 26 double (7 twin), 24 with bath, 2 with shower; one family room with bath; all rooms have central heating, TV, phone
Facilities 2 sitting-rooms, 2 dining-rooms, bar
Credit cards AE, MC, V
Children welcome; cots and special menu available
Disabled no special facilities
Pets accepted
Closed late Dec to late Jan; Sun evening and Mon
Proprietors M. and Mme Marcel Venet

Pas-de-Calais

Moulin de Mombreux

This ancient mill, converted to a hotel and restaurant in 1968, has recently expanded enormously by means of a new annexe, and at the same time has been elevated from a three-star to a four-star rating. Not good signs. But, despite these changes, the *auberge* itself still manages to preserve the charm of a picturesque old mill and the setting, alongside the River Bléquin in a large flowery park, is pleasantly rural. The standard of cuisine is well above average and a meal here makes an excellent alternative to nearby Boulogne or Le Touquet.

Nearby St-Omer (10 km); Boulogne (45 km).

Route de Bayenghem 62380 Lumbres
Tel 21.39.62.44
Location in countryside, close to N42, 30 km E of Boulogne; with 3-hectare grounds and car parking
Meals breakfast, lunch, dinner
Prices rooms 100F-550F; menus 175F-280F
Rooms 26 double, 24 with bath (19 twin); 4 single,

2 with bath; all rooms have TV, phone
Facilities dining-room, sitting-room, conference-room, 2 bars
Credit cards AE, DC, MC, V
Children accepted
Disabled one specially equipped bedroom; dining-room on first floor
Pets accepted **Closed** never
Proprietor Jean Marc Gaudry

Château de Montreuil

A substantial country house offering luxurious accommodation and lacking nothing except a French atmosphere (most of the clientele are British, as is Mme Germain). The sitting-rooms and bedrooms are immaculately decorated and furnished with taste; first-floor rooms are worth the extra cost for their space and superior views of the beautiful English-style gardens. The dining-room is decorated in the country manner, and the tables are beautifully laid. Christian Germain's cooking is ambitious and highly regarded; even breakfast is unusually delicious.

Nearby Ramparts (still intact), citadel; Le Touquet (15 km).

4 Chaussée des Capucins 62170 Montreuil-sur-Mer
Tel 21.81.53.04
Location in quiet part of town, 38 km S of Boulogne, off N1; with large garden and ample car parking
Meals breakfast, lunch, dinner
Prices rooms 480F-550F, DB&B 1,100F; menus 245F-285F
Rooms 11 double, 10 with

bath (6 twin); 3 single; 2 family rooms all with bath or shower; all rooms have central heating, phone
Facilities 2 sitting-rooms, dining-room, bar
Credit cards AE, DC, MC, V
Children welcome **Disabled** 3 ground-floor bedrooms
Pets not accepted
Closed mid-Dec to end Jan
Proprietors M. and Mme Germain

Oise/Aisne

La Bannière de France

Not far from the cathedral of Laon lies the Bannière de France, a former coaching inn dating bac† to the 17thC, and with a reputation a few years ago which Paul Lefèvre and his wife have been gradually restoring. The emphasis is on the restaurant – excellent fare (with menus to suit all budgets) served in a suitably traditional setting. There is an extensive wine list including a fine choice of Bordeaux reds. Bedrooms are standard French-flowery in style, some more than usually spacious.

Nearby Cathedral and narrow medieval streets; Reims (50 km).

11 Rue Franklin Roosevelt
02000 Laon
Tel 23.23.21.44
Location in centre of old town, with large garage
Meals breakfast, lunch, dinner
Prices rooms F95-200F; menus 95F-200F, children's 45F
Rooms 12 double, 2 with bath, 3 with shower (4 twin); 7 family rooms, 4 with bath, 2 with shower; all rooms have central heating, phone; rooms with bath or shower have TV
Facilities dining-room, breakfast room, small bar
Credit cards AE, DC, MC, V
Children welcome
Disabled no special facilities
Pets not accepted
Closed 1 May and 20 Dec to 15 Jan
Proprietors M. and Mme Paul Lefèvre

Auberge 'A la Bonne Idée'

This charming *auberge* in a sleepy village amid the Compiègne forest offers excellent food and comfortable rustic surroundings. The 18thC building has been sympathetically decorated and furnished, retaining many of the original features – old stone, beams, fireplaces. Bedrooms, in the main building or in a small annexe, are furnished simply but well, with swish bathrooms and handsome furniture – although they are not large. A lovely garden to the rear has a shady terrace with tables.

Nearby Pierrefonds (5 km) – fortress; Compiègne – château.

3 Rue des Meuniers, St-Jean-aux-Bois 60350 Cuise-la-Motte
Tel 44.42.84.09
Location in country village 10 km SE of Compiègne; with ample private car parking and large garden
Meals breakfast, lunch, dinner
Prices rooms 320F-380F; menus 140F (weekdays), 220F-350F
Rooms 23 double, 22 with bath, one with shower (5 twin); one family room with bath; all rooms have central heating, phone, TV
Facilities dining-room, sitting-room, bar, conference room
Credit cards MC, V
Children accepted if well behaved **Disabled** one bedroom specially equipped
Pets accepted if kept on lead
Closed mid-Jan to mid-Feb
Proprietor M. Royer

Aisne

La Tour du Roy

The history of this handsome, turreted building, perched on the ramparts of Vervins, goes back several centuries. It was here that Henry IV was acknowledged King of France in 1598. Today, the Tour du Roy is a hotel/restaurant of charm and individuality, largely thanks to Annie Desvignes, who skilfully converted it 17 years ago, and runs it with her husband Claude.

Bedrooms are all different in size and style, each one appropriately named – *Les amoureux, Les Cigognes, Belle Epoque, Mimi Pinson*. The most notable (and expensive) among them is 'La Tour', a quaintly furnished room on two levels – circular bedroom above, circular bathroom with a large bath below. The only drawback in some rooms is street noise, in spite of double glazing. Furnishings in the public rooms are somewhat heavy-handed.

Cuisine plays a major role at the Tour du Roy. Menus range from a simple, moderately-priced four-course meal, to a seven-course *menu dégustation* for two, which features dishes such as oysters, lobster and foie gras. And should you want a whole weekend of gluttony, there is the offer of a 'grand week-end gourmand' with a night at the hotel, breakfast, superb dinner – and bottle of champagne thrown in. The Desvignes (and their staff) are warm-hearted hosts.

Nearby 13thC church of Notre Dame, 16thC Town Hall; Laon (55 km) – 12thC cathedral and medieval architecture.

45 Rue du Général Leclerc
02140 Vervins
Tel 23.98.00.11
Location on ramparts of town; with car parking
Meals breakfast, lunch, dinner
Prices rooms 150F-400F; menus 140F-300F
Rooms 13 double, 11 with bath, 2 with shower (3 twin); one single with shower; one family room with bath; all rooms have central heating, TV, phone, minibar
Facilities dining-room, sitting-room
Credit cards AE, DC, V
Children welcome
Disabled one ground-floor bedroom
Pets accepted
Closed mid-Jan to mid-Feb
Proprietors Annie and Claude Desvignes

Bonne Idée (see opposite)

Meurthe-et-Msl. / Marne

Town hotel, Châlons-sur-Marne

Hôtel d'Angleterre

A traditional town hotel from the outside, the Angleterre has been largely modernized inside. Subtle colour schemes predominate. Deep armchairs, low tables and fresh flowers are found in the bar and sitting-room; fresh flowers also adorn the bedrooms, where they face some competition from the fabrics. The dining-room has been transformed, by means of screens, plants and mirrors, into a modern and relaxing place in which to sample Jacky's innovative and successful cooking. On summery days meals are served on a shady terrace.

Nearby Cathedral, church of Notre-Dame-en-Vaux (stained glass).

19 Place Monseigneur Tissier 51000 Châlons-sur-Marne
Tel 26.68.21.51
Location in middle of town, with terrace and small private car park
Meals breakfast, lunch, dinner
Prices rooms 260F-400F; menus 150F-300F
Rooms 16 double, 12 with bath, 4 with shower (6 twin);

2 family rooms; all rooms have central heating, phone, TV, minibar
Facilities dining-room, sitting-room, bar
Credit cards AE, DC, MC, V
Children welcome; cots available
Disabled no special facilities
Pets accepted in restaurant
Closed three weeks Jul; two weeks late Dec to early Jan
Proprietor Jacky Michel

Restaurant with rooms, Liverdun

Hôtel des Vannes et sa Résidence

The star attraction of this restaurant-with-rooms is the glassed-in terrace overlooking a great sweep of the Moselle (floodlit at night), where excellent food (emphasis on fish, highly rated by the gastronomic guides) is served with calm personal attention. A peaceful night's sleep is almost guaranteed; the bedrooms are adequately comfortable but varying in style and size – some a bit claustrophobic. Those in the annexe Résidence are larger than those in the main building. Breakfast is excellent, and promptly served.

Nearby Liverdun; Nancy – Place Stanislas (gates).

6 Rue Porte-Haute 54460 Liverdun
Tel 83.24.46.01
Location in rural setting just outside small town on D90, 16 km NW of Nancy; with private car parking
Meals breakfast, lunch, dinner
Prices rooms 210F-450F; menus 155F-360F, children's 100F
Rooms 7 rooms (3 twin) all

with bath and shower; all rooms have central heating, phone
Facilities dining-room, sitting-room, bar
Credit cards AE, DC, MC, V
Children welcome
Disabled 2 ground-floor bedrooms
Pets accepted but not in bedrooms
Closed Feb; Mon
Proprietor M. Simunic

Marne

Château des Crayères

To stay at this wonderful place for free would be heaven itself; having to pay for the experience is only slightly less perfect. Géard Boyer (who almost everyone agrees is one of the finest chefs in the land) and his wife Elyane had a good starting point: a graceful turn-of-the-century mansion (built in Louis XVI style, by a member of the house of Pommery), situated in a spacious park almost at the heart of Reims, and surrounded by the *caves* of the famous champagne names. With Elyane's exquisite taste in interior decoration, and her skill in making her grand house seem more like a cherished home than a hotel, they could hardly go far wrong.

There are a wonderful grand staircase, enormous windows, marble columns and tapestries; the dining-room is wood panelled and candle-lit, the 'English-style' bar is comfortable. Bedrooms are of two kinds: *luxe* and *grand luxe*; all are large and sumptuous, individually decorated to a theme, with views over the park, and with excellent bathrooms; two have a large balcony. The cooking is good enough to attract businessmen from Paris. Not surprisingly, it is necessary to book well ahead for the pleasure of a night or two *chez* Boyer.

Nearby Basilica, cathedral; Mont Chenot (10 km) – start of the Champagne Route.

64 Blvd Henry Vasnier
51100 Reims
Tel 26.82.80.80
Location on edge of city centre, near St-Rémi basilica; in own grounds with ample car parking
Meals breakfast, lunch, dinner
Prices rooms 980F-1530F; meals 350F-420F
Rooms 19 double, all with bath (15 twin); all rooms have air-conditioning, TV, phone, radio, minibar
Facilities dining-room, bar, function room; tennis
Credit cards AE, DC, MC, V
Children welcome
Disabled access possible, lift/elevator
Pets dogs welcome
Closed 3 weeks at Christmas/ New Year; restaurant only Mon and Tue lunch
Proprietor M. Boyer

Bas-Rhin

Village inn, Marlenheim

Le Cerf

This ancient coaching inn enjoys an excellent reputation for its cooking. Owner and chef Robert Husser and son Michel make a formidable team, their inventive dishes complemented by a distinguished wine list. Bedrooms are not luxurious, but are of a fair standard in a generally rustic style. There is a cobbled courtyard for drinks and breakfast – so, when the weather is fine, the shortage of sitting space should not be a problem.

Nearby Strasbourg (20 km) – Renaissance Chamber of Commerce, cathedral, Alsatian museum, half-timbered houses.

30 Rue du Général-de-Gaulle 67520 Marlenheim
Tel 88.87.73.73
Location on main road through village, 18 km W of Strasbourg; with courtyard and car parking
Meals breakfast, lunch, dinner
Prices rooms 190F-380F; meals 100F-400F
Rooms 17 double, 8 with bath, 7 with shower (6 twin); one single with shower; 2 family rooms, both with bath; all rooms have central heating, phone
Facilities dining-room, 2 function rooms
Credit cards AE, DC, MC, V
Children accepted
Disabled access to dining-room; 2 ground-floor bedrooms
Pets accepted
Closed school holidays in Feb; Mon, Tue
Proprietor Robert Husser

Haut-Rhin

Auberge d'Artzenheim

This is a homely *auberge* off the beaten wine track. It has a terrace for outdoor eating and a pleasant, small sitting area with log fire; but the focal point is the restaurant, all beams and polished wood. It is popular both with German tourists and locals, and the chef's repertoire is not confined to Alsatian dishes: the fixed-price menus, while not exactly cheap, are good value. Bedrooms (some small) are prettily decorated with rustic furniture and jolly fabrics.

Nearby Colmar (15 km) – Unterlinden Museum, half-timbered houses; Mulhouse (55km) – museums.

30 Rue du Sponeck 68320
Artzenheim
Tel 89.71.60.51
Location in middle of
village, 15 km E of Colmar;
in garden, with ample car
parking
Meals breakfast, lunch,
dinner
Prices rooms 165F-220F;
menus 135F-225F
Rooms 10 double, 6 with
bath, 4 with shower (2 twin);

all rooms have central
heating, phone
Facilities 3 dining-rooms,
sitting-room, garden room
Credit cards MC, V
Children accepted
Disabled access to dining-
room, but difficult to hotel
Pets not accepted
Closed Feb; restaurant only
Mon dinner and Tue
Proprietor Mme Husser-
Schmitt

Les Alisiers

The amiable Jacques and Ella Degouy have turned this secluded farmhouse, with its stunning views of the Vosges mountains, into a simple and reasonably-priced *logis*. The interior is rustic and intimate: a wood-beamed restaurant, with Ella's Alsatian speci-alities usually on the menu, and small but comfortable bedrooms, with pale wood furnishings. There is a flowery courtyard and garden, where you can admire the mountains over breakfast or early evening drinks. A beautiful, secluded spot, and good value, too.

Nearby Colmar – Unterlinden Museum, half-timbered houses.

5 Faudé 68650 Lapoutroie
Tel 89.47.52.82
Location in countryside, 20
km W of Colmar, on N415;
with courtyard and parking
for 30 cars
Meals breakfast, lunch,
dinner
Prices rooms 200F-240F;
meals 95F-150F; 30-50%
reductions for children
sharing parents' room
Rooms 11 double, 3 with

bath, 7 with shower (3 twin);
one single; one family room
with shower; all rooms have
phone
Facilities dining-room, TV
room, bar
Credit cards AE, V
Children accepted
Disabled no special facilities
Pets accepted
Closed 15 Nov to 15 Dec
Proprietors Ella and Jacques
Degouy

Haut-Rhin

Le Clos Saint-Vincent

Ribeauvillé's most elegant hotel – a chalet-style building – stands high on a hill, surrounded by vineyards, looking across to the Black Forest. The rooms are spacious and tastefully furnished: reception is a cool, tiled hall; the restaurant, renowned for its cuisine and cellar, is an airy glassed room, with a surrounding terrace. Bedrooms are quiet and comfortable and those on the ground floor have private terraces.

Nearby Vineyards; Colmar (10 km) – Unterlinden Museum, Custom's House; Mulhouse (50 km) – museums.

Rte de Bergheim 68150 Ribeauvillé
Tel 89.73.67.65
Location in vineyards on NE outskirts of town; with garden and ample car parking
Meals breakfast, lunch, dinner
Prices rooms 550F-965F; meals 200F-300F
Rooms 8 double, all with bath (5 twin); 3 family rooms, all with bath; all rooms have central heating, phone, minibar; TV on request
Facilities dining-room, bar
Credit cards V
Children accepted
Disabled no special facilities
Pets accepted
Closed mid-Nov to mid-Mar; restaurant only Tue and Wed
Proprietors Bertrand and Marie-Laure Chapotin

Les Vosges

The wine villages of Alsace are some of the most charming in France, with their streets of timbered houses, pretty fountains, and the odd stork sitting on a roof-top nest. Surprisingly, it is hard to find a hotel that reflects these idyllic surroundings. Joseph Mutter's establishment is clearly an exception. Although perfectly comfortable, this is not the most stylish of buildings, but the dining-room is restful and refined. The cooking is innovative, and certainly not confined to the usual Alsatian fare – onion tart and sauerkraut.

Nearby Colmar – Unterlinden Museum, half-timbered houses; Mulhouse (50 km); Strasbourg (50 km).

2 Grande Rue 68150 Ribeauvillé
Tel 89.73.61.39
Location on main street of village, 15 km NW of Colmar
Meals breakfast, lunch, dinner
Prices rooms 235F-330F, suites 380F, extra bed 45F; menus 130F-320F
Rooms 16 double, 6 with bath, 10 with shower (13 twin); 2 suites; all rooms have phone
Facilities dining-room, sitting-room
Credit cards AE, MC, V
Children accepted
Disabled no special facilities
Pets accepted
Closed Jan 1 to Mar 14; restaurant only Mon
Proprietor Joseph Matter

Loir-et-Cher

Converted mill, Nouan-le-Fuzelier

Moulin de Villiers

A simple hotel in a lovely secluded setting – typical of the Sologne – beside a small lake in a wooded private park, with plenty of opportunity for exploring on foot (and for fishing). For the less energetic, a sunny terrace in front of the hotel offers perfect peace.

The low-lying timbered mill building dates from the middle of the last century – some of the orginal machinery still exists in what is now the sitting-room – but there is a modern wing which blends well with the original building. It has been in Gladys Andrieux's family for many decades, and run as a hotel since 1955. It remains very much a family-run place (Gladys and Gérard are a welcoming, good-humoured couple), with good, plain cooking using fresh local produce – including, in season, the game for which the Sologne is famous.

Nearby Orléans (40 km) – cathedral, fine arts museum; Sully (45 km) – château; Chambord and Cheverny (50 km) – châteaux. Bourges (60 km).

Nouan-le-Fuziliers 41600 Lamotte-Beuvron
Tel 54.88.72.27
Location in woods, on D44 2.5 km W of village 7 km S of Lamotte-Beuvron; with garden and ample car parking
Meals breakfast, lunch, dinner
Prices rooms 100F-210F; menus 65F-160F
Rooms 20 double, 11 with bath, 5 with shower (10 twin); central heating
Facilities dining-room, bar, 2 sitting-rooms
Credit cards V
Children accepted **Disabled** no special facilities
Pets not accepted in bedrooms or dining-room
Closed 4 Jan to mid-Mar, 2 weeks early Sep
Proprietors Gladys and Gérard Andrieux

Loir-et-Cher

Hostellerie de la Caillère

The dining-room is the heart of this pretty little hotel – immaculately kept, classically French-rustic in style, with wooden furniture and stone fireplace; in fine weather you can drink and eat out in the flowery gravelled garden. Jacky Guindon's cooking – *classique* and *moderne* – is sound and satisfying (we cannot guess what has caused the withdrawal of his Michelin star), and may be familiar to residents of East Anglia – early in 1988 he did a week's stint in the kitchen of the Mill Hotel at Sudbury (somewhat to the surprise of the guests, we imagine). Charming service overseen by Mme Guindon, exceptional breakfasts and inviting bedrooms.

Nearby Château – Chaumont-sur-Loire (5 km), Blois, many others.

36 Rte des Montils 41120 Candé-sur-Beuvron
Tel 54.44.03.08
Location on edge of village, 12 km SW of Blois; with garden and car parking
Meals breakfast, lunch, dinner
Prices rooms 220F; menus 98F-290F, children's 70F
Rooms 6 double, 2 with bath, 4 with shower (2 twin); all rooms have central heating
Facilities 2 dining-rooms, sitting-room
Credit cards AE, DC, MC, V
Children welcome
Disabled no special facilities
Pets accepted
Closed mid-Jan to end-Feb
Proprietor Jacky Guindon

Château de Nanteuil

In 1975 Frédéric Théry turned his family home in the heart of château country into a hotel and restaurant. The building may not rival neighbouring Blois and Chambord, but by less elevated standards it is quite grand (it predates the revolution, just) and stands in large grounds which border the River Cosson. Inside, furnishings and decoration are in appropriately antique style, but it is essentially a simple and friendly hotel, without pretension – witness the prices. The cooking emphasises regional produce and fish.

Nearby Châteaux – Blois, Chambord, Cheverny.

Huisseau-sur-Cosson 41350 Vineuil
Tel 54.42.61.98
Location beside river, in countryside 7 km E of Blois on D33; in large grounds with ample car parking
Meals breakfast, lunch, dinner
Prices rooms 70F-320F, extra bed 40F; menus 90F-160F
Rooms 9 double, 7 with bath; one suite with bath; 2 single; all rooms have central heating
Facilities dining-room, sitting-room, bar
Credit cards MC, V
Children welcome; 50% reduction **Disabled** no special facilities **Pets** accepted in bedrooms at extra charge
Closed Jan
Proprietor Frédéric Théry

Loir-et-Cher

Hôtel du Pont d'Ouchet

Across the Loire from Chaumont, Onzain is an unremarkable village but a perfectly sensible base for exploration of château country (and conveniently close to the A10 Bordeaux motorway). For an honest, inexpensive place to stay, look no further than this neat, vaguely chalet-style restaurant-with-rooms near the middle of the village. Don't expect too much. Bedrooms are bright and cheerful, but very simply furnished. The restaurant has token timbers applied to the walls, and cloths and flowers on the tables, but canteen-style plastic chairs. What you *can* expect is a friendly welcome and a satisfying, straightforward meal.

Nearby Châteaux – Chaumont-sur-Loire (3 km), Amboise (15 km).

50 Grande Rue 41150 Onzain
Tel 54.20.70.33
Location near middle of village, 17 km SW of Blois; with car parking space and garage
Meals breakfast, lunch, dinner
Prices rooms 85F-160F; menus 70F-100F
Rooms 7 double, 2 with shower (3 twin); family room with shower; all rooms have central heating
Facilities dining-room
Credit cards MC, V
Children accepted
Disabled no special facilities
Pets accepted
Closed Nov to end Feb; Sun evening and Mon
Proprietor M Cochet

Auberge de la Croix Blanche

Souvigny is a quiet little village in the middle of the Sologne – a region of woods and ponds (largely marshes until the area was efficiently drained in the last century) much favoured for fishing and shooting. It is also big market-gardening country. This family-run *auberge* consists of adjacent buildings of brick and timber, with rustic dining-rooms – all exposed beams and whitewash – and modern bedrooms which are plain to the point of being basic, but astounding value. Mme Marois's *cuisine traditionelle et copieuse* is highly regarded.

Nearby Sully (25 km) – château; Orléans (44 km).

Rue Eugenie Labiche, Souvigny-en-Sologne 41600 Lamotte-Beuvron
Tel 54.88.40.08
Location in middle of village, 44 km SE of Orléans; with public car parking
Meals breakfast, lunch, dinner
Prices rooms 98F; menus 65F-185F
Rooms 8 double (7 twin), 1 single; all rooms have central heating
Facilities 3 dining-rooms, TV room, bar
Credit cards V
Children accepted unless noisy
Disabled no special facilities
Pets accepted if well behaved
Closed mid-Jan to end-Feb; Tue dinner, Wed lunch and dinner
Proprietor M. Marois

Loiret

Hôtel de l'Abbaye

The setting of this noble building, a 14thC abbey, is its main feature – on the banks of the Loire, facing the splendid old arched bridge of Beaugency. The style of the hotel retains a certain austerity – a lofty dining hall with black-and-white tiled floor and antlers over the tall fireplace, and a salon area in the similarly high-ceilinged reception hall (though here the squashy sofas are positively self-indulgent). Bedrooms (some duplex apartments) are spacious, and well decorated and equipped. Food has been reported as above average.

Nearby Tower of St-Firmin (keep), church of Notre-Dame.

2 Quai de l'Abbaye 45190 Beaugency
Tel 38.44.67.35
Location beside bridge over Loire in small town 25km SW of Orléans; with car parking
Meals breakfast, lunch, dinner
Prices rooms 330F-610F; menu 175F
Rooms 14 double (7 twin), 4 family rooms, all with bath and shower; all rooms have central heating, TV, phone
Facilities 2 dining-rooms, 2 sitting-rooms, bar, conference room
Credit cards AE, DC, MC, V
Children accepted
Disabled no special facilities
Pets dogs accepted
Closed never
Proprietor M. Aupetit

Hôtel du Rivage

Christian Gaillard's modern-classic cooking goes from strength to strength, but remains only one of the attractions of this unpretentious but chic hotel facing the Loire. Lovely views over the river are shared by some of the bedrooms (comfortable, and recently modernised), the terrace of the beautiful bar/sitting-room (which features a good deal of local elm), and the pretty dining-room, with its grey and pink curtains, and blue high-backed chairs. The Gaillards are ably assisted by a young staff, all anxious to please.

Nearby château (hunting museum); La Bussière (15 km).

1 Quai de Nice 45500 Gien
Tel 38.67.20.53
Location on northern bank of Loire in town, 76 km N of Bourges; with private car parking
Meals breakfast, lunch, dinner
Prices rooms 235F-285F, suites 580F; meals 135F-255F
Rooms 17 double (8 twin), all with bath; 2 single with shower; 3 family rooms/suites with bath; all rooms have central heating, TV, phone
Facilities dining-room, sitting-room, bar
Credit cards AE, DC, MC, V
Children welcome
Disabled no special facilities
Pets welcome
Closed early Feb to Mar
Proprietor Christian Gaillard

Loiret

Village hotel, Beaugency

La Tonnellerie

A former wine merchant's house dating from 1870, the Tonnellerie is now a charming creeper-covered hotel in the small village of Tavers, close to the Loire and not far from Beaugency, the medieval town which is so popular with tourists.

The hotel is set around a central courtyard-garden which is at the heart of its appeal. There is a pretty little swimming-pool, shady chestnut trees; tables for summer meals stand on the lawn and further away from the house on terrace areas. The country atmosphere extends indoors to the dining-rooms, both looking on to the garden, one with café-style furnishings, the other handsomely rustic, with tiled floor and patterned linen. The salon is not a notably comfortable or relaxing room, but the best of the bedrooms have plenty of space – and, of course, you hope to be spending most of your time in the garden. Cooking – *nouvelle* in style but recognising the traditions of the region – is good without being notably distinguished, earning a *toque* from Gault-Millau.

Nearby Beaugency – Hôtel de Ville, Tour St-Firmin, church of Notre-Dame; châteaux – Chambord (25 km), Blois (30 km).

12 Rue des Eaux-Bleues, Tavers 45190 Beaugency
Tel 38.44.68.15
Location in middle of village, 3 km W of Beaugency; with garden, and private and public car parking
Meals breakfast, lunch, dinner
Prices rooms 225F-525F; menus 150F-195F
Rooms 18 double (11 twin), 2 single and 4 family rooms, all with bath; all rooms have central heating, phone
Facilities 2 dining-rooms, sitting-room; swimming-pool
Credit cards AE, DC, MC, V
Children welcome; cots available, special meals served in room
Disabled ground-floor rooms; lift/elevator
Pets accepted if well behaved
Closed Oct to end Apr
Proprietor Mme Anne-Marie Aulagnon

Maine-et-Loire

Hôtel de la Sarthe

Don't expect too much of the bedrooms here; the modest prices reflect their simplicity. The position of the unprepossessing building, on a beautiful stretch of the River Sarthe, is the obvious attraction; there is a covered terrace beside the river, where meals are served and guests sit and relax (there is nowhere much to sit inside). The food is simple and traditional but excellent and fair value. The Houdebines are a handsome couple – hard-working, welcoming and tolerant, and they have a happy staff.

Nearby Anjou – châteaux; Angers – château (tapestries).

1 Rue du Port 49330 Châteauneuf-sur-Sarthe
Tel 41.69.85.29
Location near town bridge, 30 km N of Angers; with terrace and car parking
Meals breakfast, lunch, dinner
Prices rooms 90F-180F; menus 55F-180F
Rooms 7 double, 2 with bath, 2 with shower (one twin); all rooms have central heating

Facilities dining-room, sitting-room/bar
Credit cards MC, V
Children accepted
Disabled no special facilities
Pets accepted in public rooms only
Closed 3 weeks Oct, 2 weeks Feb
Proprietors M. and Mme Jean Pierre Houdebine

Château de Teildras

Set in acres of parkland, this aristocratic family home is a handsome creeper-clad, white-shuttered building, more approachable than many such châteaux; inside, too, it is reassuringly unpretentious, with exposed beams as well as antique furniture, pictures and tapestries. There is a large flowery terrace, with tables and comfortable chairs. Bedrooms are spacious, comfortable and reasonably stylish. Pricey traditional meals are served in the intimate dining-rooms.

Nearby Château du Plessis-Bourré (5 km); Angers (24 km).

Cheffes 49125 Tiercé
Tel 41.42.61.08
Location in large park, N of Cheffes on minor road, 24 km N of Angers; with ample car parking
Meals breakfast, lunch, dinner
Prices rooms 555F-895F; menus 200F-280F
Rooms 11 double, with shower and bath (4 twin); all rooms have central heating, TV, phone, minibar

Facilities 2 sitting-rooms, 2 dining-rooms; fishing, tennis
Credit cards AE, DC, MC, V
Children welcome; baby-sitting available
Disabled no special facilities
Pets accepted in bedrooms only, on lead in park
Closed restaurant only Nov to Apr
Proprietor Jacques de Bernard du Breil

Maine-et-Loire

Auberge Jeanne de Laval

This old-fashioned, family-run hotel with a flowery garden makes an attractive base from which to explore the Loire. The rooms are reasonably priced, furnished with antiques and overlook the garden or river. But what brings most people here is the Michelin-starred restaurant; you will not forget Michel Augereau's exquisite *beurre blanc* sauce, served with fish fresh from the Loire. About half the bedrooms are in the *auberge* itself, the rest in the nearby Ducs d'Anjou annexe – an attractive manor house with quiet rooms, large garden and views of the river.

Nearby Saumur (15 km), Angers (30 km) – cathedral, château.

54 Rue Nationale, Les Rosiers-sur-Loire 49350 Gennes
Tel 41.51.80.17
Location in middle of village, 15 km NW of Saumur; with flower gardens and car parking
Meals breakfast, lunch, dinner
Prices rooms 250F-450F; meals 150F-300F
Rooms 14 double, most with bath or shower (3 twin); all rooms have central heating; most have TV and phone
Facilities TV room, dining-room
Credit cards AE, V, DC
Children welcome
Disabled no special facilities
Pets dogs accepted in bedrooms
Closed 22 Nov to 30 Dec; Mon (except holidays)
Proprietors Augereau family

Indre-et-Loire

Château de Pray

A 13thC château steeped in history and right in the middle of château country, in a magnificent position – high up above the Loire in its own peaceful parkland, with superb views from the windows and terraces. What is more, the formality and pretension which spoil so many château hotels are here kept within reasonable bounds – as are the prices of rooms and menus. The building consists of medieval towers with a Renaissance house sandwiched in between; bedrooms in the towers have the advantage in terms of character, but not light or comfort. The dining-room shares the view, and in kind weather there is service outside.

Nearby Châteaux – Amboise, Chaumont (15 km).

37400 Amboise	with bath; all rooms have
Tel 47.57.23.67	phone
Location in park off D751,	**Facilities** dining-room,
on S bank of Loire, 3 km NE	sitting-room
of town; with car parking	**Credit cards** AE, DC, V
Meals breakfast, lunch,	**Children** accepted **Disabled**
dinner	no special facilities
Prices rooms 250F-405F;	**Pets** accepted in bedrooms
menus 145F-180F	and garden only
Rooms 8 double, 6 with bath	**Closed** 1 Jan to 10 Feb
(4 twin), 8 family rooms, all	**Proprietor** M. Farard

Le Castel de Bray et Monts

The decoration of this elegant yet friendly establishment has a lighter touch than the traditional French norm (with Laura Ashley much in evidence), and the Rochereaus are not short of ideas for keeping their rooms full – they offer week-long cookery courses with the morning spent preparing lunch under Maxime's eye and the afternoon visiting châteaux with Eliane as guide. The 18thC manor house and converted chapel sit in their own tranquil grounds beside a stream, with shaded tables next to the house and a children's play area further away.

Nearby Châteaux – Villandry (10 km), Azay-le-Rideau (10 km).

Place de L'Eglise 37130	available; all rooms have
Langeais	central heating, phone, TV,
Tel 47.96.70.47	minibar
Location in village on Loire,	**Facilities** dining-room,
5 km SW of Langeais on	sitting-room, bar
D16; with garden and ample	**Credit cards** AE, V
car parking	**Children** welcome
Meals breakfast, lunch,	**Disabled** no special facilities
dinner	**Pets** accepted at extra charge
Prices rooms 210F-540F;	**Closed** mid-Dec to end Jan;
menus 95F-180F	Wed out of season
Rooms 10 double (5 twin),	**Proprietor** Maxime and
all with bath; extra beds	Eliane Rochereau

Indre-et-Loire

Town mansion, Chinon

Hôtel Diderot

Creeper-covered and white-shuttered, this handsome town-house set in a quiet courtyard looks the epitome of 18thC elegance. Inside, it is surprisingly simple – perhaps even Spartan. Public rooms and bedrooms alike are rather sparsely furnished (though often with antiques), and our inspector complains of an entirely unheated – though otherwise well appointed – bathroom. But the Diderot has a faithful following of visitors who find it reliable and fair value. The proprietors are charming and unstintingly helpful, and breakfast (served on the shady terrace or in a rustic room with tiled floor and massive beams) is exceptionally tasty – thanks to Madame's home-made preserves.

Nearby Grand Carroi, ruined château, church of St-Maurice; châteaux – Azay-le-Rideau (20 km), Langeais (30 km); Villandry (35 km) – Renaissance gardens; Tours (48 km).

4 Rue Buffon 37500 Chinon
Tel 47.93.18.87
Location in middle of town; with courtyard and private car parking
Meals breakfast
Prices rooms 160F-270F
Rooms 17 double, 7 with bath, 8 with shower (8 twin); 3 family rooms, all with bath; all rooms have central heating, phone
Facilities bar, breakfast room
Credit cards MC, V
Children welcome
Disabled some ground-floor bedrooms
Pets not accepted
Closed 15 Dec to 15 Jan
Proprietor Theo Kazamias

Indre-et-Loire

Hôtel Hosten

This early 19thC, creeper-covered coaching inn is on a busy junction; but at night there is little through traffic, and there is the compensation of proximity to the château. The hotel has been in the Hosten family since 1904 and is now in the hands of chef Jean-Jacques. Much has been renovated recently, and the bedrooms are spacious and solidly comfortable, with good bathrooms; the sitting-room was in a state of flux when last we saw it. But the cooking remains the main feature of the place: generally traditional, with an emphasis on fish.

Nearby Loire châteaux – Azay-le-Rideaux (10 km); Tours (25 km).

2 Rue Gambetta 37130
Langeais
Tel 47.96.82.12
Location in middle of town,
20 km W of Tours; with
garage parking for 10 cars
Meals breakfast, lunch,
dinner
Prices rooms 215F-310F;
meals 165F-245F
Rooms 12 double, 10 with
bath, 2 with shower (4 twin);
all rooms have central

heating, TV, phone
Facilities sitting-room, bar,
dining-room
Credit cards AE, DC, MC, V
Children accepted
Disabled no special facilities
Pets accepted
Closed mid-Jan to mid-Feb,
mid-Jun to mid-Jul;
restaurant only Mon dinner
and Tue
Proprietor Jean-Jacques
Hosten

Château de Rochecotte

In the midst of châteaux country, here is an opportunity to stay and sample life in a château of the grandest style. Built at the end of the 18thC, Rochecotte was bought by the Prince de Talleyrand in 1882 and remained his favourite residence until his death. From the bedrooms to the dining-room, bright fabrics, elegant modern furniture and light decoration complement the classical proportions of the rooms. The cuisine is appropriately *gastronomique*. Formal terraces and an Italian garden are just part of the large grounds.

Nearby Châteaux – Langeais, Azay-le-Rideau (20 km).

St-Patrice 37130 Langeais
Tel 47.96.90.62
Location in extensive
grounds off D35, 10 km W
of Langeais; with ample car
parking
Meals breakfast, lunch,
dinner
Prices rooms 300F-480F,
suites 520F-650F; menu
160F
Rooms 14 double (2 twin),
one family room, all with

bath and shower; all rooms
have central heating, phone;
TV on request
Facilities sitting-room,
library, dining-room
Credit cards AE, DC, MC, V
Children accepted; special
meals available
Disabled no special facilities
Pets accepted
Closed never
Proprietor M. Pasquier

Indre

Château de la Vallée Bleue

This handsome château would benefit from a lick of paint on the exterior, some repairs to the drive and some attention to the grounds; but the Gasquets are barely into their stride here (they took over the hotel in 1985), and these are not serious criticisms so much as indicators that the young proprietors have their priorities right. Inside, the atmosphere of the house is warm and easy, and not in the least run-down.

Fresh flowers and a cosy log fire in the spacious entrance hall set the tone, and personal touches are in evidence in every room. The château overlooks gardens front and back, giving all the bedrooms – big, comfortably furnished with antiques – a pleasant outlook; just visible, beyond cows grazing in the fields, are the terracotta roof-tops of the village. Public rooms are gracious and charming, furnished with solid antiques and looking on to the garden. Cooking is regionally based but *nouvelle*-oriented and way above average in execution; service can be a little slow, but the food is hot when it arrives, and there are savouries with pre-dinner drinks and *petit fours* with coffee. There is a play area in the grounds for children.

Nearby Tour de la Prison (Museum of George Sand and Vallée Noire); Sarzay (10 km) – château; Nohant (5 km) – château.

Rte de Verneuil, St-Chartier
36400 La Châtre
Tel 54.31.01.91
Location just outside hamlet, on D69 9 km N of La Châtre, 26 km SE of Châteauroux; in large grounds with ample car parking
Meals breakfast, lunch, dinner
Prices rooms 150F-350F; menus 95F-225F
Rooms 11 double (3 twin), 5 with bath, 6 with shower; one single with shower; 2 family rooms with bath; all rooms have central heating, TV, phone, minibar
Facilities 2 dining-rooms, sitting-room
Credit cards MC, V
Children welcome; special menus available
Disabled 3 ground-floor rooms
Pets accepted at extra charge
Closed Feb
Proprietors Brigitte and Gérard Gasquet

Château de Rochecotte (see opposite)

Cher

Village hotel, Brinon-sur-Sauldre

Auberge de la Solognote

In an unremarkable Sologne village, at the edge of the forests that signal Alain-Fournier country, the attractions of this rather dull-looking town house are revealed only as you go through the door. Inside it is bright, airy and decorated in a simple modern style. A welcoming atmosphere in the dining-room does justice to M. Girard's excellent Sologne game. All the bedrooms face the garden (some on the ground floor open directly on to it), and are quiet and simply but charmingly furnished.

Nearby Sully (30 km) – château; Gien (40 km) – 15thC château.

Grand Rue, Brinon-sur-Sauldre 18410 Argent-sur-Sauldre
Tel 48.58.50.29
Location on main street of hamlet on D923, 4 km W of Argent-sur-Sauldre; in garden, with car parking
Meals breakfast, lunch, dinner
Prices rooms 180F–280F; menus 130F–250F
Rooms 11 double, 6 with bath, 5 with shower (4 twin);
2 family rooms, one with bath, one with shower; all rooms have phone, central heating
Facilities dining-room, sitting-room, bar
Credit cards V
Children accepted
Disabled no special facilities
Pets not accepted
Closed Feb, 10 days in May, 10 days in Sep
Proprietors M. and Mme Girard

Village inn, Nançay

Les Meaulnes

This is one of the most romantic *auberges* you are likely to come across around the Loire valley. It is quiet and secluded, lying in a small village in the moody Sologne area south of Orleans. Rooms (smaller ones in the main building, larger ones in the annexe across the pretty garden) are furnished with beautiful antiques and named accordingly – Empire Rustique, Louis XV, Louis XIII, Romantique, and so on. The dining-room, with beams, candles, fresh flowers and a roaring fire, is intimate and inviting. Daniel Prat and his wife are former Parisian journalists, and their guests include various showbiz and media personalities. Their cooking is well above average, but meals are not cheap.

Nearby Radio-astronomy station, castle, woods, lakes; Bourges (35 km) – cathedral, Palais Jacques-Coeur; Romorantin (45 km).

18330 Nançay
Tel 48.51.81.15
Location in middle of village, 35 km NW of Bourges on D944; with gardens and car parking
Meals breakfast, lunch, dinner
Prices rooms 320F–400F; meals 150F–300F
Rooms 10 double, 5 with
bath, 5 with shower (3 twin); central heating, phone
Facilities dining-room
Credit cards AE, DC, MC, V
Children accepted
Disabled no special facilities
Pets by arrangement
Closed mid-Jan to Easter
Proprietors M. and Mme Daniel Prat

Cher

Auberge du Moulin de Chaméron

Jacques and Annie Candoré converted this ancient water-mill into a restaurant in 1972, later adding bedrooms in a garden annexe; the food is still a great attraction, but no longer the only one. The dining-room is romantic and intimate, with old beams and fireplace, and in summer you can eat on the terrace beside the stream. Bedrooms differ in size and style; all are modest, but calm and comfortable.

Nearby Meillant castle (25 km); Noirlac abbey (30 km).

Bannegon 18210
Charenton-du-Cher
Tel 48.61.83.80
Location in countryside between Bannegon and Neuilly, 40 km SE of Bourges; with garden and ample car parking
Meals breakfast, lunch, dinner
Prices rooms 180F-420F; menus 110F-175F, children's 50F
Rooms 13 double, 8 with bath, 5 with shower (5 twin); one family room with bath; all rooms have central heating, phone
Facilities 2 dining-rooms, bar, 2 sitting-rooms; swimming-pool, fishing
Credit cards V
Children welcome
Disabled no special facilities
Pets accepted in bedrooms; charge
Closed 15 Nov to 15 Dec, 4 Jan to 4 Mar
Proprietors M. Candoré and M. Merilleau

Deux-Sèvres / Charente-Mtme.

Au Marais

The Marais in question is the Poitevin – a huge area of salt marshes west of Niort, reclaimed from the sea since the 17thC. The part of the area between Niort and Damvix, known as La Venise Verte, is laced with shady canals, once the only main form of local transport but now a tourist curiosity. Coulon is the main point of departure for boat trips, and this friendly little inn on the banks of the Sèvre-Niort river makes a peaceful and pleasant stop-over. The rooms, neatly furnished in rustic style and immaculately kept, are accommodated in a separate building from the two-level restaurant, where Alain Nerrière's inventive but regional-based cooking attracts a steady trade. Martine Mathé serves with a smile.

Nearby Boat trips; Fontenay-le-Comte (26 km).

46-48 Quai Louis-Tardy
79510 Coulon
Tel 49.35.90.43
Location in village 6 km W of Niort
Meals breakfast, lunch, dinner
Prices rooms 230F-260F; menu 150F
Rooms 11 double, all with

bath; all rooms have central heating, phone, TV
Facilities dining-room
Credit cards V
Children accepted
Disabled no special facilities
Pets accepted at extra charge
Closed never
Proprietors Martine Mathé and Alain Nerrière

Auberge Pontoise

Most travellers who have a choice would prefer to stay in a village or in the countryside rather than in a town hotel like this, set on a noisy, smelly through-road. Philippe Chat has the answer that keeps the customers coming: ambitious and competent cooking, lately recognized with the award of a Michelin star. For the moment, at least, the hotel remains simple and unpretentious, relying heavily on the honest virtue of good housekeeping for its appeal – though the rooms are of a fair size and attractively decorated, and there is a pleasant courtyard.

Nearby Castle (12thC keep); Saintes (22 km).

23 Ave Gambetta 17800 C
Pons
Tel 46.94.00.99
Location on narrow through-road in middle of town; with limited private car parking
Meals breakfast, lunch, dinner
Prices rooms 180F-300F; menus 140F-250F
Rooms 21 double, all with bath or shower (some twin);

one suite; all rooms have central heating, phone, TV
Facilities sitting-room/bar, 2 dining-rooms, small conference room
Credit cards MC, V
Children accepted
Disabled access difficult, outside steps
Pets not accepted
Closed 5 weeks Dec to Jan; Sun and Mon out of season
Proprietor Philippe Chat

Charente-Maritime

Village hotel, Tonnay-Boutonne

Le Prieuré

Tonnay-Boutonne is a small, quiet village lying between the old military town of Rochefort and St-Jean-d'Angély, a former wine port. Set slightly back from the (not very busy) main road is this typical Charentaise building: handsome, symmetrical, with white shuttered windows. It was the family home of the proprietors before they opened it as a hotel, and retains that friendly atmosphere – making it an attractive base for a family holiday. Le Prieuré has an excellent reputation for food and the dining-rooms are light and unpretentious. Although comfortable, the bedrooms don't have any particularly distinguishing features, and the decoration is sometimes garish.

Nearby Rochefort – 17thC Corderie Royale, Navy Museum; La Roche Courbon (25 km) – château; Saintes (30 km).

17380 Tonnay-Boutonne
Tel 46.33.20.18
Location in village 21 km E of Rochefort; with large garden and ample car parking
Meals breakfast, lunch, dinner
Prices rooms 180F-250F, menus 85F-125F
Rooms 16 double (6 twin), 2 family rooms; all with bath; all rooms have phone, TV
Facilities reception/sitting-area, TV/sitting-room, 2 dining-rooms
Credit cards V
Children welcome
Disabled no special facilities
Pets accepted
Closed Dec to Feb
Proprietor M. and Mme Paul Vernoux

Charente-Maritime

Restaurant with rooms, St-Léger

Le Rustica

The inimitable style of Le Rustica is undoubtedly due to the charming and effusive Mme Rivière, who runs the dining-room and eight bedrooms of this restaurant-with-rooms with admirable attention to detail: at the end of dinner, four types of sugar will be offered with coffee and, despite the small scale of the place, someone will usually materialise to carry your bags.

This attention to detail does not extend to the decoration and furnishings. The bedrooms often have uneven and/or creaky floors, poor lighting, thin walls and curtains that are too small for the windows – but they are cheap, spotlessly clean, and have a cosy feel which is relaxing. (When all the bedrooms are occupied, the one shower and lavatory could prove inadequate, although each room has a wash basin and *bidet*.) There is not much garden – a terrace with tables and a wild patch of ground, which merges with the adjacent farm.

It is in the restaurant that Le Rustica and Mme Rivière really come into their own. It remains resolutely popular with the locals as a place to eat, despite the odd blast of piped music. The food is superb and there is plenty of choice from five menus, all served in a friendly yet unintrusive way.

Despite its drawbacks, Le Rustica found favour with our inspector: 'about the most friendly welcome I've experienced – I could almost feel myself unwinding'.

Nearby Pons – 12thC Keep; Usson (10 km); Saintes (15 km); Cognac (25 km); Royan (30 km) – beaches; Rochecourbon Château (40 km).

St-Léger 17800 Pons
Tel 46.96.91.75
Location in tiny hamlet, off N137, 5 km NW of Pons; with garden and car parking
Meals breakfast, lunch, dinner
Prices rooms 90F-110F; DB & B (for one) 160F; menus 50F-220F
Rooms 8 double

Facilities TV-room, bar, 2 dining-rooms
Credit cards MC, V
Children accepted
Disabled access difficult
Pets accepted
Closed 3 weeks in Oct, one week in Feb; Tue evening and Wed, out of season
Proprietor Mme Rivière

Charente

Converted mill, Hiersac

Moulin du Maine Brun

Despite the inescapable scale of the place and the existence of a room with dance-floor for functions, M. and Mme Menagers keep the running of Le Moulin very much *en famille*, and the 40 hectares of grounds that surround this attractive 16thC mill, would be hard to beat – the deer park, stream, woods and sunny terrace make a tranquil setting for the hotel. The bedrooms are beautiful: all have a south-facing terrace, the first-floor rooms are furnished with 18thC antiques and the second-floor ones with 19thC pieces, and each room has its own colour scheme. Appropriately, the mill has its own cognac distillery.

Nearby Angoulême; St-Michel-d'Entraygues (6 km); Cognac.

La Vigerie 16290 Hiersac	central heating, TV, phone,
Tel 45.90.83.00	minibar
Location on RN 141, in	**Facilities** 3 dining-rooms,
countryside 8 km SW of	bar, sitting-room,
Angoulême; in grounds with	conference room;
car parking	swimming-pool
Meals breakfast, lunch,	**Credit cards** AE, DC, V
dinner	**Children** accepted
Prices rooms 475F; menus	**Disabled** no special facilities
165F-270F, children's 50F	**Pets** accepted
Rooms 20 double, all with	**Closed** Nov and Dec
bath (8 twin); all rooms have	**Proprietors** Menager family

Converted mill, St-Fort-sur-le-Né

Moulin de Cierzac

The ivy-clad walls and tall, white-shuttered windows give this 17thC mill a rather formal look. But inside the atmosphere is unpretentious and friendly, the style reassuringly rustic – tiled floors, stone walls, exposed beams and solid, comfortable chairs. Bedrooms are vividly decorated, but neat and spacious. The grounds are shady, lush and tranquil; often the only sound is the water running in the stream, which used to power the mill. The food has a reputation and is made more enjoyable by the lovely view of the garden from the simple but attractive dining-room.

Nearby Cognac – cellar tours; Pons (20 km) – 12thC keep; Usson (20 km) – Renaissance château; Angoulême (45 km).

St-Fort-sur-le-Né 16660	phone
Cognac	**Facilities** dining-room,
Tel 45.83.01.32	sitting-room (with TV, bar)
Location on edge of village,	**Credit cards** AE, V
14 km S of Cognac; in quiet	**Children** accepted
grounds, with car parking	**Disabled** no special facilities
Meals breakfast, lunch,	**Pets** accepted
dinner	**Closed** end Jan to end Feb,
Prices rooms 190F-390F	25 Jul; Mon and Sun
Rooms 10 double, 5 with	evenings in winter
bath, 5 with shower; all	**Proprietors** M. and Mme
rooms have central heating,	Patrick Labouly

Charente

Hostellerie Ste-Catherine

The stately approach to the Hostellerie Ste-Catherine – through a stone archway and along a winding drive – is imposing and grand. The house, too – built in a pale, irregular stone, dating back to the 17thC, and once a residence of the Empress Joséphine – looks handsome but austere, and exudes an aura of formality. But inside it is a different story: despite fine furnishings and immaculate housekeeping, there is none of the expected pretension, but a relaxed and easy atmosphere – largely thanks to the charm and good spirits of Mme Chupin.

Rooms are decorated and furnished with proper regard for both style and comfort: the dining-rooms (one leads in to the other) have tapestries on the walls, and a carved-wooden mantlepiece stands over an old fireplace; the two sitting-rooms are inviting and relaxing (one has board games, the other an open fireplace and a TV). Most of the individually furnished and thoroughly comfortable bedrooms have views of the extensive surrounding parkland; they do vary in size, and the prices reflect this. A choice of three interesting menus is offered, and the reassuring sound of satisfied lunchtime guests lingers well into the afternoon.

For good living in secluded surroundings at modest prices, this is hard to beat.

Nearby Angoulême (30 km) – cathedral, walk along ramparts; châteaux – de Brie (40 km), Rochechouart (40 km); Montbrun (45 km) – fortress.

16220 Montbron
Tel 45.23.60.03
Location in park off D16, 4 km SW of Montbron, 28 km E of Angoulême; with ample car parking
Meals breakfast, lunch, dinner
Prices rooms 180F-420F; menus 135F-220F
Rooms 14 double and 4 family rooms, most with bath or shower; all rooms have central heating, phone
Facilities 2 dining-rooms, 2 sitting-rooms, bar; swimming-pool
Credit cards AE, DC, MC, V
Children accepted
Disabled no special facilities
Pets accepted
Closed never
Proprietor Mme Chupin

Haute-Vienne/Creuse

Moulin de la Gorce

A tranquil setting and renowned cooking (2 stars from Michelin, 2 *toques* from Gault-Millau) are the primary attractions of this 16th century mill – a neat, low-lying, white-painted building beside a lake in the middle of wooded grounds. Within are two dining-rooms (one delicately decorated, the other more rustic) and a comfortable, unassuming salon. The bedrooms – some richly furnished, some rather plain – are split between the main building and a nearby annexe. Reproduction tapestries are a recurring feature. Mme Bertranet greets guests warmly.

Nearby St-Yrieix (10km); Coussac-Bonneval (10 km) – château.

La Roche l'Abeille 87800 Nexon
Tel 55.00.70.66
Location in countryside 2 km S of village, 35 km S of Limoges; with large grounds and ample car parking
Meals breakfast, lunch, dinner
Prices rooms 230F-450F, with 4 beds 700F; menus 160F-400F
Rooms 9 double (2 twin), all with bath; phone, TV
Facilities 2 dining-rooms, sitting-room/bar
Credit cards AE, DC, MC, V
Children welcome; special meals available
Disabled 2 ground-floor rooms
Pets if kept on leash
Closed Jan; Mon lunch Oct to Dec
Proprietors Jean and Annie Bertranet

Hôtel du Thaurion

We classify this unpretentious 18thC hotel as a restaurant-with-rooms not only because there is nowhere to sit except in the bar, but also because some of the bedrooms are uncomfortably small and overdue for redecoration. One attraction is Gérard Fanton's *nouvelle*-but-not-insubstantial cooking – rated by our inspector as the best of a week-long tour of duty, despite the lack of recognition from Michelin. Another is the warm welcome of the Fantons – a charming and hardworking young couple who took over the family enterprise about a decade ago.

Nearby Bourganeuf – Tour de Zimzim; Moutier d'Ahun (25 km).

St-Hilaire-le-Château 23250 Pontarion
Tel 55.64.50.12
Location in middle of rural village, on D941 14 km NE of Bourganeuf; with terrace and car parking
Meals breakfast, lunch, dinner
Prices rooms 120F-250F, suite 500F; menus 60F-320F
Rooms 11 double (2 twin), 1 suite, all with bath; all rooms have central heating, TV, phone, minibar
Facilities 2 dining-rooms, bar
Credit cards AE, DC, MC, V
Children accepted
Disabled no special facilities
Pets accepted
Closed Nov to Apr; restaurant only, Wed, and Thu lunch out of season
Proprietor Gérard Fanton

Yonne

Town mansion, Auxerre

Parc des Maréchaux

This substantial 1850s house was restored from near-dereliction by Espérance Hervé and her doctor husband, and is now run with great enthusiasm by her. They have cut no corners: the welcoming ambiance, confident style and solid comfort of the house would do credit to any professional hotelier. For a bed-and-breakfast establishment, the public rooms are exceptionally comfortable, and the large bedrooms are beautifully done out in restrained colours and handsomely furnished. The garden – the park from which the hotel takes its name – is leafy and secluded, and breakfast and drinks may be had there in good weather.

Nearby Cathedral, abbey church of St-Germain; Chablis (20 km).

6 Ave Foch 89000 Auxerre	central heating, phone; TV
Tel 86.51.43.77	available (small charge)
Location close to middle of	**Facilities** sitting-room, bar,
town; with gardens and car	breakfast room
parking	**Credit cards** AE, V
Meals breakfast	**Children** welcome
Prices rooms 180F-320F;	**Disabled** 3 ground-floor
extra bed 40F, free for under 7s	bedrooms; lift/elevator
Rooms 19 double (7 twin), 2	**Pets** accepted at extra charge
single, 3 family rooms, all	**Closed** 24 Dec to 3 Jan
with bath; all rooms have	**Proprietor** Espérance Hervé

Converted mill, Avallon

Moulin des Templiers

The little River Cousin burbling merrily past is virtually the only sound to disturb the peace of this pretty old mill, yet it is close enough to the motorway to make a splendid stop-over on the way through Burgundy. To sip a drink on the shady riverside terrace after a long day on the road is worth waiting for; breakfast is served here on fien days – otherwise in a tiny room – there may be a queue. The bedrooms are freshly decorated and well kept, but most are small and the smallest is minute. If planning to stay more than a night or two, book well ahead and ask for a larger room. There are good restaurants in Avallon, and nearer to hand in Pontaubert; the courteous Mme Hilmoine will make reservations.

Nearby Avallon – ramparts, St-Lazare; Vézelay (10 km).

Vallée du Cousin,	2 single, all with shower; all
Pontaubert 89200 Avallon	rooms have phone
Tel 86.34.10.80	**Facilities** breakfast room
Location in secluded valley,	**Credit cards** not accepted
4 km SW of Avallon on	**Children** accepted
D427; with garden and	**Disabled** no special facilities
separate car park	**Pets** accepted at extra
Meals breakfast	charge
Prices rooms 180F-270F	**Closed** Nov to mid-Mar
Rooms 12 double (3 twin),	**Proprietor** Mme Hilmoine

Yonne

Village mansion, Mailly-le-Château

Le Castel

This charming old *maison bourgeoise* makes an excellent base for a touring holiday, or a convenient and welcoming stopover on the way to the south of France. Built at the end of the last century, it is a large shuttered house lying in the shadow of the village church, with a well kept garden and a flowery terrace shaded by lime trees, where you can have breakfast and drinks on warm days.

Since 1979 the hotel has been run by the exceptionally friendly and courteous Breerettes. Michel speaks English (he worked at Gleneagles Hotel in Scotland and spent 15 years as a chef on ocean-going liners) and is in charge of the kitchen. Food is taken seriously here, and is both excellent and inexpensive – whether you opt for the cheapest set menu or the *carte*. There are two dining-rooms, separated by a small salon with Empire-style furnishings and a handsome fireplace. Bedrooms vary widely – from spacious ones with touches of grandeur, such as chandeliers and drapes over bedheads, to much smaller and simpler rooms.

The hotel is a *Relais du Silence*, and since the silencing of the church bells (which used to ring twice every hour from 10pm to 7am) it has almost literally lived up to the classification.

Nearby Vézelay (30 km) – Romanesque buildings; Avallon (30 km) – ramparts; Chablis (45 km) – vineyards.

Place de l'Eglise 89660 Mailly-le-Château
Tel 86.40.43.06
Location in church square of village, 30 km S of Auxerre; with garden, terrace and car parking
Meals breakfast, lunch, dinner
Prices rooms 135F-260F; meals 75F-135F
Rooms 10 double, 7 with bath, 2 with shower (5 twin); 2 family rooms with bath; all rooms have central heating, phone
Facilities 2 dining-rooms, sitting-room
Credit cards MC, V
Children accepted
Disabled no special facilities
Pets accepted
Closed Wed
Proprietors M. and Mme Breerette

Yonne

Moulin des Pommerats

In many ways, the Moulin des Pommerats is the ideal French country hotel: an ancient mill set in peaceful riverside gardens, with pretty rooms at modest prices and a restaurant serving honest Burgundian fare. What is more, the patron/chef, Paul Reumaux d'Equainville, is a great Anglophile and fought as an RAF officer in World War II.

The floral-decorated bedrooms are mostly situated in an attractive annexe close to the main mill. Public rooms consist of a large sitting-room with open fire, a bar, a small salon decorated with English hunting scenes, and a dining-room with large windows that look out on to a garden full of apple trees. If there is a criticism to be made it is that the furnishing of these rooms is uninspired. There is an excellent-value three-course menu (served on weekdays only) with the emphasis on prime basic ingredients. Typical dishes are Burgundy snails, quail with bilberries, pancakes sautéd in brandy and an excellent selection of local cheeses.

There is no shortage of things to do in the area, but many tourists just stay for the night, stopping off *en route* to the south. The Moulin certainly merits the 22 km detour from the motorway.

Nearby Chablis (30 km) – vineyards; Auxerre (35 km) – cathedral; Tanlay (40 km) – château.

Venizy 89210 St-Florentin
Tel 86.35.08.04
Location in countryside on D129, 4 km N of St-Florentin; in gardens, with ample car parking
Meals breakfast, lunch, dinner
Prices rooms 200F-420F; meals 120F-280F
Rooms 20 double, 18 with bath, 2 with shower (9 twin); one family room; all rooms have central heating, phone
Facilities dining-room, bar, sitting-room
Credit cards DC, MC, V
Children welcome
Disabled access easy to 2 bedrooms and to dining-room
Pets accepted
Closed 8 days in Feb
Proprietors M. and Mme Reumaux d'Equainville

Yonne

Town mansion, Vézelay

Le Pontot

There is only one hotel inside the walls of the old town of Vézelay, and that is Le Pontot. Just a short walk from the famous basilica, it is a fine fortified mansion, thought to have been rebuilt on 11thC cellars after the Hundred Years War, and added to in the 18thC.

It has existed as a hotel only since 1984. The American owner, architect Charles Thum, and manager Christian Abadie have skilfully converted the building into an expensive, but rather special, B&B. (Who needs a restaurant when l'Espérance (page 000) lies just down the road?) The bedrooms include a large Louis XVI apartment, with canopied beds, fireplace and private dressing room; and another with stone paving, 16thC beamed ceiling and antique, country-style, furnishings.

Breakfast is quite a sumptous affair, served as it is on gold-encrusted, royal blue Limoges porcelain. On cool days, it is eaten in front of a blazing fire in the handsome, panelled, Louis XVê salon; but in summer you sit outside in the delightful walled garden.

Among the amusements offered by this rather exclusive hotel are cruises on the Canal du Nivernais, and hot-air balloon rides over the rolling Burgundian hills.

Nearby St-Père-sous-Vézelay (5 km) – church; Avallon (15 km); Auxerre (50 km); Pouilly and Sancerre (50 km) – vineyards.

Place du Pontot 89450 Vézelay
Tel 86.33.24.40
Location in middle of town; with small walled garden, public car parking
Meals breakfast
Prices rooms 450F-800F, child sharing room 100F
Rooms 10 double all with bath and shower (6 twin); all rooms have phone, radio
Facilities sitting-room, bar, breakfast room
Credit cards AE, MC, V
Children accepted
Disabled not suitable for wheelchairs
Pets accepted; 50F charge
Closed Nov to Mar
Manager Christian Abadie

Yonne

L'Espérance

The reputation of the l'Espérance is based first on its cuisine. Marc Meneau is considered one of the finest chefs in France, and his culinary skills have earned the restaurant three Michelin stars. Indulging in specialities such as foie gras, roast turbot and hot *feuilleté de fromages*, while admiring the garden, with its streams and abundant roses, is an experience hard to forget.

Graciously supervised by Françoise Meneau, the dining-room is impeccable – tables are immaculately laid with pink linen cloths, gleaming crystal and silver, and beautiful flowers; a glassed-in extension gives the best view of the garden. M. Meneau can often be seen leaving the kitchens to greet his guests, and to join them for coffee.

The l'Espérance lies below the town of Vézelay, famed for its beautiful Romanesque basilica. Bedrooms in the main building – a mellowed old manor house standing back from the Avallon road – are romantically decorated. There are more in a renovated mill 300 metres down the road, furnished in a simpler style, with beams and antiques, and cooler, quieter and larger than those in the manor house.

Nearby Vézelay – Romanesque buildings; Avallon (15 km); Auxerre (50 km); Pouilly and Sancerre – wine villages (50 km).

89450 St-Père-sous-Vézelay
Tel 86.33.20.45
Location in small village, 3 km S of Vézelay; with grounds and ample car parking
Meals breakfast, lunch, dinner
Prices rooms 580F-950F, suites 1,050F-1,950F; menus 250F-500F
Rooms 21 double, all with bath (5 twin); all rooms have TV, phone
Facilities dining-room, bar, sitting-room
Credit cards AE, DC, V
Children welcome
Disabled 3 ground-floor rooms
Pets welcome; no charge
Closed Jan and early Feb; Tue, Wed lunch
Proprietor Marc Meneau

Yonne

L'Abbaye St-Michel

Not everyone likes the way Daniel and Denise Cussac have elevated this ancient abbey to Relais & Château status – using plate glass or stainless steel as readily as stone and wood. But there is no disputing the achievements of their son Christophe, whose innovative cooking has earned countless *toques* and stars from the gastronomic guides. The focal point is the dining-room, a stone vault dating from the 12thC, stylishly but simply furnished. There are several sitting areas decorated in a mix of styles, and bedrooms also blend old and new successfully.

Nearby Tonnerre – Fosse Dionne (spring), Uzès Museum.

Montée de St-Michel 89700 Tonnerre
Tel 86.55.05.99
Location in countryside on edge of village, 35 km E of Auxerre; in large garden with ample car parking
Meals breakfast, lunch, dinner
Prices rooms 600F-900F, suites from 1200F; meals 270F
Rooms 15 double (9 twin), all with bath; all rooms have central heating, phone, TV, minibar
Facilities dining-room, 2 sitting-rooms, bar; tennis court
Credit cards AE, DC, MC, V
Children welcome **Disabled** no special facilities **Pets** accepted
Closed Oct to May; Mon and Tue lunch out of season
Proprietor Daniel Cussac

La Grande Chaumière

The small town of St-Florentin makes a pleasant stop-over if you are touring northern Burgundy or making your way south through France, and La Grande Chaumière is an attractive pink turn-of-the-century building close to the middle. The Bonvalots have steadily improved the place year-by-year since their arrival in 1975; most recently, all the bedrooms have been entirely redecorated in an essentially modern style. But the emphasis is on the restaurant – a light, smartly furnished room; Jean-Pierre cooks, while Madame manages the front of house with charm and enthusiasm.

Nearby Chablis (30 km) – wine; Auxerre (31 km) – cathedral.

3 Rue des Capucins 89600 St-Florentin
Tel 86.35.15.12
Location on quiet road in middle of town; with gardens and ample car parking
Meals breakfast, lunch, dinner
Prices rooms 250F-350F; meals 90F-260F
Rooms 11 double, 10 with bath, one with shower (2 twin); all rooms have central heating, phone, TV
Facilities dining-room, bar, sitting-area, breakfast room
Credit cards AE, DC, V
Children special meals and extra beds available
Disabled no special facilities
Pets if well behaved
Closed first week Sep, mid-Dec to mid-Jan; Wed out of season
Proprietor J-P Bonvalot

Côte-d'Or

Manor house hotel, Aloxe-Corton

Hôtel Clarion

The tiny village of Aloxe-Corton is a place of pilgrimage for lovers of great white wine. Its symbol is the château of Corton-André, a picturesque building of gleaming coloured tiles and tidy tunnels full of *premier crus*. Next to it lies the Hôtel Clarion, a 17thC mansion which has been cleverly converted into a small and exclusive hotel.

The style is a mix of modern and old, namely art deco furnishings set against old timberwork and beamed ceilings. Bedrooms are stylish and well co-ordinated, mainly in matching fabrics of pastel shades. Although varied in size and price, all are thoroughly comfortable and well equipped (leave yours for an hour or two and you may well come back to a bowl of fresh fruit or plate of gateaux). Bathrooms, in marble, are large and luxurious.

Other merits of the hotel are the comfortable salon (beams, open fireplace) opening out on to the park and vineyards, the free wine-tasting for guests in the impressive 18thC vaulted cellars, the large garden and the excellent breakfasts, which include eggs, cheese and fresh fruit in addition to the usual coffee and croissants.

Nearby Vineyards; Beaune – infirmary, wine museum; Le Rochepot (25 km) – château; Dijon (35 km).

21420 Aloxe-Corton
Tel 80.26.46.70
Location in middle of village, 3.5 km N of Beaune on N74; in large garden with ample car parking
Meals breakfast
Prices rooms 375F-685F
Rooms 10 double, all with bath (7 twin); one family room with bath; all rooms have central heating, phone, TV, minibar

Facilities sitting-room; bicycles
Credit cards AE, DC, MC, V
Children welcome; cots, special meals, baby-sitting available
Disabled one ground-floor bedroom specially equipped
Pets accepted
Closed never
Proprietor Christian Voarick

Côte-d'Or

Hôtel la Côte d'Or

In the past it has been the glorious classic cooking of Jean Crotet which has drawn people to this splendid traditional little hotel in the famous wine village of Nuits-St-Georges. Gastronomes should be warned that M. Crotet has taken himself off to run another establishment nearer Beaune, leaving the Côte d'Or in the hands of M. Guyot – so whether the cuisine will in future merit two stars from Michelin and two *toques* from Gault-Millau must be in doubt. But you can count on the virtues of the place as a hotel – spacious, airy rooms, traditionally decorated and kept with proper attention to detail.

Nearby Vineyards of the Côte de Nuits.

37 Rue Thurot 21700 Nuits-St-Georges
Tel 80.61.06.10
Location in town 22 km S of Dijon; with public car parking
Meals breakfast, lunch, dinner
Prices rooms 320F-600F; menus 140F-260F
Rooms 7 double, (4 twin) all with bath; all rooms have central heating, phone, TV
Facilities dining-rooms, sitting-room/bar
Credit cards AE8tSC, V
Children accepted; special meals on request
Disabled no special facilities
Pets not accepted
Closed Feb; Sun dinner and Wed
Manager M. Guyot

Hostellerie du Val-Suzon

The Hostellerie Val-Suzon, a country inn situated in a large flower-filled park, was originally an 18thC mill. It is now a charming little hotel with beams and flowery prints in the bedrooms and above-average cuisine. The modern annexe, known as the Chalet de la Fontaine aux Geais, is a short walk up the hillside. It is the more peaceful of the two buildings, but the less charming. Guests at both establishments eat in the dining-room of the Hostellerie or in the shady garden.

Nearby Château de Vantoux (10 km); Lake Kir (15 km).

RN 71, Val-Suzon 21121 Fontaine-lès-Dijon
Tel 80.35.60.15
Location in countryside 15 km NW of Dijon; with large gardens and ample car parking
Meals breakfast, lunch, dinner
Prices rooms 250F-320F; menus 120F-280F
Rooms 16 double, 10 with bath, 6 with shower (9 twin); one single with shower; all rooms have central heating, phone, alarm
Facilities 2 dining-rooms, bar, sitting-room
Credit cards MC, V
Children accepted; special meals available
Disabled no special facilities
Pets accepted in bedrooms; 35F charge
Closed Jan; Wed and Thu lunch, except Jun to Aug
Proprietors Yves and Chantal Perreau

Côte-d'Or

Restaurant with rooms, Bouilland

Hostellerie du Vieux Moulin

Jean-Pierre Silva and his wife Isabelle have worked hard for the last eight years, and there is no sign of any weakening. Since 1981, when this young couple took over the stream-side restaurant-with-rooms in the hamlet of Bouilland (where there are almost four times as many cows as people), much has changed; not least the restaurant itself.

Inevitably, some mourn the old place – simple and cheap – and regret the rather cold formality of the new. But few will fail to appreciate the cooking; Jean-Pierre is undoubtedly one of the most skilful chefs in the region – and the competition is tough. It is natural for him to want the accommodation to be impeccable, although some may feel that it is now a touch *too* elegant for its bucolic surroundings. The large dining-room looks out, through huge picture windows, over the stream and garden, which are dramatically illuminated at night. Bedrooms (some in a newly built annexe) are comfortable, and facilities include an intercom for anxious parents, who have no need to divert their attention from eating in order to check up on their offspring. What will the thoughtful Silvas think of next?

Nearby Ruins of Ste Marguerite abbey; Beaune.

Bouilland 21420 Savigny-lès-Beaune
Tel 80.21.51.16
Location on edge of village, 15 km N of Beaune; with gardens and car parking
Meals breakfast, lunch, dinner
Prices rooms 350F-700F; menus 140F-310F
Rooms 12 double, 8 with bath, 4 with shower (6 twin); all rooms have central heating, TV, phone, radio
Facilities breakfast room, sitting-room, dining-room
Credit cards MC, V
Children welcome; special meals, baby alarms available
Disabled access easy to dining-room; one ground-floor bedroom
Pets accepted
Closed mid-Dec to Jan; restaurant only Thu lunch and Wed, except public holidays
Proprietors M. and Mme Jean-Pierre Silva

Côte-d'Or

Hostellerie du Château

From the A6 you can see the medieval village of Chateauneuf-en-Auxois perched on a hilltop, but once you are there you feel a million miles from any modern motorway. The picturesque Hostellerie, cleverly converted from a 15thC presbytery close to the château, is almost entirely in keeping with the village around it: old stone walls, quiet rustic rooms, a delightful beamed restaurant (where wholesome Burgundian dishes are the order of the day) and charming terraced gardens.

Nearby Castle; Commarin (10 km) – château; Beaune (35 km).

Chateauneuf 21320 Pouilly-en-Auxois
Tel 80.49.22.00
Location overlooking château in hill village, 42 km SW of Dijon and 35 km NW of Beaune; with small garden
Meals breakfast, lunch, dinner
Prices rooms 130F-450F; menu 120F-250F, children's 55F
Rooms 9 double, 2 single; 9 with shower, 2 with bath; all rooms have central heating, phone
Facilities 2 dining-rooms, sitting-room, billiards room, bar
Credit cards AE, MC, V
Children welcome
Disabled no special facilities
Pets dogs not accepted in dining-room
Closed mid-Nov to mid-Mar
Proprietors M. and Mme Truchot

Les Grands Crus

Quarry-tiled floors, old beams, lime-washed walls, tapestry fabrics and a carved-stone fireplace all add to the illusion that this handsome Burgundian house was built far less recently than 1977; it combines the charm of the old with the comfort of the new – with perhaps too much emphasis on the latter in the small salon. The bedrooms, too, lack style in decoration, but they are peaceful, spacious and thoughtfully furnished, and look out over the famous Gevrey-Chambertin vineyards which you will doubtless have come here to admire. Breakfast is served in the small flowery garden in fine weather. There is no shortage of good restaurants in the area for other meals.

Nearby Dijon – Grand Duke's palace, Place de la Libération.

Rte des Grands Crus 21220 Gevrey-Chambertin
Tel 80.34.34.15
Location in middle of village, 10 km SW of Dijon; with garden and ample car parking
Meals breakfast
Prices rooms 245F-305F; children under 5 free
Rooms 24 double (8 twin) all with bath; all rooms have phone
Facilities sitting-room
Credit cards not accepted
Children welcome
Disabled no special facilities
Pets accepted but not to be left in rooms
Closed mid-Dec to end Feb
Proprietors M. and Mme Mortet

Côte-d'Or

Chez Camille

Armand Poinsot's excellent cooking (traditional but light, Michelin-starred) is only one attraction of this captivating little hotel. The bedrooms (the best of them quite spacious) are taste-fully decorated and furnished with antiques, and effectively double-glazed against noise from the RN6. Downstairs there is a cute little salon with enormous open fireplace, as well as the focus of the hotel – the conservatory-style dining-room. Created in an inner courtyard with stone walls and floor, wicker chairs, trellis and plants, it has an outdoor feel. Monique works front-of-house with charm and good humour.

Nearby Châteaux – Sully-sur-Loire (20 km), Le Rochepot.

1 Place Edouard-Herriot
21230 Arnay-le-Duc
Tel 80.90.01.38
Location in middle of town on RN6, 28km SE of Saulieu; with car parking and garage
Meals breakfast, lunch, dinner
Prices rooms 350F-325F; menus 118F-156F
Rooms 12 double, all with bath (6 twin); 2 family rooms with bath; all rooms have central heating, phone, TV
Facilities dining-room, sitting-room
Credit cards AE, DC, V
Children welcome; special menu available
Disabled no special facilities
Pets welcome
Closed Jan
Proprietors Monique and Armand Poinsot

Le Parc

As the centre of Burgundy's wine trade, Beaune is liberally endowed with wine-tasting cellars, and is also a fine town in its own right. Its only drawback as a stopping-off spot for motorists is the dearth of reasonably priced accommodation – at least in the middle of the town. But for those prepared to stay 6 km away, the Parc at Levernois offers excellent value and a pleasant rural setting. It is a simple hotel, converted from an old farmhouse, larger than many in this book but retaining the atmosphere of a small *auberge* thanks largely to the amiable owner, Mme Moreau. She runs the Parc rather like a private home, drawing many regular visitors year after year.

Nearby Beaune; Archèodrome (5 km); Dijon (45 km).

Levernois 21200 Beaune
Tel 80.22.22.51
Location on edge of village 5 km SE of Beaune; with garden and ample car parking
Meals breakfast
Prices rooms 120F-180F
Rooms 20 double, 3 with bath, 16 with shower (6 twin); all rooms have central heating, phone
Facilities bar, breakfast room
Credit cards AE, DC, MC, V
Children accepted
Disabled several ground-floor bedrooms
Pets accepted
Closed 2 weeks late Nov, 2 weeks early Mar
Proprietor Mme Jacqueline Moreau

Saône-et-Loire

Hostellerie du Château de Bellecroix

This creeper-covered château combines 12thC and 18thC architecture to magical effect. There is a grand spiral staircase, round bedrooms in the turrets and other rooms, in an annexe, which make up in grace what they lack in novelty. All are furnished with a sensible blend of antique, reproduction and modern furniture, and enjoy views over the mature surrounding parkland. The main dining-room is plain but pleasant – wood-panelled, with a stone fireplace, simple wooden chairs and crisp white tablecloths. Modest prices by château standards.

Nearby Archéodrome (10 km); Beaune (15 km) – wine tasting.

71150 Chagny
Tel 85.87.13.86
Location just SE of town on RN6; in large grounds with ample car parking
Meals breakfast, lunch, dinner
Prices rooms 300F-750F; menus 95F-280F
Rooms 19 double, 16 with bath, 3 with shower (5 twin); all rooms have central heating, phone

Facilities dining-room, sitting-room, bar, conference room; swimming-pool
Credit cards AE, DC, MC, V
Children accepted if well behaved
Disabled no special facilities
Pets accepted at extra charge
Closed mid- to end Dec; Wed
Proprietor Mme Evelyne Gautier

Hôtel Lameloise

In an ancient house, in the rather dull heart of Chagny, Jacques Lameloise carries on his father Jean's reputation for excellent cooking. The house lacks the public rooms to be considered a proper hotel – apart from the elegant restaurant, there is only a small bar and a sitting area by reception – and has no garden or terrace. But there are compensations: all is beautifully decorated and serene, and the bedrooms are thoroughly comfortable, with well-equipped bathrooms. And of course the food is the thing – about the best in a region noted for its excellent cuisine. In case over-indulgence leaves you incapable of motion, a lift/elevator has been newly installed.

Nearby Beaune (15 km) – medieval infirmary, wine tasting.

36 Place d'Armes 71150 Chagny
Tel 85.87.08.85
Location in middle of town
Meals breakfast, lunch, dinner
Prices rooms 280F-950F; menus 250F-400F
Rooms 21 double, 19 with bath, 2 with shower (7 twin); all rooms have TV, phone

Facilities sitting-room, dining-room, bar, lift/elevator
Credit cards V
Children accepted
Disabled no special facilities
Pets accepted in bedrooms, but not in dining-room
Closed 20 Dec to 20 Jan; Wed, and Thu until 5 pm
Proprietors Lameloise family

Saône-et-Loire

Hôtel de la Poste

A prime example of an unassuming provincial hotel – in the heart of beef-cattle country – doing a sound job. Flowers and shrubs crowd the pavement outside; the white-painted building is immaculately maintained, as is the smart bar-salon; and the dining-room has been made positively Ritzy by small-town standards, so as not to undermine Daniel Doucet's culinary ambitions – though they remain firmly rooted in *cuisine bourgeoise*. (Naturally, *entrecôte charolaise* is among his specialities.) Bedrooms are unremarkable but comfortable.

Nearby Paray-le-Monial (15 km); Cluny (40 km).

2 Ave de la Libèration 71120 Charolles **Tel** 85.24.11.32 **Location** in middle of small town, 55 km W of Mâcon; with garage and car parking opposite **Meals** breakfast, lunch, dinner **Prices** rooms 175F-250F; menus 90F-260F **Rooms** 9 double, 6 with bath, 3 with shower (4 twin);	3 family rooms; all rooms have central heating, TV, phone **Facilities** sitting-room, dining-room **Credit cards** AE, MC, V **Children** very welcome **Disabled** no special facilities **Pets** very welcome **Closed** Nov; Sun evening and Mon **Proprietors** M. and Mme Daniel Doucet

Hôtel de Bourgogne

Run by the Gosse family for over three decades, the Hôtel de Bourgogne is the most comfortable and central hotel in Cluny. An attractive stone mansion, dating from 1817, it is built around a garden and courtyard. Most of the bedrooms look out on to the remains of the abbey, or over surrounding green hills, and the elegant setting and Burgundian specialities of the Michelin-starred restaurant draw many non-residents.

Nearby Abbey ruins; Azé caves (10 km); St-Point château and church (15 km).

Place de l'Abbaye 71250 Cluny **Tel** 85.59.00.58 **Location** in middle of town, 27 km NW of Mâcon; with small courtyard and parking **Meals** breakfast, lunch, dinner **Prices** rooms 185F-900F; lunch 120F-350F, dinner 190F-350F **Rooms** 16 double, 15 with bath or shower (12 twin); all rooms have phone, central	heating **Facilities** dining-room, sitting-room, bar/breakfast room **Credit cards** AE, DC, MC, V **Children** welcome; special meals available **Disabled** access difficult **Pets** accepted in bedrooms (at a charge), not in restaurant **Closed** various weeks between Nov and Mar **Proprietor** J-C Gosse

Saône-et-Loire

Village inn, Mercurey

Hôtellerie du Val d'Or

This early 19thC coaching inn, on the main street of the rather dull wine village of Mercurey, continues to delight visitors. It is easy to see why: in a region of culinary excellence and exhorbitant prices, many are daunted by the over-formal (or even pretentious) style of most hotels in the area, and long to find some village-inn simplicity. The Val d'Or obliges, and combines this with excellent cooking and comfortable (but smallish) bedrooms.

Nearby Château Germolles (10 km); Buxy (20 km); wine tasting.

Grande-Rue 71640 Mercurey
Tel 85.45.13.70
Location in middle of village, 9 km S of Chagny; with garden and car parking
Meals breakfast, lunch, dinner
Prices rooms 190F-280F; meals 130F-280F, children's 50F-60F
Rooms 8 double (3 twin), one single, 2 family rooms; all with bath or shower; all

rooms have central heating, TV, phone
Facilities 2 dining-rooms, lounge/bar
Credit cards V
Children accepted
Disabled no special facilities
Pets not accepted
Closed 13 Dec to 13 Jan, first week in Sep; restaurant only Mon and Tue lunch (Sun dinner in winter)
Proprietor Jean Claude Cogny

Saône-et-Loire

Château de Fleurville

Unlike so many châteaux hotels, this is not a formal, luxury establishment – the atmosphere is pleasantly relaxed (you can feel at ease with children) and it is reasonably priced. It is well placed for touring, or for a stop-over on the way south (close to the A6 and N6, though in a large, quiet park). Dating from the 16thC, it retains many of the original features – old stone fireplaces, timbered ceilings, quarry-tiled floors – and despite various modernizations there is still a medieval atmosphere. Bedrooms are simply furnished with a variety of antiques. There are mixed reports about the food, though most people seem to enjoy the fish.

Nearby Azé caves (10 km); Tournus – abbey (15 km).

71260 Fleurville
Tel 85.33.12.17
Location 17 km N of Mâcon, off N6; with gardens and ample car parking
Meals breakfast, lunch, dinner
Prices rooms 330F; meals 120F-230F
Rooms 14 double, all with bath (7 twin); one family room with bath; all rooms have central heating, phone
Facilities sitting-room, bar, dining-room
Credit cards AE, DC, MC, V
Children welcome
Disabled no special facilities
Pets accepted
Closed 15 Nov to 25 Dec
Proprietors Naudin family

Hotel de la Halle

The façade of La Halle is undistinguished – with its slightly grubby white-shuttered windows and glass-fronted bar – and furniture and decoration in both the dining-room and the bedrooms are distinctly basic. What captivates a steady stream of British visitors – as well as the large band of local regulars in the restaurant – is the scrupulous housekeeping, Christian Renard's excellent traditional Burgundian cuisine, the exceptionally low prices for both rooms and meals and (most of all) the Renards' good-hearted welcome. The one notable feature of the building is a splendid 12thC spiral staircase.

Nearby Chalon (10 km) – photography museum; Beaune (35 km).

Place de la Halle 71640 Givry
Tel 85.44.32.45
Location in middle of village, 10 km W of Chalon-sur-Saône; with car parking
Meals breakfast, lunch, dinner
Prices rooms 100F-165F; menus 50F-165F
Rooms 10 double (3 twin), most with bath or shower; all rooms have central heating, phone
Facilities sitting-room, dining-room, bar
Credit cards AE, DC, MC, V
Children accepted
Disabled access to restaurant only
Pets not accepted
Closed Nov
Proprietor Christian Renard

Saône-et-Loire

Les Récollets

The Brionnais is a rural region, with gently rolling hills and lush meadows where Charollais cattle graze. It is a part of Burgundy that few French, let alone foreigners, are really familiar with, and even in summer months you can drive for miles without meeting another tourist.

The small market town of Marcigny provides an excellent base for touring – it is close to the Loire, and not far from the famous cattle market of St-Christophe-en-Brionnais. It is also the location of one of the most delightful hotels in the region, and one which has (up to now) escaped the notice of any guidebook. Converted from an ancient convent, Les Récollets is an ideal combination of French chic and home comforts. There are log fires, home-made *brioches* for breakfast, hand-made chocolates by the bedside (along with sleeping tablets, indigestion pills and painkillers). Indeed, every need is catered for, and the only house-rule is 'do as you please'.

Josette Badin, who runs the place with Burgundian *bon-homie*, has furnished the rooms superbly, from the dining-room with its hand-painted cupboards to the antique-laden bedrooms. Officially, only breakfast is served, but ask in advance and Josette will be happy to prepare a simple meal: soup or omelette – even foie gras, followed by Charollais beef.

Nearby Mill Tower Museum; La Clayette (25 km); Charlieu Abbey (30 km); Château Drée (30 km).

Place du Champ de Foire
71110 Marcigny
Tel 85.25.05.16
Location in small town 22 km S of Paray; in grounds with ample car parking
Meals breakfast; lunch and dinner on request
Prices rooms 300F (with breakfast for 2)
Rooms 4 double, all with bath (2 twin); 3 family rooms, all with bath; all rooms have central heating, phone
Facilities TV room, library, breakfast/dining-room
Credit cards not accepted
Children accepted
Disabled one ground-floor bedroom
Pets accepted
Closed never
Proprietor Mme Josette Badin

Saône-et-Loire

Converted mill, St-Gervais-en-Vallière

Moulin d'Hauterive

The wheels of this ancient watermill were still turning less than 30 years ago; only for the last decade or so has it been enjoying a new lease of life as a country hotel – offering an unusual blend of rural seclusion (it is a *Relais du Silence*), good living and sporty activities.

It is a handsome creeper-clad building, four storeys high, surrounded by lower outbuildings. The interior is the epitome of rustic chic. The building contributes beams, smooth stone-flagged floors, whitewashed or pale rough stone walls. Against this backdrop are placed bright fabrics, delicate mellow antiques, gleaming ornaments, extravagant bowls of flowers. Bedrooms are romantically done out – beds are often draped or canopied with lacy fabrics.

The Moilles are a young couple who were new to hotel keeping when they set up the Moulin. Madame came new to professional cooking, too, but has gained a formidable reputation for her essentially simple but inventive dishes.

The swimming-pool has a lift-off cover/roof which is doubtless a great aid to energy conservation but diminishes the pleasure of swimming.

Nearby Archéodrome (10 km) – archeological centre; Beaune (15 km) – medieval infirmary, wine museum.

Chaublanc 71350
St-Gervais-en-Vallière
Tel 85.91.55.56
Location in countryside beside river, 16 km SE of Beaune, off D970; in grounds with car parking
Meals breakfast, lunch, dinner
Prices rooms 360F–600F; menus 180F–230F; children under 3 free
Rooms 16 double, 10 with bath, 6 with shower; one single with shower; 5 family rooms, with bath; all rooms have central heating, TV, phone, minibar
Facilities 2 dining-rooms, bar, 4 seminar rooms; swimming-pool, tennis, health spa, billiards, heliport
Credit cards AE, DC, V
Children accepted
Disabled no special facilities
Pets dogs accepted in bedrooms at extra charge
Closed Dec, Jan
Proprietors Christiane and Michel Moille

Jura

Chez Yvonne

This modest, family-run *logis* lies in the quiet, untamed region of the Jura, beside the River d'Ain and is a real haven of peace. The accommodation is simple and cosy, but the real reason for coming here is the food. For years it has been serving excellent regional fare, at reasonable prices: *morilles* fresh from the forests, trout from the rivers and streams, and corn-fed chickens from Bresse. In summer, the riverside terrace makes an ideal spot for lunch or dinner.

Nearby Abbey of Baume-les-Messieurs (15 km); Pin Château (20 km); Hérisson Falls (20 km).

Châtillon 39130 Clairvaux-les-Lacs
Tel 84.25.70.82
Location in countryside 20 km E of Lons-le-Saunier; with ample car parking and garages
Meals breakfast, lunch, dinner
Prices rooms 70F-160F; meals 95F-195F
Rooms 10 double, 8 with shower (2 twin); all rooms have central heating
Facilities 2 dining-rooms, breakfast-room, ping-pong room
Credit cards AE, DC, MC, V
Children accepted
Disabled no special facilities
Pets accepted
Closed 15 Nov to 15 Jan
Proprietor Richard Routhier

Auberge du Rostaing

A completely peaceful and relaxed *auberge* in an attractive and unspoiled area west of the Jura. It is a simple place, but well run by the charming Eckerts and with more to offer than most competitors – an inviting sitting-room with music, games and books, and a shady courtyard-garden for drinks. The airy dining-room is stylishly rustic, the bedrooms fresh – some of them in an adjacent building with an outside staircase. Madame cooks well; and just look at the prices.

Nearby Château-Chalon (5 km); Cirque de Ladoye (10 km).

Passenans 39230 Sellières
Tel 84.85.23.70
Location on outskirts of hamlet, 11 km SW of Poligny on D 57; with garden
Meals breakfast, lunch, dinner
Prices rooms 70F-145F (extra bed 25F-35F); menus 50F-125F
Rooms 9 double (3 twin), 3 with bath, 2 with shower; one family room with bath; all rooms have central heating
Facilities 2 dining-rooms, sitting-room; bicycles for hire
Credit cards DC, MC, V
Children accepted; reductions by arrangement
Disabled no special facilities
Pets accepted
Closed Dec, Jan
Proprietor Félix Eckert

Doubs/Rhône

Chalet hotel, Goumois

Hôtel Taillard

The wooded Doubs valley is a paradise for fishermen, and this fine traditional chalet hotel is where to come and eat trout or salmon (and much else besides – the restaurant earns a Michelin star), and then to linger over the peaceful view towards Switzerland. With its wide picture windows, the chalet is light and airy; there is a comfortable sitting-room, and for fine days a splendid terrace. Bedrooms are thin on style but comfortable enough, some with balconies. Guests in this rather remote spot are generally regulars or guidebook-led; few are disappointed. The Taillard family are excellent hosts.

Nearby Doubs valley, mountains, forests: walking, fishing.

25470 Goumois
Tel 81.44.20.75
Location in fields above village, 14 km E of Maîche, on Swiss frontier; with ample car parking and garage
Meals breakfast, lunch, dinner
Prices rooms 80F-280F; menus 90F-260F
Rooms 17 double, 10 with bath, 7 with shower (7 twin);
all rooms have central heating, TV, phone
Facilities bar, sitting-room, 2 dining-rooms
Credit cards AE, DC, MC, V
Children accepted; special meals available
Disabled access easy to dining-room
Pets accepted
Closed end Nov to Mar
Proprietor M. Taillard

Riverside hotel, Condrieu

Hôtellerie Beau Rivage

The *beau rivage* is that of the Rhône, though these days it is not an entirely appropriate description, given the nearby chemical works. But Paulette Castaing – now in her seventies – continues to win the praise of most visitors for the precision and care of her traditional cooking (still earning 2 stars from Michelin and 2 *toques* from Gault-Millau, and described as 'outstanding' by our most recent reporter). The hotel remains solidly comfortable, the shady dining terrace more attractive than the plain modern dining-room. Spacious bedrooms.

Nearby Vineyards; Malleval (10 km); Vienne (10 km).

Rue du Beau Rivage 69420 Condrieu
Tel 74.59.52.24
Location beside the river Rhône in Condrieu, 40 km S of Lyon on RN86; with garden terrace, and garage by arrangement
Meals breakfast, lunch, dinner
Prices rooms 260F-550F, suites 700F; menus 215F-330F
Rooms 22 double, 4 suites, all with bath or shower; all rooms have central heating, phone
Facilities sitting-room, dining-room
Credit cards AE, DC, MC, V
Children accepted
Disabled no special facilities
Pets accepted at extra charge
Closed Jan to mid-Feb
Proprietor Mme Castaing

Ain

Restaurant with rooms, Montmerle-sur-Saône

Castel de Valrose

For motorists, the location of the Castel de Valrose could not be better. It is only 6.5 km from the A6, but the peaceful setting, just 100 metres from the River Saône, seems far removed from the hurly-burly of the *autoroute*. What is more, it is a friendly, comfortable place to stay and the cuisine is better than average. But this is no castle. It is a large 1930s house, with modern decoration. Even if you are not intending to stay the night, the food, with the emphasis on fish from the river, is reason enough for a deviation from the motorway.

Nearby Villefranche-sur-Saône – wine centre; Trévoux (20 km).

12 Blvd de la République
01090 Montmerle-sur-
Saône
Tel 74.69.30.52
Location S of village, close to
river Saône, 30 km S of
Mâcon; in garden, with car
parking
Meals breakfast, lunch,
dinner
Prices rooms 190F-280F;
menus 95F-230F
Rooms 6 double, 5 with
bath, one with shower (2
twin); 4 family rooms, all
with bath; all rooms have
central heating, phone
Facilities 2 dining-rooms,
banquet room
Credit cards V
Children accepted
Disabled no special facilities
Pets dogs welcome if well
behaved **Closed** Jan
Proprietor Christian
Birgolotti

Ain

Restaurant with rooms, Meximieux

Claude Lutz

Claude Lutz's restaurant-with-rooms stretches our terms of reference, but is ideal if you need a stop-off near the motorway to Geneva and are more interested in good food than in stylish bedrooms. The comfortable dining-room (in Louis XIII style) is naturally the focal point. Bedrooms (including a couple of family-sized ones) face the street and there is some traffic noise in the morning.

Nearby Pérouges – medieval village; Villars-les-Dombes (30 km) – bird sanctuary; Lyons (35 km); Bourg (45 km).

17 Rue de Lyon 01800 Meximieux
Tel 74.61.06.78
Location in middle of town, 1 km E of Pérouges; with enclosed garden and ample car parking
Meals breakfast, lunch, dinner
Prices rooms 130F-270F; meals 125F-265F, children's menu 70F
Rooms 15 double, 5 with bath, 10 with shower (2 twin); 2 family rooms, both with shower; all rooms have central heating, phone, TV
Facilities 2 dining-rooms, bar
Credit cards AE, MC, V
Children welcome
Disabled no special facilities
Pets dogs accepted
Closed 2 weeks Jul, 3 weeks Oct/Nov; Sun evening and Mon
Proprietors M. and Mme Claude Lutz

Restaurant with rooms, Mionnay

Alain Chapel

Gastronomy has always been the forte of the Chapel family. Alain's father was *maître d'hôtel* in one of the most famous restaurants of Lyon, then in 1930 bought the Mère Charles at Mionnay – an old village bistro which 30 years later was to become the famous luxury restaurant-with-rooms it is today. A meal here is a truly memorable experience – from the succulent appetizers to the irresistible plate of *petits fours*.

Bedrooms, all of which were renovated in 1986 and decorated in Laura Ashley fabrics, are the height of luxury (as they should be at the price).

Nearby Lyon – Textile Museum, church of St-Marin-d'Ainay.

01390 Mionnay
Tel 78.91.82.02
Location in countryside, 18 km NE of Lyon on N83; with garden and public car parking
Meals breakfast, lunch, dinner
Prices rooms 600F-750F; meals 475F-580F
Rooms 13 double, all with bath (4 twin); all rooms have central heating, phone, TV
Facilities 3 dining-rooms, bar
Credit cards AE, DC, MC, V
Children welcome; special menu available
Disabled no special facilities
Pets accepted; extra charge in hotel
Closed Jan; restaurant only Mon and Tue lunch (except holidays)
Proprietor Alain Chapel

Ain

Ostellerie du Vieux Pérouges

Pérouges is a perfectly preserved medieval village and at its heart, on the main square, is the Ostellerie du Vieux Pérouges, an irresistible timbered building. Both village and hotel have, not surprisingly, an eye to the tourist, but not offensively so. In the restaurant, the theme is medieval: meals on copper dishes, aperitifs in pewter goblets. Food is essentially regional and a speciality is the *galette Pérougienne*, a sort of sweet tart, served with plenty of thick cream. The bedrooms (some are in two nearby annexes) are mostly furnished with handsome antiques, including four-poster beds, and a few have small terraces.

Nearby Rue des Rondes; Villars-les-Dombes (30 km) – bird sanctuary; Lyons (35 km); Bourg (45 km).

Place du Tilleul, Pérouges
01800 Meximieux
Tel 74.61.00.88
Location in middle of medieval town; with car parking and garage
Meals breakfast, lunch, dinner
Prices rooms 390F-750F; meals 150F-320F
Rooms 25 double, all with bath (14 twin); 4 family rooms, all with bath; all rooms have phone
Facilities dining-room, sitting-rooms, bar
Credit cards V
Children accepted
Disabled no special facilities
Pets accepted
Closed Wed out of season
Proprietor Georges Thibaut

Hôtel du Rhône

Seyssel is a small town split in two by the upper Rhône; the main part is on the left bank, in Haute-Savoie, the minor part across the river in Ain – which is where the Hôtel du Rhône is found, separated from the river bank only by its sunny elevated dining terrace and a minor road. The setting apart, what distinguishes the hotel – which is a modest place, with no pretensions to luxury or style – is Robert Herbelot's cooking. His cuisine is classic with a regional emphasis (which, with Bourg not far away, naturally means plenty of *poulets*), and good enough to earn a Michelin star.

Nearby Le Grand-Colombier (20 km); Abbaye de Hautecombe (30 km).

Quai de Gaulle 01420
Seyssel
Tel 50.59.20.30
Location outside town beside Rhône, 37 km W of Annecy; with garage and car parking
Meals breakfast, lunch, dinner
Prices rooms 150F-290F; meals from 125F
Rooms 16 double (6 twin – 2 with double beds), 10 with bath or shower; all rooms have central heating
Facilities dining-room, sitting-room
Credit cards DC, MC, V
Children welcome
Disabled no special facilities
Pets welcome
Closed mid-Nov to mid-Feb
Proprietor Robert Herbelot

Haute-Savoie

Chalet hotel, Chamonix

Auberge du Bois Prin

The Auberge du Bois Prin is a superior chalet-style hotel close to the foot of the Brévent cable-car, with a magnificent panorama of the snow-capped dome of Mont Blanc. The friendly Carriers have run the hotel since it was built in 1976; Denis's brother also runs a hotel in Chamonix, whose facilities can be used by guests at the Bois Prin. Bedrooms are luxuriously furnished, with flowery fabrics and carved woodwork (much of it Denis's own work); nine have a private terrace.

Nearby Mt Blanc and Le Brévent – walking, rock climbing.

69 Chemin de l'Hermine, Les Moussoux 74400 Chamonix
Tel 50.53.33.51
Location on hillside, NW of town; with garden and ample car parking
Meals breakfast, lunch, dinner
Prices rooms 760F-790F (with breakfast for 2); meals 130F-340F
Rooms 9 double, all with bath (5 twin); 2 family rooms, with bath; all rooms have TV, phone, minibar
Facilities dining-room, seminar room
Credit cards AE, DC, V
Children welcome; special meals, high-chair available
Disabled no special facilities
Pets accepted
Closed 10 May to 5 June, 10 Oct to 18 Dec
Proprietors Monique and Denis Carrier

Haute-Savoie

Pavillon de l'Ermitage

One day we shall find a captivating small hotel in the lovely old town of Annecy. Until then, our summer strategy will remain one of staying out of the town (and so escaping its traffic and parking problems) on the shores of the splendid lake. It is only a summer strategy because, to be frank, Maurice Tuccinardi's villa lacks character and style, and it is only in summer that the pleasures of its lakeside garden and dining-terrace can compensate. M. Tuccinardi's cooking (worthy of a Michelin star) is what the place is all about: *cuisine classique* making use of lake fish and Bresse poultry.

Nearby Annecy – old town, château, boat trips.

79 Rte d'Annecy, Chavoire 74290 Veyrier-du-Lac **Tel** 50.60.11.09 **Location** beside lake, 3 km E of Annecy; with gardens and ample car parking **Meals** breakfast, lunch, dinner **Prices** rooms 155F-430F; menus 170F-310F **Rooms** 10 double, 9 with bath (4 twin); 3 family	rooms, one with bath; all rooms have central heating, phone **Facilities** dining-room, sitting-room **Credit cards** AE, DC, V **Children** accepted **Disabled** no special facilities **Pets** accepted **Closed** Oct to Mar **Proprietors** Maurice Tuccinardi

Chalet Hôtel de la Croix-Fry

Mountain chalets come in many styles, but the pretty-as-a-cuckoo-clock variety is all too rare in France. This cosy modern hotel is about as close as you get; it has kept a rustic style even in its modern annexe-chalets, which offer flexible and comfortable accommodation (with kitchenettes) for all sizes of family. Style apart, the peaceful setting is the attraction, with superb views across the valley from the flowery terrace. The tennis court and swimming-pool are further pluses; and the welcoming owners have prepared detailed information about things to do.

Nearby Vallée de Manigod; Thônes (10 km); Annecy (30 km).

Rte du Col de la Croix-Fry, Manigod 74230 Thônes **Tel** 50.44.90.16 **Location** at the col, 5 km NE of Manigod, on D16 10 km S of La Clusaz; in countryside, with ample car parking **Meals** breakfast, lunch, dinner **Prices** DB&B 300F (for one) **Rooms** 15 double with bath (5 twin); all rooms have central heating, phone	**Facilities** dining-room, sitting-room, bar; swimming-pool, tennis **Credit cards** MC, V **Children** accepted **Disabled** no special facilities **Pets** not in dining-room **Closed** mid-Sep to mid-Dec, mid-Apr to mid-Jun **Proprietor** Mme Marie-Ange Guelpa-Veyrat

Isère

Domaine de Clairefontaine

In sharp contrast to the nearby Marais St-Jean, this rather austere stone mansion in peaceful parkland has an old-fashioned, essentially French appeal. Bedrooms are in the main solid and spacious, with huge wardrobes and chests, and large bathrooms with somewhat erratic plumbing. Public rooms consist of two formal dining-rooms and a baronial salon (which acts as the main sitting-room if it is not warm enough to sit in the garden). The cooking is variable, but affluent gastronomes can opt for the Marais St-Jean or one of several Michelin-starred restaurants.
Nearby Condrieu (5 km) – vineyards; Malleval (15 km).

Chonas l'Amballan 38121
Reventin-Vaugris
Tel 74.58.81.52
Location in countryside
9 km S of Vienne, just off
N7; with large grounds and
ample car parking
Meals breakfast, lunch, dinner
Prices rooms 110F-300F;
menus 95F-210F
Rooms 13 double, 9 with
bath (5 twin); 5 single, 3 with
bath; 4 family rooms, 2 with
bath, one with shower; all
have central heating, phone
Facilities sitting-room,
dining-room; tennis
Credit cards MC, V
Children accepted **Disabled**
access possible to 5
bedrooms **Pets** accepted but
not in dining-room
Closed Dec to Feb; Mon lunch
Proprietor Mme Girardon

Le Marais St-Jean

Christian and Suzette Heugas are enthusiastic hosts who make every effort to run their 'hostellerie' more like a private house than a stereotyped hotel. Christian is the chef, and his cooking is among the best you will come across in the area. There are set menus to suit most pockets, plus a 'carte' with specialities such as fresh salmon grilled with sorrel sauce and guinea fowl stuffed with fresh onion. There is also an excellent selection of Rhône wines. The location, above the Rhône valley, is quiet and rural.
Nearby Condrieu (5 km) – river port, vineyards; Malleval (10 km) – medieval village above gorge; Lyon (40 km).

Chonas-l'Amballon 38121
Reventin-Vaugris
Tel 74.58.83.28
Location just outside village,
10 km S of Vienne; with
garden and car parking
Meals breakfast, lunch,
dinner
Prices rooms 420F; menus
120F-280F
Rooms 10 double, all with
bath and shower (5 twin); all
rooms have phone
Facilities 2 sitting-rooms,
bar, dining-room,
conference room
Credit cards AE, DC, MC, V
Children welcome; extra
bed and special menu
Disabled one ground-floor
bedroom
Pets welcome
Closed Feb, 1 Nov to 10
Nov; Tue evening and Wed
Proprietors Suzette and
Christian Heugas

Isère/Hautes-Alpes

Le Cucheron

This roadside chalet occupies a beautiful spot, on the summit of the Col du Cucheron, surrounded by firs and Alpine meadows, ideal for mountain hikes and skiing – the *pistes* are only 20 metres away. Don't expect too much from the hotel. It is no more than a simple, family-run restaurant, with basic rooms and a cosy sitting-room. The food complements the setting: mountain hams, fresh trout, local cheeses and Savoie wines; finishing, inevitably, with a glass (or two) of the famous local liqueur.

Nearby Grenoble (25 km) – art museum, Fort de la Bastille (by cable-car); Voiron (25 km) – Chartreuse liqueur.

St-Pierre-de-Chartreuse
38380 St-Laurent-du-Pont
Tel 76.88.62.06
Location on roadside 3 km S of St-Pierre-de-Chartreuse; with ample car parking
Meals breakfast, lunch, dinner
Prices rooms 95F-150F; meals 65F-125F
Rooms 6 double, 3 with bath (2 twin); one family room with bath; all rooms have central heating
Facilities dining-room, bar, games and TV room
Credit cards AE, MC, V
Children welcome; special meals available
Disabled no special facilities
Pets dogs accepted in bedrooms only
Closed 15 Oct to 15 Dec; Tue, except in school holidays
Proprietor André Mahaut

Auberge du Choucas

The Auberge de Choucas re-opened in July 1988 after a thorough refurbishing, but the charm of this old farmhouse in the heart of an Alpine village has reportedly been retained. Downstairs the vaulted rooms, old beams and fireplaces create a warm atmosphere. Equally inviting are the bedrooms – although these are newer in style with light wood furnishings, terraces (in the case of eight rooms) and, in some, kitchenettes.

Nearby Parc des Ecrins – walks and climbing; Briançon – walled citadel, Pont d'Asfeld, Grand-Rue; high mountain passes.

17 Rue de la Fruitière 05220 Monêtier-les-Bains
Tel 92.24.42.73
Location in middle of village, 16 km NW of Briançon; with small garden and public car parking
Meals breakfast, lunch, dinner
Prices DB&B 355F (for one); full board 395F
Rooms 8 double, all with bath (4 twin); 4 family rooms, all with bath; all rooms have TV, phone
Facilities dining-room, cellar bar; sauna
Credit cards AE, DC
Children accepted if well behaved
Disabled access possible
Pets accepted
Closed restaurant only, spring and autumn
Proprietors Yves Gattechaut and Nicole Sanchez-Ventura.

Gironde

Auberge de la Commanderie

St-Emilion is much the most attractive base for exploration of the vineyards of Bordeaux. Were the Commanderie located elsewhere, it might not appear here: it lacks space in which to relax – there is neither a sitting-room nor a garden – and its corridors and some bedrooms are rather gloomy. But it is the best in town, and has several plus points: other bedrooms are light and pleasantly decorated in vivid flowery prints, the position (only a short stroll up from the central square) is convenient for exploration of the beautiful town, the staff are friendly, breakfast is excellent (warm croissants and rolls) though other meals do not earn high marks from recent visitors.

Nearby various sights in St-Emilion; Bordeaux vineyards.

Rue des Cordeliers 33330 St-Emilion
Tel 57.24.70.19
Location in middle of town, on main road; public car parking nearby
Meals breakfast, lunch, dinner
Prices rooms 150F-250F; menus 90F-250F
Rooms 15 double, 12 with bath, one with shower (6 twin); all rooms have central heating, phone
Facilities dining-room, bar
Credit cards AE, DC, MC, V
Children accepted
Disabled access difficult
Pets not accepted
Closed Dec, Jan
Proprietor Mme Hannequin

Domaine de Loselly

This handsome brick-built house, in gardens that sweep down to the River Dordogne, is largely unchanged from the days when it was a family home, and some of the simply furnished bedrooms will take four people comfortably. The particularly attractive and relaxing sitting-room is furnished in a happily mixture of antique styles; the dining-room is much simpler – wooden tables covered with red cloths. Michel Macq and his wife are a charming couple who share the job of running the hotel – cooking included. The food tends to be simple – one four-course set menu – but unlimited wine is included in the fixed price.

Nearby Ste-Foy-la-Grande – *bastide*; Montcaret (15 km).

38 Ave Georges Clémenceau, Pineuilh 33220 Ste-Foy-la-Grande
Tel 57.46.10.59
Location on main road through small village, 2 km SE of Ste-Foy, 22 km W of Bergerac; with gardens and private car parking
Meals breakfast, dinner
Prices rooms 150F-320F; menu 90F
Rooms all rooms have central heating, phone, alarm
Facilities dining-room (residents only), sitting-room, small conference room
Credit cards AE, DC, MC, V
Children accepted
Disabled access difficult
Pets accepted in first-floor rooms only **Closed** never
Proprietors M. and Mme Michel Macq

Dordogne

Auberge du Noyer

We tend to shy away from places run by British *emigrés*, but this lovely old farmhouse run by Paul and Jenny Dyer – who 12 years ago gave up their wine bar in Southend to come here – is irresistible. They have made it a perfect place to unwind, where you are encouraged to make yourself at home and enjoy the luxury of being looked after. Tucked away, high in the hills above Le Bugue, the house has nothing in view except wooded hills. The swimming-pool is particularly delightful: reached by steps leading behind from the house, it is secluded and sunny, but surrounded by trees to give shade when you want it. The farmhouse and its outbuildings, dating from the 18thC, have been completely restored with panache and sensitivity. Some of the prettiest bedrooms are in the converted barn (decorated with Laura Ashley prints) but all the rooms are large and full of character.

Two French chefs are responsible for the excellent food served in the atmospheric dining-room, dominated by a large stone fireplace, with masses of fresh flowers and candles. This is an excellent hotel for children – the Dyers have two of their own and are happy to baby-sit, and if the weather is bad there is plenty of space in the large sitting-room.

Nearby Bara-Bahau cave – engravings; Les Eyzies-de-Tayac (15 km) – National Prehistoric Museum; Beynac (30 km).

Le Reclaud de Bouny-Bas
24260 Le Bugue
Tel 53.07.11.73
Location in hilly countryside, off D703 4 km W of Le Bugue; in gardens, with ample car parking
Meals breakfast, lunch, dinner
Prices rooms 160F-320F; meals from 85F
Rooms 10 double, all with bath; all rooms have central heating, phone
Facilities dining-room, sitting-room/bar; swimming-pool
Credit cards MC, V
Children very welcome; meals available with proprietors' children
Disabled access difficult
Pets not welcome
Closed end Dec to mid Mar
Proprietors Paul and Jenny Dyer

Dordogne

Hôtel de L'Esplanade

Like many other busy tourist villages, Domme is best enjoyed in the evening and early morning; if that is your aim, the place to stay is the Esplanade, with the splendid view over the Dordogne that is one of the village's chief attractions. The hotel is beautifully furnished with taste and flair, and well run – housekeeping is immaculate and service (under the uncompromising eye of the charming Mme Gillard) is efficient and pleasant. Some bedrooms are in an annexe, some have private terraces; all are comfortable and the best are very spacious. René Gillard is the chef, and has earned a Michelin star.

Nearby Beynac (10 km); Les Eyzies-de-Tayac (40 km).

24250 Domme
Tel 53.28.31.41
Location on edge of village 12 km S of Sarlat; with garden
Meals breakfast, lunch, dinner
Prices rooms 200F-400F, DB&B (encouraged) 250F-370F; menus 110F-300F
Rooms 19 double (6 twin), 15 with bath, 4 with shower; all rooms have central heating, phone
Facilities dining-room, sitting-room, bar
Credit cards AE, MC, V
Children accepted **Disabled** access difficult **Pets** accepted
Closed Nov to Feb; Mon out of season
Proprietor M. René Gillard

Hostellerie Les Griffons

This handsome 16thC house occupies a prime position in the attractive little medieval town of Bourdeilles – on the banks of the Dronne, next to the splendid old bridge and only yards from the dominant 14thC fortress. Modernized with style and taste, but without ostentation, it feels very much in harmony with its surroundings. The original timber and stone – including grand fireplaces – are complemented by floral prints in the furnishings and decoration. Bedrooms are a fair size and well furnished, and many have lovely river views. Madame's cooking, based on fresh local ingredients, attracts a thriving non-resident trade, which perhaps interferes somewhat with the hotel's atmosphere.

Nearby Château; Brantôme (10 km); Merlande priory (20 km).

Bourdeilles 24310 Brantôme
Tel 53.03.75.61
Location in middle of town, 10 km SW of Brantôme; with terraces
Meals breakfast, lunch, dinner
Prices rooms 280F-350F; menus 110F-200F
Rooms 10 double (4 twin), all with bath; all rooms have central heating, phone, TV
Facilities 2 sitting-rooms, 2 dining-rooms
Credit cards AE, DC, MC, V
Children welcome
Disabled no special facilities
Pets accepted
Closed Nov to end Mar
Proprietor Mme Deborde

Dordogne

Hostellerie Moulin du Roc

The perfect upmarket French hotel? Not far from it, in the view of many visitors to this delectable old walnut-oil mill, for many years a favourite halt for foreign holidaymakers.

Its setting on the banks of the Dronne (a few miles upstream of Brantôme) is wonderfully romantic and rural; the waterside gardens are lush, secluded, shady and bursting with colour – and, with the addition of a brand-new heated swimming-pool, more difficult than ever to leave. Inside the rough-stone 17th-century building, old beams, fireplaces, mill machinery, fine old carved furniture and massive oil paintings – together with plenty of ornaments and flower arrangements – create a style far removed from the designer-decorated pastel look that is creeping into French luxury hotels. Some may find it rather heavy. The same cannot be said of the food: in an area dominated by foie gras and *confit*, Solange Gardillou manages to build on culinary traditions to produce remarkably light and inventive dishes which earn high praise from the gastronomic guides. Breakfasts are a treat, with home-made rolls and jams, beautifully served. The Gardillou's two sons are now helping their parents in this splendid family enterprise.

Nearby Brantôme; Bourdeilles (15 km) – château.

24530 Champagnac-de-Belair	suites, all with bath; all rooms have central heating, phone, TV, minibar
Tel 53.54.80.36	
Location in hamlet, on D82 and D83, 6 km NE of Brantôme; with large garden and ample car parking	**Facilities** sitting-room, dining-room; swimming-pool, tennis court
	Credit cards AE, DC, MC, V
Meals breakfast, lunch, dinner	**Children** welcome **Disabled** two ground-floor rooms
Prices rooms 380F-620F; menus 190F-350F, children's 100F	**Pets** accepted
	Closed mid-Nov to mid-Dec, mid-Jan to mid-Feb
Rooms 10 double (2 twin), 4	**Proprietors** M. and Mme Gardillou

Griffons (see opposite)

Dordogne

Manor house hotel, Brantôme

Le Chatenet

Brantôme is one of the most popular tourist towns in Périgord, so Le Chatenet comes as a pleasant surprise – 'quite a find', to quote our captivated inspector: it is only a short drive outside the town, down a country track off the busy riverside road, but blissfully far removed from the tourist bustle.

The appeal of this well restored 17thC manor house stems not only from its rural surroundings but also from its informal atmosphere: despite evidently heavy investment in rich furnishings, the Laxtons attach importance to maintaining the family-home feel, and it shows. Inside there are vases of freshly cut flowers on low tables, deep armchairs, and country antiques in both the sitting-room and breakfast room. Bedrooms are spacious, and verging on the luxurious. Outside, there are flower-beds bursting with colour (and lush fields of wild flowers beyond), deck-chairs scattered invitingly around the garden beneath shady trees, and plenty of space for children.

Ample breakfasts (with a choice of 12 sorts of *confiture*, among other attractions) are served on a covered terrace in fine weather, and Philippe is talking about the possibility of picnic lunches around the pool. But for the moment you have to look elsewhere for lunch and dinner – a tolerable hardship, given the several excellent restaurants nearby.

Nearby Brantôme – monks' garden, belfry; Bourdeilles (10 km) – château; Chancelade (30 km) – abbey.

24310 Brantôme
Tel 53.05.81.08
Location 1.5 km SW of town, off D78; in large grounds with ample car parking
Meals breakfast (served until 1 pm)
Prices rooms 360F–390F, suites 400F–580F
Rooms 8 double, all with bath (6 twin); one cottage with 2 double rooms; all rooms have central heating, phone; TV on request
Facilities sitting-room, breakfast room, clubhouse; heated swimming-pool, tennis
Credit cards MC, V
Children welcome if well behaved
Disabled access easy; 2 ground-floor bedrooms, one specially equipped
Pets welcome if well behaved
Closed never
Proprietors Philippe and Magdeleine Laxton

Dordogne

Converted mill, Brantôme

Moulin de l'Abbaye

It used to be possible to grumble about the parking arrangements at this exquisite little mill; but the excavation of a cave across the road has dealt with that problem, leaving nothing to deter the visitor except the Relais & Château prices and the ever-present muted roar of the adjacent River Dronne tumbling over the nearby weir.

The setting is the thing. The shady riverside terrace, illuminated in the evening, is an idyllic place for a drink or a meal while admiring Brantôme's unusual angled bridge, the tower of the eponymous abbey or the swans gliding by. Wonderful views over the river and the old houses of one of the prettiest villages in France are also to be had from many of the bedrooms – all beautifully decorated and comfortably furnished (some have four-poster beds and antiques, others are more modern).

Traditional Périgord dishes with a *nouvelle* touch earn the restaurant 2 *toques* from Gault-Millau and a star from Michelin, and the dining-room is nearly as lovely as the terrace. Well-spaced round tables covered in lacey cloths stand on a tile floor beneath a beamed ceiling and before a pale stone fireplace. There are fresh-flowers, sparkling glass and silverware, and soft lighting in the evening. Staff are correct and courteous; service is efficient.

Nearby Monk's garden, belfry; Antonne-et-Trigonant (3 km) – 15thC Périgord manor; Bourdeilles (10 km) – château.

1 Rte de Bourdeilles 24310 Brantôme
Tel 53.05.80.22
Location on edge of town, 20 km N of Périgueux; with garden, and ample car parking across road
Meals breakfast, lunch, dinner
Prices rooms 420F-750F, extra bed 100F; menus 240F-350F
Rooms 12 double, all with bath (9 twin); all rooms have central heating, TV, radio, minibar
Facilities dining-room, sitting-room
Credit cards AE, V
Children welcome; special meals available **Disabled** no special facilities **Pets** dogs accepted
Closed Nov to May
Proprietors M. and Mme Bulot

Dordogne

Les Glycines

The name means wisteria, and that lovely flower is to be found in abundance behind this handsome, creeper-covered 19thC house in the beautiful landscaped gardens that are the hotel's chief attraction. There is also a swimming-pool and a dining-terrace. On a wet day, these outdoor plus points might not weigh heavily enough in the balance to counter the rather formal atmosphere – it is larger than most of our hotels, and the grand entrance hall and the smartly furnished sitting-rooms can be intimidating. But the pink dining-room has a softer air, and all the bedrooms are comfortable; those at the bact are superior and less affected by daytime noise from the busy through-road (and more expensive).

Nearby Château de Fages (15 km); Sarlat (21 km); Lascaux caves (25 km); Beynac (30 km) – village and castle.

24620 Les Eyzies-de-Tayac
Tel 53.06.97.07
Location on edge of town, on main road; with large gardens and car parking
Meals breakfast, lunch, dinner
Prices rooms 210F-340F
Rooms 25 double, all with bath or shower (12 twin); all rooms have central heating
Facilities 2 sitting-rooms, dining-room, bar; swimming-pool
Credit cards AE, DC, MC, V
Children accepted
Disabled access difficult
Pets accepted
Closed Nov to Easter
Proprietors M. and Mme Henri Mercat

Moulin de la Beune

Of all the hotels in Les Eyzies, the Moulin de la Beune has the best location, on the bank of the River Beune. M. and Mme Dudicourt are a charming and enthusiastic couple (he is a painter) and take great pride in their hotel, which is a peaceful place to stay despite the business of the town. The bedrooms are all excellent, decorated with co-ordinating fabrics and colour schemes, the majority with a view over the river. The large fireplace in the sitting-room is turned to good use at the slightest excuse. Only breakfast is served, but there are plenty of restaurants in the town (Le Vieux Moulin is near).

Nearby Caves, here and further afield – Lascaux (25 km).

24620 Les Eyzies-de-Tayac
Tel 53.06.94.33
Location in middle of town, off main road, next to river; with small garden and car parking
Meals breakfast
Prices rooms 185F-250F
Rooms 13 double and 7 family rooms, 14 with bath, 6 with shower; all rooms have phone
Facilities sitting-room, breakfast room; riverside garden
Credit cards MC, V
Children accepted
Disabled 4 ground-floor bedrooms
Pets accepted in some bedrooms
Closed Nov to Mar
Proprietors M. and Mme Dudicourt

Dordogne

Country house hotel, Mauzac

La Métairie

The pretty, creeper-covered, old stone building of La Métairie is oozing with French country style: its unlandscaped grounds merge into rolling fields, and the hotel's own sheep graze quietly nearby. Madame Vigneron and her son Bruno (the chef) have taken care to create a comfortable and charming establishment – the perfect 'get away from it all' hotel.

Each of the bedrooms (most are on ground level) is evocatively named after flowers and it is obvious that thought has gone into their stylis decoration. Some open on to a private terrace, and they all have large, modern bathrooms. The dining-room is a successful mixture of old stone walls and Louis XIIê furnishings. Bruno plans the menu to make the best of local produce and his dishes are original – traditional Pèrigord fare influenced by his experience abroad. Light snacks are served on the lawns by the pool in the summer. The family uses the sitting-room in winter so it has a cosy air, with large comfy chairs and a big open fireplace.

This is not the cheapest of hotels, but the prices are justified by the peace, style and standard of comfort provided.

Nearby Les Eyzies (35 km) – National Prehistoric Museum; Beynac (40 km) – castle; Montpazïer (40 km) – *bastide*.

Mauzac-et-Grand-Castang 24150 Lalinde **Tel** 53.22.50.47 **Location** in countryside 23 km E of Bergerac, between Mauzac and Trèmolat; with garden and car parking **Meals** breakfast, lunch, dinner **Prices** rooms 500F-750F (reduction for children under 6 years); menus 120F-280F **Rooms** 10 double, all with	bath (2 could be family rooms); all rooms have central heating, minibar, phone **Facilities** dining-room, sitting-room, bar; swimming-pool, ping-pong, tennis, boules **Credit cards** MC, V **Children** welcome **Disabled** no special facilities **Pets** accepted; charge 35F **Closed** mid-Nov to end Dec **Proprietor** Françoise Vigneron

Dordogne

Village inn, Saint-Saud-en-Périgord

Hostellerie St-Jacques

The front of the creeper-clad 18thC building on the main road through the hamlet of St-Saud gives little clue to what lies within – or, more to the point, what lies behind: lovely sloping gardens, with masses of colourful flowers, a modest pool, tennis court and plenty of space for children.

Inside there is an unusually spacious dining-room/bar, with crisp blue linen and big windows which open on to the terrace above the garden. All the bedrooms are comfortable, spacious and attractively decorated, but they vary in style, and second-floor rooms are preferable to first-floor ones, with better views over the garden and beyond.

The food, cooked by Madame, is rich and excellent, with Périgord specialities in abundance – even the basic menu is probably enough to satisfy most appetites. Brunch is served in the garden under the shade of the trees, or by the pool. Occasionally there are lively evenings with dancing and games.

The really outstanding feature of this hotel, though, is the consideration M. and Mme Babayou give to their guests' needs – everyone has a *chaise longue* reserved by the pool, for example. Their friendly and relaxed attitude makes this an ideal hotel for families.

Nearby Montbrun (15 km) – fortress; Brantôme (35 km) – monks' garden, château de Richemont; Rochechouart (45 km).

24470 Saint-Saud-en-Périgord
Tel 53.56.97.21
Location in quiet village, 50 km SW of Limoges; with garden and car parking (public and private)
Meals breakfast, brunch, lunch, dinner
Prices rooms 180F-320F, suites 600F; menus 90F-220F
Rooms 22 double (7 twin), 2 suites, all with bath or shower; all rooms have central heating, phone; 10 have TV and minibar
Facilities 2 dining-rooms, bar, TV room; swimming-pool, tennis
Credit cards MC, V
Children very welcome
Disabled no special facilities
Pets accepted
Closed Mon out of season
Proprietor Jean Pierre Babayou

Dordogne

La Hoirie

M. and Mme Sainneville-de-Vienne bought this former hunting-lodge six years ago, only to discover that three centuries ago it had belonged to the same family. Spurred on, no doubt, by their special affinity with the place, they have created a delightful country house retreat, redolent of a past era.

Dating back to the 13thC, it is a building of character, spacious and comfortable, superbly decorated and furnished – 'really quite a gem' in our inspector's view. All the bedrooms (some are in an attractive annexe) have individual features: one a huge fireplace (not in use), another (the old pigeon loft) a private staircase. The dining-room is small but not cramped, with pretty table settings against a stone backdrop. Fortunately, the small conference room does not detract from the air of privacy surrounding the hotel.

Mme Sainneville-de-Vienne is in charge of the kitchen, and has won a high reputation locally my making imaginative use of the regional delicacies: truffles, foie gras, *cèpes*. The large grounds are shady and tranquil, with a swimming-pool to relax by. For the less sedentary, there is the French capital of walnuts and foie gras to explore – the ancient town of Sarlat.

Nearby Sarlat – Renaissance/medieval town; Beynac (10 km) – village and castle; Domme (10 km) – *bastide* town; Les Eyzies (20 km) – caves and National Prehistoric Museum.

'La Giragne' 24200 Sarlat
Tel 53.59.05.62
Location in countryside 2 km E of the middle of Sarlat; with gardens and ample car parking
Meals breakfast, lunch, dinner
Prices rooms 250F-400F; meals 160F-250F
Rooms 13 double, 8 with bath, 5 with shower (5 twin); 2 family rooms, both with bath; all rooms have central heating, phone
Facilities dining-room, sitting-room/bar, small conference room; swimming-pool
Credit cards AE, DC, MC, V
Children dogs accepted
Disabled no special facilities
Pets accepted
Closed mid-Nov to mid-Mar
Proprietors M. and Mme Sainneville-de-Vienne

Dordogne

L'Abbaye

The rooms in this friendly hotel are not uniformly recommend-able – those facing the main road may be noisy, and one or two others are a bit gloomy – but the best rooms (including the first-floor ones in the more recently opened of the two annexes) are very attractive indeed. There is a private-house atmosphere: the interior is civilized and relaxing, and in the sitting-room you can see the abbey's pastry oven and *potager* dating from the 18thC. Meals are served on the terrace in the summer.

Nearby Château de Fages (1 km); Les Eyzies (15 km) – caves, National Prehistoric Museum; Montpazier (30 km) – *bastide*.

24220 St-Cyprien **Tel** 53.29.20.48 **Location** near middle of village, on main road; with gardens and car parking **Meals** breakfast, lunch, dinner **Prices** rooms 230F-550F; DB&B (for 2 persons) 550F-850F; menus 120F-285F **Rooms** 23 double, 13 with bath, 10 with shower; one suite with bath; all rooms	have phone **Facilities** sitting-room, dining-room; swimming-pool **Credit cards** AE, DC, MC, V **Children** welcome; baby-listening **Disabled** no special facilities **Pets** dogs accepted **Closed** early Nov to early Apr **Proprietors** Y and M Schaller

Auberge du Vieux Moulin

M. Tournier – a young, friendly chap from Paris – now plies his trade as a chef in a glorious setting: an old mill, half-hidden by trees and flowers, and set beside a bubbling stream. His menu is short, making good use of whatever is fresh at the time, and he aims to lighten many traditionally rich Périgord dishes. From the dining-room – prettily laid tables with pink linen contrasting with the rough walls and floor – you look out on to the stream and the verdant and unlandscaped garden. M. Tournier takes pains to stress that until he can afford to renovate them his bedrooms are simple; indeed they are – though all have a basin and bidet, and there are two communal bathrooms. But look at the price.

Nearby Montbrun (15 km) – fortress; Brantôme (35 km).

24470 St-Saud-Lacoussière **Tel** 53.56.97.26 **Location** outside village, 14km W of La Coquille, at end of riverside track; with gardens and car parking **Meals** breakfast, lunch, dinner **Prices** rooms 70F; DB&B 185F for one; menus 95F	**Rooms** 8 double; all rooms have central heating **Facilities** dining-room, bar **Credit cards** V **Children** accepted **Disabled** no special facilities **Pets** accepted **Closed** 2 weeks at end of year **Proprietor** M. Tournier

Dordogne

Village hotel, Trémolat

Le Vieux Logis

The Giraudel-Destords, an old Perigordian family, have lived in this complex of farm and village houses for nearly 400 years. The part which is now the dining-room was a barn for tobacco drying, and also housed pigs and wine barrels; upstairs they kept fodder.

None of this can be detected now, of course, in what has for decades been one of the region's most civilized country hotels, now in the hands of Bernard Giraudel, a natural host. All has been designer-decorated to produce comfort of a high degree. The bedrooms are particularly delightful, individually furnished and very cosy in a sophisticated rustic style, with fine materials and furniture; some have four-poster beds. Public rooms are elegant and comfortable, and there are plenty of nooks where you can enjoy after-dinner chess or a quiet read; the small salon has an open fire, and there are fine antiques throughout. The galleried dining-room is very attractive, and looks out on to the green and flowery garden, where you can choose to take breakfast. The classic and modern cooking of Pierre-Jean Duribreux is excellent (*toques* from Gault-Millau) and the wine list extensive. All of which makes for a very pleasant stay indeed.

Nearby Les Eyzies-de-Tayac (25 km) – National Prehistoric Museum; Monpazier (30 km) – *bastide*; Beynac (30 km).

24510 Trémolat
Tel 53.22.80.06
Location in village 15 km SW of Le Bugue; with garden and private car parking
Meals breakfast, lunch, dinner
Prices rooms 560F-750F; menus 160F-220F, children's 60F
Rooms 19 double (8 twin), all with bath; all rooms have central heating, phone, TV, minibar
Facilities 2 dining-rooms, sitting-room, bar, conference room
Credit cards AE, DC, MC, V
Children welcome
Disabled no special facilities
Pets welcome
Closed never
Proprietors M. Bernard Giraudel

Dordogne

Hôtel Bonnet

Beynac-et-Cazenac is one of the showpiece villages of the Dordogne – a cluster of honey-coloured stone houses lying in the shadow of a castle and commanding glorious views over the valley. The Bonnet (named after the family who have run it for almost a century) has been a favourite with foreign visitors for years. They are attracted by the setting, the friendly welcome and the reasonably priced (though far from luxurious) rooms. One of the great assets is the delightful terrace where on warm days you can admire the views while enjoying competent regional cuisine under an arbour of vines.

Nearby Sarlat; Domme (10 km) – *bastide*; Les Eyzies (25 km).

Beynac-et-Cazenac 24220 St-Cyprien	**Rooms** 22 rooms, all with bath or shower
Tel 53.29.50.01	**Facilities** dining-room
Location on main road beside Dordogne, on edge of village, 11 km SW of Sarlat; with terrace	**Credit cards** MC, V
	Children accepted
	Disabled no special facilities
	Pets not accepted
Meals breakfast, lunch, dinner	**Closed** mid-Oct to mid-Mar
	Proprietors Bonnet family
Prices rooms 190F-210F; menus 90F-175F	

La Daille

British *emigrés* Barbara and Derek Vaughan Brown have been running this unusual establishment just south of the Dordogne for over a decade now – long enough to have built up a local clientele for their set dinners. It is a small-scale *pension* (half board obligatory, minimum stay three days, weekly terms available) catering for no more than 7 guests, so you get to know your hosts (and fellow inmates) well. The bedrooms are in a modern single-storey building – thoroughly comfortable, with big bathrooms – across the neat, flowery garden from the original farmhouse, which contains the cool, rustic dining-room.

Nearby Domme (15 km) – *bastide*; Sarlat (25 km).

Florimont-Gaumiers 24250 Domme	one single, all with bath or shower; all rooms have central heating
Tel 53.28.40.71	
Location in countryside, 2 km S of Gaumiers (signposted from village); in large grounds with ample car parking	**Facilities** dining-room
	Credit cards not accepted
	Children accepted over 7
	Disabled access difficult
	Pets not accepted
Meals breakfast, dinner	**Closed** Nov to Easter
Prices DB&B (with wine) 310F for one	**Proprietors** Mr and Mrs Derek Vaughan Brown
Rooms 3 double (2 twin),	

Dordogne/Corrèze

Manoir Hôtel Rochecourbe

This 15thC manor house, in the same family for over 100 years and open as a hotel since 1978, offers an unusual and entirely peaceful place to stay in the popular Dordogne valley. Outside it is informal and rural, partly creeper-covered, with the air of an old farmhouse, though a grander note is added by the single round tower housing the spiral staircase which you climb to reach the bedrooms. Inside there is space in plenty, and solid antique furnishings in harmony with the massive carved stone chimneypieces, great old beams and bare-board ceilings. Arrangements for dinner are informal – Madame offers to make light meals according to what is available and how well disposed she is towards you. Breakfast is excellent.

Nearby Beynac (5 km) – village and castle; Sarlat (10 km).

Vézac 24220 St-Cyprien	central heating, phone
Tel 53.29.50.79	**Facilities** sitting-room,
Location in countryside, off	dining-room
D57 6 km SW of Sarlat; with	**Credit cards** V
garden and car parking	**Children** welcome
Meals breakfast; other meals	**Disabled** no special facilities
may be available	**Pets** by arrangement
Prices rooms 215F-380F	**Closed** 1 Nov to 15 Apr
Rooms 7 double, 6 with	**Proprietors** M. and Mme
bath, one with shower (5 twin);	Roger

Relais St-Jacques de Compostelle

The medieval village of Collonges never fails to amaze – whether you come upon it by chance or primed by a guidebook. It is built entirely of red sandstone, and decades or even centuries of neglect seem merely to have preserved it; it is all as pretty as a picture. The fact that there is a pleasing *auberge* in the village comes as a bonus. The St-Jacques has a terrace where satisfying lunches are served, a simple stone-walled dining-room, a salon and a bar; bedrooms are small, simple and bright (some have fine views); and the Casteras are welcoming hosts.

Nearby Turenne (10 km) – white limestone village; Aubazines (20 km) – abbey church; Argentat (45 km) and Dordogne gorges.

Collonges-la-Rouge 19500	one single; all rooms have
Meyssac	central heating, phone
Tel 55.25.41.02	**Facilities** dining-room,
Location in middle of	sitting-room, bar
village, 14 km SE of Brive;	**Credit cards** AE, DC, V
with some private and ample	**Children** accepted; special
public car parking	meals available
Meals breakfast, lunch, dinner	**Disabled** no special facilities
Prices rooms 85F-210F;	**Pets** small ones accepted
menus 70F-200F	**Closed** 1 Nov to 31 Jan
Rooms 11 double, 5 with	**Proprietor** Jean-Pierre
bath, 2 with shower (5 twin);	Castera

Lot-et-Garonne

Château-Hôtel des Jacobins

In a quiet square in the middle of Agen, this large 1830s house with shuttered windows and a walled garden makes a peaceful haven. The bedrooms are, without exception, beautifully decorated, large, elegant and well equipped. The two fine sitting-rooms are furnished with antiques and the atmosphere is one of refined elegance. The welcome from the Bujans is friendly, but they have high standards which they expect guests to share (this is not a place for boisterous children). There is no alcohol licence, but you are welcome to bring your own (glasses and ice provided). Breakfast is served in your room or on the terrace.
Nearby Museums (5 Goya paintings); Condom (35 km).

1 ter Place des Jacobins
47000 Agen
Tel 53.47.03.31
Location in middle of town; with garden and car parking
Meals breakfast, light lunch, light supper
Prices rooms 180F-400F; meals 40F-100F
Rooms 13 double, all with bath (4 twin); 2 single, with shower; all rooms have central heating, TV, phone,
Facilities 2 sitting-rooms, writing-room
Credit cards not accepted
Children accepted
Disabled 3 ground-floor bedrooms
Pets accepted if well behaved
Closed never
Proprietors M. and Mme Serge Bujan

Château de Monviel

This solid old manor house is a world away from the pretensions of many Relais & Château hotels. Although there is ambitious food to be had (regionally based, with much emphasis on fish), the essence of the place is simplicity, space and peace – coupled with the sincere welcome of the Leroy family. The grand hall sets the tone, with its pale stone walls and stairs leading from the polished floor of the sitting-area up to a gallery giving access to the bedrooms – which are vast, and individually furnished in simple good taste.
Nearby Monflanquin (25 km) – *bastide*; Biron (35 km) – castle.

Monviel 47290 Cancon
Tel 53.01.71.64
Location in countryside off D124, 2 km NW of Cancon, 30 km S of Bergerac; in gardens with ample car parking
Meals breakfast, lunch, dinner
Prices rooms 390F-800F; menus 120F-250F
Rooms 9 double (all twin), one family room, all with bath; all rooms have central heating, phone; TV on request
Facilities 2 dining-rooms, sitting-room
Credit cards AE, DC, V
Children welcome **Disabled** access difficult; many steps
Pets very welcome
Closed mid-Nov to Apr
Proprietors M. and Mme Leroy

Lot

Country house hotel, Cabrerets

La Pescalerie

Despite its natural beauty and proximity to the Dordogne, this area of the Lot valley is not well endowed with outstanding hotels. La Pescalerie is an exception – one of the most delightful hotels in the whole of France.

An 18thC manor house with towers and dormer windows, it lies in the wooded valley of the Célé, close to the little village of Cabrerets. It was opened in 1980 by Hélène and Roger Combette, who are both doctors. Hélène gave up medicine to devote herself entirely to the hotel; Roger still practices as a surgeon, but is to be found serving in the restaurant in the evenings. Meals are prepared in the original 18thC kitchen and all the ingredients (which include foie gras, goose, duck, trout and delicious salads) are fresh each day from the market. There are ten luxurious bedrooms; no two are alike but each is a charming blend of old and new, with handsome four-poster beds, wardrobes and chests, offset by creamy-coloured rugs and light modern fabrics. The top rooms are particularly popular, with their exposed beams, quarry tiles and windows which overlook the flowered garden and river. Breakfast on the terrace, with freshly-squeezed orange juice, and home-made croissants and jam, makes a happy start to the day.

Nearby Pech-Merle caves and museum; Cahors (35 km) – medieval bridge.

46330 Cabrerets	central heating, phone, TV
Tel 65.31.22.55	on request
Location on D41, 2 km E of	**Facilities** dining-room,
village, 44 km W of Figeac;	sitting-room, bar
in own grounds with ample	**Credit cards** AE, DC, V
parking	**Children** accepted
Meals breakfast, lunch,	**Disabled** no special facilities
dinner	**Pets** dogs accepted
Prices rooms 430F-560F;	**Closed** 1 Nov to 1 Apr
menus 195F-225F	**Proprietor** Hélène
Rooms 10 double, all with	Combette
bath (7 twin); all rooms have	

Lot

Village inn, Dégagnac

Auberge sans Frontière

For over 200 years this little *auberge* has been an integral part of the life of sleepy Dégagnac, and in the caring hands of the engaging Hauchecornes it remains so. Run along simple lines, the hotel is a little old-fashioned, but friendly and decorated in a pretty style, with Laura Ashley-style prints and antiques in evidence. Bedrooms are smallish – there are four attic rooms – but comfortable and inviting. The dining-rooms serve also as bar and sitting-room. Mme cooks excellent regional food.
Nearby Domme (20 km) – *bastide*; Sarlat (25 km).

Dégagnac 46340 Salviac
Tel 65.41.52.88
Location in village on D6, 10 km SW of Gourdon; with ample public car parking
Meals breakfast, lunch, dinner
Prices rooms 100F-140F; menus 45F-105F
Rooms 5 double, one with bath, 4 with shower (4 twin); 2 single; one family room with shower; all rooms have
central heating
Facilities 2 dining-rooms, bar, sitting-room
Credit cards DC
Children accepted if well behaved **Disabled** access to restaurant only **Pets** accepted if well behaved
Closed mid-Nov to end Dec; Mon out of season
Proprietors Gisèle and Alain Hauchecorne

Country hotel, Gluges

Hôtel des Falaises

There is nothing particularly remarkable about the Hôtel des Falaises, and the setting beneath the cliffs after which it is named may be a little severe. But it makes a convenient stop-over (just off the N140 where it crosses the Dordogne), offering a friendly welcome from Madame and traditional Périgord cuisine from the kitchen of M. Dassiou – served in one of two attractive restaurants (one opening on to a shady terrace). And in an area where bargains are becoming hard to find, the prices are modest. The bedrooms, although variable in their decoration, are pleasant, comfortable and, like the rest of the hotel, spotlessly clean.
Nearby Martel – town hall, Raymondie Palace; Rocamadour (15 km) – 'vertical village'; Carennac (15 km) – village around priory.

Gluges 46600 Martel
Tel 65.37.33.59
Location in countryside, off N140 5 km S of Martel; with terrace and car parking
Meals breakfast, lunch, dinner
Prices rooms 130F-260F; menus 75F-125F
Rooms 11 double (5 twin), 4 family rooms, all with bath or shower; all rooms have
central heating, phone
Facilities 2 dining-rooms, 2 sitting-rooms (one in annexe)
Credit cards V
Children accepted
Disabled no special facilities
Pets not accepted
Closed Dec to Feb
Proprietors M. and Mme Dassiou

Lot

Farmhouse hotel, Mauroux

Hostellerie Le Vert

Finding the entrance to the Hostellerie Le Vert may take a little time: this solid 17thC farmhouse has been little changed in its recent conversion (first to a restaurant, then to a hotel), and there is just a small side door to lead you inside.

Within, all is original stone walls and beams. The dining-room, with elegantly laid tables, opens out on to a terrace with spectacular views of the countryside; through an arch at one end of the room is the small sitting-room – fine for an aperitif, but not a place to relax for the evening. The bedrooms are all comfortably and tastefully modernized, and have lovely views from their small windows. The largest are quite grand; one particularly striking room is decorated in apricot and pale green and another is contained in a separate long, tunnel-shaped building, with stone walls and intriguing peep-hole windows. The garden is lush, with chairs and tables, but plain and colourless when our inspector visited.

The Philippes are an 'exceedingly friendly' and hard-working couple – he cooks (interestingly and competently), she serves – whose enterprise deserves to succeed.

Nearby Bonaguil (15 km) – château; Biron castle (35 km); Monpazier (50 km) – *bastide*; Cahors (50 km) – medieval bridge.

Mauroux 46700 Puy-l'Evêque
Tel 65.36.51.36
Location in countryside, off D5 10 km SW of Puy-l'Evêque; in garden, with ample car parking
Meals breakfast, lunch, dinner
Prices rooms 160F-230F; menus 90F-170F
Rooms 6 double; 4 rooms with bath or shower; one family room with shower in separate building; all rooms have central heating, phone
Facilities dining-room, sitting-room
Credit cards AE, V
Children accepted
Disabled no special facilities
Pets accepted
Closed Jan, Feb
Proprietors M. and Mme Philippe

Lot

Hôtel du Pont de L'Ouysse

The *raison d'etre* of this small *auberge* is its stunning dining terrace overlooking the little River Ouysse, shaded by a lime tree and a large horse-chestnut. It is wonderfully peaceful, as there is no nearby through-road, only an access road to the hotel. The bedrooms have recently been done up with Laura Ashley fabrics and papers, and there is a simple dining-room for cool days and evenings. The cooking is good, and makes use of local produce (including eel from the Ouysse), but is not confined to the ubiquitous *confit* and foie gras of which it is easy to tire in this area. The Chambons – he in the kitchen, she in charge of the front of the house – are improving their little hotel all the time.

Nearby Souillac – abbey church; Martel (20 km) – town hall, Raymondie Palace; Autoire (30 km) – gorges.

Lacave 46200 Souillac
Tel 65.37.87.04
Location in countryside
9 km SE of Souillac; with
terrace and car parking
Meals breakfast, lunch,
dinner
Prices rooms 250F-450F;
meals 120F-250F
Rooms 12 double, all with

bath (4 twin); all rooms have
phone, TV
Facilities dining-room,
sitting-room
Credit cards V
Children accepted
Disabled no special facilities
Pets accepted
Closed mid-Nov to end Feb
Proprietor Daniel Chambon

Auberge du Sombral

A beautifully restored house in a spectacular setting at the heart of the lovely medieval village, perched high above the Lot Valley. There is a pretty dining-room with a tiled floor and rural colours – cream walls, browns, rusts and fresh flowers. Housekeeping is excellent – bedrooms are fresh and spotlessly clean, with crisp linen and lots of hot water on tap. Some bedrooms are on the small size though. Sadly, the Hardevelds could not raise a smile between them on the occasion of our visit, and the food seemed limited – menus remained from day to day and offered little choice.

Nearby Pech-Merle – caves; Cahors (35 km) – medieval bridge.

St-Cirq-Lapopie 46330
Cabrerets
Tel 65.31.26.08
Location on village square,
with public car parking
nearby
Meals breakfast, lunch,
dinner
Prices rooms 180F-230F;
menus 70F-220F
Rooms 10 double, 5 with
bath, 5 with shower (2 twin);

all rooms have phone
Facilities sitting-room,
dining-room
Credit cards MC, V
Children accepted
Disabled access difficult
Pets accepted at extra
charge
Closed mid Nov to Apr; Tue
dinner and Wed except in
school holidays
Proprietor Gills Hardeveld

Lot

La Pélissaria

It is a long drive up to St-Cirq-Lapopie – far longer than the maps would have you believe – but it is also a beautiful one, and at the end is not only a lovely medieval hill-top village but also this archetypal charming small hotel.

Lovingly restored by the proprietor, M. Matuchet, the 13thC house clings to the side of the mountain. Its quirky character is such that you descend the stairs to the bedrooms – which look out on to the tiny garden and enjoy stunning views over the Lot valley. The bedrooms vary in size, and some are rather cramped; they have tiled floors which are chilly in anything other than summer weather, but they are, nevertheless, light, airy and comfortable.

Dinner, a set menu cooked by Mme Matuchet and served by Monsieur in the elegant and intimate beamed dining-room (with roaring log fire on cold, wet nights) is adventurous, delicious and extremely good value. M. Matuchet is a musician, and tapes of his music provide a pleasant background to dinner. Breakfast is served al fresco or in your room if you prefer.

Happily, M. Matuchet has recently completed building two extra rooms in the garden. So the excellent service and aura of tranquility that surrounds this enchanting hotel (only occasionally marred by difficulty in finding a parking place) can now be enjoyed by a few more travellers.

Nearby Pech-Merle caves and museum; Cahors – medieval bridge.

St-Cirq-Lapopie 46330
Cabrerets
Tel 65.31.25.14
Location in middle of
village, 30 km E of Cahors;
with garden; parking
difficult
Meals no lunch
Prices rooms 220F-300F;
menu 120F
Rooms 6 double, 3 with
bath, 3 with shower (4 twin);
2 single, both with shower;
all rooms have phone
Facilities dining-room,
sitting-room
Credit cards not accepted
Children welcome
Disabled no special facilities
Pets accepted
Closed 3 Nov to 1 Apr
Proprietor Marie-Françoise
Matuchet

Lot

Relais les Vieilles Tours

Rocamadour – the 'vertical village' – can claim the dubious honour of being the second most visited tourist sight in France; but, despite the hordes who descend upon it in season, complete seclusion and tranquillity can be had only a couple of miles away in this splendid manor-house.

It is a beautifully restored stone building, dating from the 13thC and 17thC, with its medieval atmosphere largely preserved. The dining-room is in the oldest part of the building, with rich pink and floral fabrics contrasting with the original stone and brick walls, bare floors and old timbers. The cosy sitting-room occupies the first floor of an interesting circular turret-wing. The views across open countryside are completely uninterrupted, and all the bedrooms have large windows, the vast panoramas giving a feeling of privacy and isolation to the spacious, attractively furnished rooms. The Zozzolis are a friendly couple who generate a relaxed but refined atmosphere. He is an artist, and his paintings (for sale) are hung throughout the hotel. Madame cooks, making full use of fresh local produce in her short dinner menus.

Our inspector, desperate to balance her praise with some criticism, observes that the Vieilles Tours is 'very isolated, with nothing to do except read or walk'. Some problem.

Nearby château; Moulin de Cougnaguet (10 km); Autoire (20 km) – village, mouth of Autoire Gorges; Carennac (20 km).

Lafage 46500 Rocamadour
Tel 65.33.68.01
Location in countryside 2.5km outside Rocamadour, on D673 to Calès; with grounds and ample car parking
Meals breakfast, dinner; lunch by arrangement
Prices rooms 200F; menus 90F-115F
Rooms 8 double (one twin), all with bath; 2 family rooms; all rooms have phone
Facilities 2 sitting-rooms, dining-room, swimming-pool
Credit cards MC, V
Children accepted
Disabled access difficult
Pets accepted
Closed Christmas to Easter
Proprietors M. and Mme Zozzoli

Lot

La Source Bleue

Displayed in the dining-room of La Source Bleue, the original watermark dates this wonderful old paper-mill to the 11thC. The buildings have been in the Bouyou family for six centuries, and now Jean-Pierre and his Welsh wife Siân – a thoroughly friendly couple who make natural hosts – have converted it into a romantic and captivating hotel. Set on the bank of a beautiful stretch of the River Lot, the gardens creep down to the water through a bamboo forest and past the spring of the hotel's name.

The first-floor sitting-room has tiny windows dotted around the walls in a disorderly fashion. Most of the bedrooms enjoy lovely views, and all are comfortable; one has its own private garden. The Bouyous look after their guests without much help – although they do employ a chef. Of course, fresh salmon and trout feature as specialities on the menu.

Although La Source Bleue is not undiscovered by other guidebooks, it is not yet over-run by British visitors; its tranquillity remains a relatively private pleasure. More bedrooms are being added in another mill next door, but even so the scale of the place will remain small.

Nearby Bonaguil (15 km) – Château Bonaguil; Monpazier (45 km).

Moulin de Leygues, Touzac
46700 Puy-l'Evêque
Tel 65.36.52.01
Location in countryside on banks of the Lot, 7 km E of Fumel; with gardens and private car parking
Meals breakfast, lunch, dinner
Prices rooms 200F-350F; meals 95F-195F
Rooms 12 double, all with bath (5 twin); all rooms have phone

Facilities TV room, dining-room, sitting-room, gym; children's garden
Credit cards V
Children welcome; special meals available
Disabled no special facilities
Pets welcome at extra charge, but not in dining-room
Closed Nov to end Mar; Tue lunch
Proprietors M. and Mme Jean-Pierre Bouyou

Landes

Les Huitrières du Lac

Hossegor is an attractive family resort amid pine forests, spreading between a lake and the nearby Atlantic coast. Les Huitrières, on the lakeside, is primarily a restaurant, specializing (of course) in excellent fish and seafood. The large dining-room (with terrace) has a superb view over the lake and, despite its size, a pleasantly intimate feel. Service is prompt and efficient, proper without being stuffy. Bedrooms are simply furnished but large, with fair-sized bathrooms, and most have balconies overlooking the lake – well worth the small extra charge; the sun rising over the lake provides a spectacular awakening. Mme Cotis can be slightly crusty, but underneath is friendly and helpful, and speaks English.

Nearby Bayonne (20 km); Biarritz (30 km).

1187 Ave du Touring Club 40150 Hossegor **Tel** 58.43.51.48 **Location** on edge of lake, just outside village, with car parking **Meals** breakfast, lunch, dinner **Prices** rooms 160F-200F; menus 90F-230F **Rooms** 8 double (3 twin),	one family room, all with bath; central heating, phone **Facilities** sitting-room, dining-room **Credit cards** not accepted **Children** accepted **Disabled** no special facilities **Pets** accepted **Closed** Dec to Mar **Proprietor** Mme Cotis

Auberge des Pins

If you spend any time travelling with children, the major asset of this hotel will quickly become apparent: it is eminently suitable for families looking for a relaxing place to stay, with plenty of entertainment value. The gardens have swings and a sand-pit, and there is a miniature railway nearby. The dining-room is large and attractively rustic, the food satisfying rather than ambitious. The other public rooms are not so captivating (the bar has a TV and gaming machines), but the bedrooms are pleasant and there is an easy-going quality about the place.

Nearby Marquèze Ecomuseum; Landes Forest; beaches (40 km).

Rte de la Piscine 40630 Sabres **Tel** 58.07.50.47 **Location** amid forests, 40 km NW of Mont-de-Marsan; with large gardens and private car parking **Meals** breakfast, lunch, dinner **Prices** rooms 95F-220F; menus 65F-195F **Rooms** 14 double, 12 with bath or shower (2 twin); all	rooms have central heating, phone **Facilities** dining-room, bar, TV/conference room **Credit cards** V **Children** very welcome **Disabled** access to restaurant **Pets** not accepted **Closed** mid-Jan to mid-Feb; Mon out of season **Proprietors** Lesclauze family

Landes

Lakeside hotel, Mimizan

Au Bon Coin du Lac

Jean-Pierre Caule is the third generation of his family to run Au Bon Coin, and is rightly proud of it. The two-storey, stone and painted-wood house has a superb lakeside setting, with neat little footpaths inviting you to walk around the grounds. But the hotel's *raison d'être* is its Michelin-starred restaurant, and M. Caule's culinary skill as head chef (seafood is his speciality). The generally expensive feel of the place is reflected in the menu – and the prices. The dining-room has an uncluttered view of the lake and is charmingly furnished: round tables, white table-cloths, floral china and floral-covered chairs. The service is formal, as you would expect in a restaurant in this price range, but nevertheless friendly, and not overpowering.

The bedrooms are large and luxurious; not impersonal, but rather uniform. Despite the many activities on the lake – sailing, fishing – the swings nearby and the special children's menu, this is not really a place for a family holiday. But it is ideal for those who want four-star treatment, a relaxed and friendly atmosphere and excellent food.

Nearby Lakes; beaches (5 km); Landes forest (30 km); Sabres (40 km) – railway to Marquèze Ecomuseum.

34 Ave du Lac, Mimizan
40200 Landes
Tel 58.09.01.55
Location amid forests, 2 km N of Mimizan; on edge of lake, with garden and car parking
Meals breakfast, lunch, dinner
Prices rooms 320F-560F; DB&B (for one) 400F-520F; menus 120F-290F; reduced rates for children
Rooms 5 double, all with bath and shower; 4 suites, all with bath and shower; all rooms have central heating, TV, phone, radio, minibar
Facilities sitting-room, dining-room
Credit cards AE, V
Children welcome; special meals, baby-listening available
Disabled ground-floor bedrooms
Pets not welcome
Closed Feb; restaurant only Sun dinner, and Mon in low season
Proprietor Jean-Pierre Caule

Landes/Gers

Le Ripa Alta

Set on the main square of a quiet town recently invigorated by an ambitious scheme to equip the church with a massive organ, the Ripa Alta (itself recently renovated) is a simple hotel which revolves around the restaurant – and the cooking of Maurice Coscuella, which manages to combine innovation, respect for regional tradition and honest value. He also dispenses samples from a mightily impressive selection of fine Armagnacs. His wife and daughter manage the hotel – furnished simply and without frills, but with fresh flowers in evidence.

Nearby Aire-sur-l'Adour (30 km) – church of Ste-Quitterie.

3 Place de l'Eglise 32160 Plaisance
Tel 62.69.30.43
Location in middle of village, 43 km N of Tarbes; with ample car parking
Meals breakfast, lunch, dinner
Prices rooms 135F-280F; menus 70F-260F, children's 45F
Rooms 15 double, some with bath or shower (5 twin); all rooms have central heating, phone
Facilities sitting-room, dining-room, bar, banqueting-room
Credit cards AE, DC, V
Children welcome
Disabled no special facilities
Pets accepted at extra charge
Closed Jan
Proprietor Maurice Coscuella

La Bergerie

It may take a while to take your leave of the talkative Mme Clavier and her husband, but you probably will not be in any hurry. Their immaculate white-washed house – built in southern single-storey style – is a calm and civilized haven where the slow pace of life is infectious. M. Clavier used to be a wine merchant and, naturally enough, tends the cellar; Madame does the cooking, and the (obligatory) set dinner is based on whatever is fresh and good at the time – she makes a point of not owning a freezer. The dining-room is small, but attractively furnished with antiques, the adjacent sitting-room cool and elegant. The bedrooms – recently redecorated, and all with fair-sized bathrooms – look on to the neat gardens.

Nearby Beaches (15 km); Léon (20 km) – boat trips.

Ave du Lac 40140 Soustons
Tel 58.41.11.43
Location close to middle of village, 37 km NW of Biarritz; with large garden and ample car parking
Meals breakfast, dinner
Prices DB&B 250F for one
Rooms 12 double, all with bath (8 twin); all rooms have central heating, phone
Facilities sitting-room, dining-room
Credit cards AE, DC, MC, V
Children accepted
Disabled access difficult
Pets not accepted
Closed Oct to end Mar
Proprietors M. and Mme Clavier

Gers

Country hotel, Segos

Domaine de Bassibé

Le charme d'un vrai relais de campagne and *une cuisine sincère et raffinée*, to quote from the Domaine de Bassibé's brochure, are exactly the attractions of this tastefully renovated old farmhouse. It offers complete comfort and relaxation without any pomp or stuffiness.

Jean Pierre Capelle's innovative and essentially simple cooking (largely self-taught) has earned deserved awards from Michelin and Gault-Millau, and attracts a strong local trade. Neither the menus nor the *carte* offer much choice. The dining-room is in the old stable block, interestingly converted and pleasantly informal in its decoration, with simple furnishings and a warm colour scheme – and a modern 'island' fireplace. On summer days, tables are placed outside on the shady terrace, or you can take lunch beside the pool. The few bedrooms are decorated with great flair by Mayi Capelle, using rich fabrics and bold colours – and the same style is evident throughout the house. Staff are friendly and helpful; the countryside is lovely; and serenity as well as space around the swimming-pool are easy to find.

Nearby Aire-sur-l'Adour – church of Ste-Quitterie; château de Morlanne (35 km); Pau (45 km) – château, Blvd des Pyrénées.

Segos 32400 Riscle
Tel 62.09.46.71
Location in countryside 8 km S of Aire-sur-l'Adour, off N134; with large garden and ample car parking
Meals breakfast, lunch, dinner
Prices rooms 420F-570F, suites 720F; menus 150F-250F
Rooms 9 double, all with bath and shower (4 twin); all rooms have central heating, phone; suites have TV
Facilities dining-room, sitting-room, bar; swimming-pool, golf practice
Credit cards AE, DC, MC, V
Children accepted if well behaved **Disabled** no special facilities **Pets** accepted
Closed late Nov to Easter
Proprietor Jean-Pierre Capelle

La Bergerie (see opposite)

Pyrénées-Atlantiques

Village hotel, Aînhoa

Hôtel Ohantzea

Aînhoa is an attractive mountain village, close to the Spanish border but with adequate roads to Bayonne. Set on the main through-road, the timbered Ohantzea has been in the Ithurria family for three centuries, and old family furniture is scattered throughout the house, which is satisfyingly rustic and tasteful throughout – uneven wooden floors, beamed ceilings. The bedrooms are notably spacious, and some have balconies. The menu may disappoint those expecting some Spanish influence but it is fair value and the dining-room is pleasant enough, looking out on to a terrace and the apple trees in the garden beyond. M. and Mme Ithurria are a charming, outgoing couple who make everyone feel at home.

Nearby St-Pée-sur-Nivelle (10 km) – old houses, galleried Basque church; Sare (10 km) – cog railway up La Rhune.

Aînhoa 64250 Cambo-les-Bains
Tel 59.29.90.50
Location in middle of village, 10 km SW of Cambo-les-Bains; with garden and car parking behind
Meals breakfast, lunch, dinner
Prices rooms 120F-250F; menus 75F-160F
Rooms 10 double, 9 with bath and shower (3 twin); all rooms have central heating, phone
Facilities sitting-room, 2 dining-rooms
Credit cards AE, DC, MC, V
Children welcome
Disabled no special facilities
Pets accepted
Closed Jan and Feb
Proprietor M. Ithurria

Pyrénées-Atlantiques

Relais des Voyageurs

This former presbytery – its pretty, flower-filled garden used to be the cemetery of the next-door church – has been sympathetically converted into a welcoming small hotel. It is not perfect – it suffers from noise from the road (as well as from the church bells), and some of the bedrooms are cramped. But the best of the rooms are spacious and have balconies overlooking the garden; the dining-room (with a small sitting-area by the huge fireplace) is light and warm, with bare stone walls; and the Gonders are an amiable young couple.

Nearby Bidache (15 km) – château de Gramont; Orthez (28 km).

Place de l'Eglise, Escos
64270 Salies-de-Bèarn
Tel 59.38.42.39
Location in grounds of
village church, on D936
30 km NW of Navarrenx;
with garden, and car
parking in square nearby
Meals breakfast, lunch,
dinner
Prices rooms 80F–175F;
menus 60F–150F
Rooms 9 double, 3 with
bath, 5 with shower (2 twin);
all rooms have central
heating
Facilities dining-room with
sitting-area
Credit cards AE, DC, MC, V
Children accepted
Disabled no special facilities
Pets accepted
Closed 15 Dec to 15 Jan
Proprietors M. and Mme
Gonder

Le Vieux Logis

This jolly little *auberge* is not particularly *vieux* in style or in fact, but it attracts a brisk trade in lunchtime visitors on their way to or from the nearby caves of Bétharram – its traditional regional cuisine earning a red R from Michelin for quality combined with moderate prices. It is an attractive spot to stay in while exploring the foothills of the Pyrenees. With its large lawned garden dotted with wooden chalets (accommodation is in these or in the main hotel) it is particularly appealing for families.

Nearby Grottes de Bétharram; Lourdes (15 km); Pau (30 km).

Rte des Grottes 64800
Lestelle-Bétharram
Tel 59.71.94.87
Location in countryside on
RN637, 3 km E of village,
12 km W of Lourdes; with
garden and car parking
Meals breakfast, lunch,
dinner
Prices rooms 120F–180F;
menus 80F–150F
Rooms 11 double with
shower (6 twin); one single; 2
family rooms, one with
shower; all rooms have
central heating; most have
phone
Facilities 4 dining-rooms
Credit cards MC, V
Children welcome
Disabled no special facilities
Pets accepted if small and
well behaved
Closed 1 Nov to 1 Apr
Proprietor Pierre Gaye

Pyrénées-Atlantiques

La Fayette

This little family-run hotel occupies a prime spot (in a pedestrian zone) in the very heart of the animated port and resort of St-Jean, only yards from the beach and from the Place Louis XIV, lined with cafés and buzzing with activity. The building is unusual – in Dutch style, all arches and red brick; it has a street terrace for outside meals, and a charming rustic dining-room. There is a small, neat and formal TV room, and small, simple but cheerful bedrooms. Guests on *pension* terms enjoy a choice of dishes; Peyo Colombet's repertoire includes his wife's special recipe for scallop and monkfish casserole (called *co'lotte*).

Nearby Church of St-Jean-Baptiste; Ciboure; Biarritz (15 km); Ascain (10 km) – Basque church; Sare (15 km) – cog railway.

18-20 Rue de la République
64500 St-Jean-de-Luz
Tel 59.26.17.74
Location in middle of old town, near beach; with free car parking 400m away
Meals breakfast, lunch, dinner
Prices rooms 190F-240F; meals 75F-200F
Rooms 18 double, 10 with bath, 7 with shower (10 twin); all rooms have central heating, phone
Facilities dining-room, TV room, conference room, bar
Credit cards AE, DC, MC, V
Children accepted
Disabled no special facilities
Pets dogs accepted
Closed 2 to 31 Jan
Proprietor Mme Mayie Colombet

La Forestière

Despite its situation close to the main Laruns-Pau road (front-facing rooms could be noisy), its slightly staid atmosphere and its airport-lounge-style sitting room, this neat little hotel deserves consideration either as a stop-over or as a touring base for families. The elderly Mme Decart is ably assisted in running the hotel by friendly young people, while her husband's kitchen produces reliable traditional dishes, served in a simple but attractive room with splendid views of the Pyrenees. These views are shared by many of the tastefully decorated and notably spacious bedrooms, and of course by the pleasant grassy garden.

Nearby Pau (26 km) – Blvd des Pyrénées, château.

Rte de Laruns 64260
Louvie-Juzon
Tel 59.05.62.28
Location just outside village on N134bis Laruns to Pau road; with garden and car parking
Meals breakfast, lunch, dinner
Prices rooms 220F-260F (suites 460F); menus 75F-150F
Rooms 10 double (4 twin), 5 family rooms; all with bath; all rooms have central heating, phone
Facilities sitting-room, dining-room/bar
Credit cards AE, DC, MC, V
Children accepted
Disabled no special facilities
Pets accepted
Closed never
Proprietors M. and Mme Decart

Pyrénées-Atlantiques

Hôtel Arraya

With its timbered, white-painted houses, Sare can claim to be the prettiest of all the extremely pretty Basque villages – altogether captivating, provided the weather is right and the surrounding pastures merely lush, emerald and gleaming (not rain-sodden). In the heart of the village, this 16thC house was once a hostel for religious pilgrims on their way across the Pyrenees to Santiago de Compostella; now it houses, among others, stylish Parisians who have no wish to hurry away, despite the charms of the coast (less than 16 km away) or the high mountains (a little further).

Behind the slightly severe frontage on the main square lies a country-house hotel of great character. Sitting-room, bar and dining-room – not to mention every nook and cranny on stairways or landings – are filled with glorious old Basque furniture; sofas and chairs are comfortable and inviting, and flowers are everywhere. There are more antiques in the individually decorated bedrooms (not especially spacious, but bright and beautiful); some look out over the fine garden. As if all this is not enough, the cooking is good and there is a particularly well-chosen wine list; and there is even a splendid Gâteau Basque for tea.

Nearby Cog railway up La Rhune; Aìnhoa (10 km) – Basque village; Ascain (5 km) – Basque church; St-Jean-de-Luz (14 km).

64310 Sare
Tel 59.54.20.46
Location in middle of village, 14 km SE of St-Jean-de-Luz; with garden and ample public car parking (private parking nearby)
Meals breakfast, lunch, dinner
Prices rooms 240F-350F; meals 100F-250F
Rooms 20 double, 17 with bath, 4 with shower (12 twin); one single with shower; all rooms have central heating, phone; TV on request
Facilities sitting-room, bar, dining-room
Credit cards AE, MC, V
Children welcome; special menu available
Disabled no special facilities
Pets accepted in restaurant only
Closed early Nov to mid-May
Proprietor Paul Fagoaga

La Forestière (see opposite)

Haute-Garonne / Ariège

L'Oustal

Perched high above the valley of the Ariège, the Oustal is a simple rustic *auberge* where food takes priority – a place worth noting in an area not over-equipped with attractive hotels. The restaurant's traditional regional dishes – straightforwardl but wholesome and generous – are popular with locals, especially at weekends. The bedrooms are simply furnished, but they are all prettily decorated and well kept – as are the communal bathrooms (the two private bathrooms are a recent improvement). The little bar doubles as reception, and the sitting-room (with TV) is distinctly primitive. But if you are intending to spend your time out and about, this is a delightful spot to stay – and a reasonably priced one, too.

Nearby Ax-les-Thermes – spa, winter sports; Grotte de Lombrives (15 km) – underground lake; Montségur (45 km).

Unac 09250 Luzenac
Tel 61.64.48.44
Location on edge of village, 9 km NW of Ax-les-Thermes; car parking nearby
Meals breakfast, lunch, dinner
Prices rooms 145F-310F; menus 140F-210F
Rooms 5 double, 2 with bath (2 twin); central heating
Facilities dining-room, sitting-room, bar
Credit cards AE, V
Children accepted
Disabled access difficult
Pets dogs accepted
Closed Jan
Proprietor M. Descat

Auberge du Poids Public

The Lauragais is the rolling upland that forms the watershed between Aquitaine and the Midi, and St-Félix, on top of a hill, gives views in all directions, not the least impressive of them from the windows of this thoroughly well run inn. Bernard Augé is the life-and-soul of the place, never confined for long to the kitchen wherein he concocts excellent regional dishes which are outstanding value. The dining-room is rustic and jolly, with a blazing fire when appropriate; bedrooms are rather grander in style. A TV apparently spoils the cosy little sitting-room.

Nearby Castres (37 km); Toulouse.

31540 St-Félix-Lauragais
Tel 61.83.00.20
Location on edge of village, on D2, 40 km SE of Toulouse; with small garden, car parking and garages
Meals breakfast, lunch, dinner
Prices rooms 190F-210F; menus 50F-160F
Rooms 13 double, 8 with bath, 5 with shower (4 twin); all rooms have central heating, phone
Facilities dining-room, bar, sitting-room
Credit cards AE, V
Children welcome; special meals available
Disabled no special facilities
Pets dogs accepted
Closed early Jan to early Feb; restaurant only Sun dinner in winter
Proprietor Bernard Augé

Allier

Château hotel, Target

Château de Boussac

The Château de Boussac lies between Vichy and Moulin, tucked away in the Bourbonnais – a region rarely included on foreign visitors' itineraries – and is quite difficult to find. There are no prominent signs or roadside posters, because this is not a hotel in the ordinary sense. Solid, turreted and moated, the château could be a tourist sight in its own right; it is built around a courtyard, and the main reception rooms, furnished with Louis XV antiques and chandeliers, open on to a vast terrace with an ornamental lake and formal gardens.

But this is no echoing monument devoid of furnishings – on the contrary, the château is very much lived-in. It is a private home where you stay as paying guests of the aristocratic owners, whose family have owned the château since the middle of the 18thC. By day the Marquis dons his overalls and works on the estate, but comes in to cook at least one course of the *table d'hote* evening meal and chat to his guests. His wife looks after the rooms with care – there are fresh flowers everywhere and the antiques are highly polished. Dinner *en famille* can be a rather formal affair, but the food is hard to fault and the Marquis, who speaks English, will make you feel at home.

Nearby Souvigny (35 km) – Gothic/Romanesque church; Vichy (40 km) – spa town; Moulins (50 km) – half-timbered houses.

Target 03140 Chantelle
Tel 70.56.63.20
Location in countryside, off D42 (on D282), 12 km NW of Chantelle, 50 km W of Vichy; in large park, with ample car parking
Meals breakfast, dinner
Prices rooms 525F-790F; menus 250F-300F
Rooms 4 double (3 twin), 1 suite, all with bath; all rooms have central heating

Facilities dining-room, sitting-room (hosts' own rooms)
Credit cards not accepted
Children accepted if well behaved
Disabled no special facilities
Pets accepted if well behaved
Closed Nov to Feb
Proprietors Marquis and Marquise de Longueil

Auberge du Poids Public (see opposite)

Allier

Country hotel, Coulandon

Le Chalet

It is the setting that lifts this *Relais du Silence* out of the ordinary – in a secluded, wooded garden (park-like in style) of which the main feature is a big fish pond perfect for strolling around, drink in hand, before dinner. Rooms (some in the chalet-style building itself, others in converted outbuildings) vary in style and size; none is notably stylish, but the best are cheerfully comfortable (with exposed beams and bright wallpaper) and sound value. There are regional specialities in the traditional-style dining-room, and the service is amiable. The kitchen is the province of M. Hulot (no relation).

Nearby Moulins – timbered houses, cathedral.

Coulandon 03000 Moulins
Tel 70.44.50.08
Location in countryside
6 km W of Moulins, off
D945; with large grounds
and ample car parking
Meals breakfast, dinner
Prices rooms 140F–290F;
menus 62F–100F
Rooms 16 double, 4 with
bath, 12 with shower (5
twin); 9 family rooms, 6 with
bath, 3 with shower; all

rooms have central heating,
phone; 15 rooms have TV
Facilities dining-room,
sitting-room; fishing
Credit cards AE, DC, V
Children accepted
Disabled 6 ground-floor
bedrooms
Pets accepted at extra
charge
Closed 1 Nov to 31 Jan
Proprietor M. H Hulot

Cantal

Auberge Fleurie

This delightful creeper-covered *auberge* was first opened as a hotel in 1919 by Yvonne Barral's parents. After 30 years at the helm, and at the stove, she is now joined by her son, fully trained in the schools of cooking and hotel-keeping. Bedrooms are comfortable enough, but the two attractive dining-rooms (polished wood dressers, gleaming copper, red-check table-cloths) are the focal point; there is a bar, which is well patronised by locals (and a sitting-room in a cottage annexe, a km or so away). You are assured of a thoroughly friendly welcome.

Nearby Entraygues (15km) – medieval bridge; Lot valley.

Place du Barry 15120 Montsalvy
Tel 71.49.20.02
Location on edge of village, 35 km S of Aurillac; garden and private car parking at cottage annexe, 1 km away
Meals breakfast, lunch, dinner
Prices rooms 100F-140F; meals 50F-105F
Rooms 13 double, 5 with shower (3 twin); 2 family rooms, both with shower; all rooms have central heating
Facilities 2 dining-rooms, bar; sitting-room in annexe
Credit cards AE, DC, MC, V
Children welcome; special meals available
Disabled no special facilities
Pets accepted
Closed restaurant mid-Nov to mid-Mar
Proprietor Mme Yvonne Barral

Hostellerie de la Maronnne

Set in a beautiful peaceful valley in the Auvergne, with a small modern swimming-pool, this 1880 country house makes a fine retreat whether you are in search of peace or of outdoor exercise. There is a glorious view down the valley of the nearby Maronne. The rooms – some in the main house, some in rustic annexes – are pleasant and well looked after; but for stylish decoration, look elsewhere. There is a set menu only but the cooking is careful and traditional.

Nearby Salers (10 km); Anjony (20 km) – château.

Le Theil 15140 St-Martin-Valmeroux
Tel 71.69.20.33
Location in countryside 3 km E of St-Martin, on D37; with gardens and ample car parking
Meals breakfast, lunch, dinner
Prices rooms 210F-280F; menu 100F
Rooms 19 double, 16 with bath, 3 with shower (12 twin); 5 family rooms, all with bath; all rooms have central heating, phone, minibar
Facilities dining-room, sitting-room, seminar room; swimming-pool, tennis, archery, pétanque
Credit cards MC, V
Children welcome **Disabled** no special facilities **Pets** accepted but not in dining-room
Closed mid-Oct to Apr
Proprietor Alain de Cock

Lozère

Château hotel, La Malène

Château de la Caze

This is a medieval château in the true fairytale tradition, with turrets and vaults in abundance. Converted sympathetically, it still retains an ancient atmosphere although the chapel is now the dining-room, and modern bathrooms have been added to the bedrooms. Furnishings are antique and grand, bedrooms are large. A barn annexe in the lush garden provides space for further bedrooms, and there is a sunny terrace for summer breakfasts which looks down over the moat. Cooking is traditional, and of a high standard. And then there is the setting, right by the glorious River Tarn, the steep valley sides rearing above.

Nearby Gorges du Tarn; Florac; Parc National des Cévennes.

La Malène 48210 Ste-Enimie
Tel 66.48.51.01
Location beside river in Tarn gorge, on D907 48 km NE of Millau; with ample car parking and large garden
Meals breakfast, lunch, dinner
Prices rooms 450F-750F; menus 130F-380F
Rooms 19 double (10 twin) all with bath; all rooms have TV, phone
Facilities sitting-room/bar, dining-room
Credit cards AE, DC, MC, V
Children welcome; special meals available **Disabled** 3 ground-floor rooms in annexe **Pets** accepted but not in dining-room
Closed mid-Oct to May
Proprietors Simone and Martine Roux

Manor house hotel, Meyrueis

La Renaissance

Meyrueis is a pleasant village, well placed for exploration of various gorges cutting through the causses or of the upland scenery of the Cèvennes national park. The Renaissance is an exceptionally captivating old manor house – in the Bourguet family for two and a half centuries, furnished with great character and obviously looked after with affection. Simple antiques fill the sitting room and some of the bedrooms (others are simpler and more modern); the beamed dining-rooms are more consciously elegant. Food is excellent and regionally based, and there is an impressive wine list.

Nearby Aven Armand (10 km) – stalagmites; Gorges du Tarn.

Rue de la Ville 48150 Meyrueis
Tel 66.45.60.19
Location in middle of village, 42 km E of Millau and 35 km SW of Florac; with large garden
Meals breakfast, lunch, dinner
Prices rooms 200F-390F; menus 80F-170F, children's 40F
Rooms 19 double, (4 twin), 1 suite, all with bath; all rooms have phone, TV
Facilities 3 dining-rooms, sitting-room
Credit cards AE, DC, MC, V
Children welcome
Disabled no special facilities
Pets accepted
Closed mid-Nov to mid-Mar
Proprietor Henry Bourguet

Haute-Loire

Village inn, Moudeyres

Auberge Pré Bossu

Moudeyres is a remote village high (1,200 metres) in the volcanic hills of the Mézenc massif, surrounded by fields of wild flowers (in the spring) and mushrooms (in the autumn). The village consists almost entirely of thatched rough-stone houses, many now beautifully restored. The *auberge* is no exception, although it was built as recently as 1969, but with old materials; from a distance, there is little to make you suspect it is a hotel, and inside all is appropriately simple and charming. The young Flemish owners have worked hard to create an attractive and comfortable house. Starting with beams, wood floors and ingle-nook fireplace, they have added fine antique dressers, lace curtains, wild flowers, plants, books – and a budgerigar. It is all fresh and well-kept. Bedrooms are rustic, too – clean and simple, with good shower rooms; tranquillity is assured.

Carlos Grootaert's cooking skills have been discovered by guidebook writers (not only in France), and he will, therefore, not have to worry about the lack of passing trade in this isolated spot. Certainly this small hotel deserves to be known, and as yet there is little sign that the steady stream of discerning visitors has spoilt the peace of the village. For the moment at least, the fixed-price menus offer remarkable value.

Nearby Restored 18thC farm; Le Puy–volcanic rock formations.

43150 Moudeyres
Tel 71.05.10.70
Location on edge of village, 25 km E of Le Puy; in garden, with ample car parking
Meals breakfast, lunch, dinner
Prices rooms 195F-260F; menus 95F-150F
Rooms 10 double, 5 with bath, 5 with shower (4 twin); one family room; all rooms have central heating, phone
Facilities bar, TV room, dining-room
Credit cards AE, DC, MC, V
Children accepted
Disabled no special facilities
Pets accepted in bedrooms, but not in dining-room
Closed 11 Nov to Easter
Proprietor Carlos Grootaert

Aveyron

Manor house hotel, Castelpers

Château de Castelpers

This family-home-turned-hotel makes a relaxing retreat. The house dates from the 17thC and ranges from the purely rustic to the Gothic in style, with a tower, arched windows and rooms of character furnished comfortably with antiques. But it is not a château hotel in the grand manner; families can feel at ease, with swings and spacious lawns (dotted with ancient trees) for children to play on and trout streams to explore, and prices that reflect the modest size of the bedrooms. The food is good (nearby Naucelle is known particularly for *charcuterie*).

Nearby Château du Bosc (10 km); Sauveterre-de-Rouergue (20 km).

Castelpers 12170 Requista
Tel 65.69.22.61
Location in countryside
9 km SE of RN88, 10 km S of
Naucelle; in wooded park
with private car parking
Meals breakfast, lunch,
dinner
Prices rooms 165F-350F;
menus 100F-180F
Rooms 7 double (4 twin), 2
family rooms; 2 with bath, 7
with shower; all rooms have
phone

Facilities sitting-room, 2
dining-rooms; fishing
Credit cards AE, MC, V
Children welcome if well
behaved
Disabled one specially
equipped ground-floor
bedroom
Pets accepted, but not in
dining-room
Closed 1 Oct to 1 Apr
Proprietor Mme Yolande
Tapie de Celeyran

Aveyron

Hôtel Ste-Foy

Conques is a lovely old village which was an important port of call for Santiago-bound pilgrims, and at its heart is the great abbey church from which this hotel – a sturdy medieval house directly opposite – takes its name. It is an unassuming, relaxing place, furnished in suitably plain style and beautifully kept, with much polished wood. There is a courtyard behind where meals are served in summer. Rooms vary somewhat in size and comfort, but not in price. Food is not notably ambitious, but soundly cooked and excellent value.

Nearby Church of Ste-Foy (remarkable tympanum and treasury).

Conques 12320 St-Cyprien-sur-Dourdou
Tel 65.69.84.03
Location in heart of village, 40 km N of Rodez; with private car parking
Meals breakfast, lunch, dinner
Prices DB&B 300F-350F for one; lunch 100F
Rooms 19 double, 12 with bath, 7 with shower (10 twin); 2 single, one with bath, one with shower; all rooms have central heating, phone
Facilities 2 dining-rooms, sitting-room, bar, interior patio, conference room
Credit cards MC, V
Children accepted
Disabled no special facilities
Pets accepted
Closed end Oct to Easter
Proprietors M. and Mme Garcenot

Lou Mazuc

If you happened by chance upon Michel and Ginette Bras's modest hotel, in the middle of the out-of-the-way town of Laguiole, and found a room free, you would be happy enough with your accommodation – in a neat bedroom (possibly studio-style, with a mezzanine) equipped with solid wooden furniture designed by Michel himself. But you would be positively bowled over when you went down to dinner, because here, in these inauspicious surroundings, resides one of France's best chefs. Like no one else in France, the young Michel will transport you to the heights of your gastronomic dreams at prices which remain resolutely earth-bound. Go soon, before all the awards go to his head.

Nearby Aubrac (20 km) – former priory, in Aubrac mountains; Espalion (25 km) – Pont Vieux, Lot Valley, Eglise de Perse.

Place Prat 12210 Laguiole
Tel 65.44.32.24
Location in middle of town, 65 km SW of St-Flour; with private garages
Meals breakfast, lunch, dinner
Prices rooms 190F-400F; menus 130F-380F
Rooms 13 double, 6 with bath, 7 with shower (2 twin); all rooms have phone, TV
Facilities dining-room, sitting-room
Credit cards AE, V
Children accepted
Disabled no special facilities
Pets not accepted
Closed mid-Oct to Apr; Sun dinner and Mon
Proprietor Michel Bras

Aveyron

L'Oustal del Barry

High up in the pretty old village of Najac – justly renowned for its medieval fortress towering above the winding River Aveyron – is this unassuming little country hotel offering an honest welcome and notably good value, both for meals and rooms. The hotel (sometimes known as the Miquel) has been in the family for five generations, and for the last 15 years in the hands of Jean-Marie, whose cooking – modern, but regionally based – has a high local reputation. The lush little garden has swings for children, and there is a sunny terrace in front of the hotel.

Nearby Castle, Gorges de l'Aveyron; Cordes (25 km).

Place du Bourg 12270 Najac
Tel 65.29.74.32
Location in middle of village, 54 km NW of Albi and 24 km S of Villefranche-de-Rouergue; with garden and car parking
Meals breakfast, lunch, dinner
Prices rooms 130F-210F; meals 95F-240F
Rooms 20 double, 7 with bath, 10 with shower (5 twin);
one family room with shower; all rooms have central heating, phone
Facilities dining-room, sitting-room; boules
Credit cards MC, V
Children welcome; special menus available
Disabled lift/elevator
Pets accepted
Closed Nov to Apr
Proprietor M. and Mme Jean-Marie Miquel

Hôtel du Midi

The rural *logis* at its best: a village inn amid grand countryside, carefully run by the same family for four generations, offering welcoming rooms and excellent honest food at irrestible prices. It is very much a family-run place, with Mme overseeing the dining-room while Jean-Michel cooks (his background includes time with the revered Michel Bras at Lou Mazuc). Most of the vegetables come from the garden, poultry is home-raised, jams and croissants home-made. The dining-room is plain – bentwood chairs on a tiled floor – but spick-and-span, and the bedrooms too are simple but comfortable.

Nearby Gorges de la Dourbie (10 km); Montpellier-le-Vieux.

12230 St-Jean-du-Bruel
Tel 65.62.26.04
Location in village on D991, 40 km SE of Millau; with ample car parking
Meals breakfast, lunch, dinner
Prices rooms 65F-205F; menus 60F-160F
Rooms 12 double, 8 with bath (3 twin); 2 single; 5 family rooms, 3 with bath, 2 with shower; all rooms have
central heating, phone
Facilities 3 dining-rooms, bar, sitting-room, TV room
Credit cards V
Children welcome; special menus available **Disabled** access to dining-room only
Pets accepted
Closed mid-Nov to week before Easter
Proprietor Jean-Michel Papillon

Aveyron

Village inn, St-Sernin-sur-Rance

Hôtel Carayon

St-Sernin is a handsome medieval village in attractive hilly countryside not far from the Tarn, of which the Rance is a tributary. The Carayon (once called the France but, after a century in the same hands, now known by the family name) is an undistinguished building – white painted, shuttered, with cars parked directly in front – and the accommodation it offers is simple. But it enjoys a lovely view over the valley of the Rance (shared by the restaurant and its terrace and many of the rooms), the welcome is warm and – last but not least – Pierre Carayon's cooking is excellent. What is more, the menu prices are modest, earning a prized red R rating from Michelin. The reputation of the Carayon is for good honest regional fare, fresh ingredients and large portions – nothing *nouvelle* about it, although if you want a light dish Pierre will oblige.

The Carayons are an attractive and friendly couple (Pierre speaks good English, having spent a couple of years in London hotels). Some bedrooms are in a modern annexe.

Nearby Vallée du Tarn (20 km); Monts de Lacaune (30 km).

Place du Fort 12380 St-Sernin-sur-Rance
Tel 65.99.60.26
Location in village, 50 km E of Albi, 63 km SW of Millau; with garden, car parking
Meals breakfast, lunch, dinner
Prices rooms 99F-250F; menus 55F-215F
Rooms 26 double, 14 with bath, 10 with shower (8 twin); 10 family rooms/ suites, 5 with bath, 3 with shower; all rooms have central heating, phone, minibar; 10 rooms have TV
Facilities 2 dining-rooms, TV room, games room
Credit cards AE, DC, MC, V
Children welcome **Disabled** 3 bedrooms specially equipped **Pets** accepted
Closed Sun dinner and Mon out of season
Proprietor Pierre Carayon

Tarn

Le Grand Ecuyer

Cordes is a glorious medieval village on an isolated hill, its main street lined by fine Gothic mansions. Le Grand Ecuyer is scarcely less impressive – a former hunting lodge of the Comte de Toulouse and a classified historic monument, transformed into a comfortable, elegant and atmospheric hotel.

For many visitors, the food is the thing. Yves Thuriès, the *chef-patron*, is an excellent cook in general but as a *pâtissier* he has few equals. The dining-room is medieval in style, with old stone walls and tiled floors, dark beamed ceiling, old prints and so on blending well with the lacey white table-cloths, shining silver, painted plates and tapestry chairs. The sitting-room and bar are more domestic, with deeply upholstered armchairs, low tables and potted plants. Bedrooms are grand but inviting – beamed ceilings, monumental stone fireplaces, rugs on expanses of polished floor – and are beautifully furnished with antiques (four-poster beds, antiques chests and so on). Bathrooms are modern.

It could easily be too heavy and pompous, but M. Thuriès and his charming wife Pascale ensure that a graciously informal atmosphere prevails.

Nearby Rue Droite (14thC houses); Fôret Grésigne (15 km) – marked trails; Albi – *la ville rouge*.

Rue Voltaire 81170 Cordes
Tel 63.56.01.03
Location in middle of village, 25 km NW of Albi; with public car parking nearby
Meals breakfast, lunch, dinner
Prices rooms 450F-700F, suite 1,200F; menus 160F-340F
Rooms 12 double, one suite, all with bath; all rooms have central heating, phone, radio
Facilities 2 dining-rooms, breakfast room, sitting-room, bar
Credit cards DC, MC, V
Children accepted **Disabled** no special facilities **Pets** accepted
Closed Nov to Easter
Proprietor Yves Thuriès

Tarn

Hostellerie du Vieux Cordes

If you want a simpler base than the Grand Ecuyer in the old town of Cordes, here is the answer. Also owned by the exacting M. Thuriès, and managed by his brother-in-law, it compromises only slightly on his high standards of comfort and cuisine. Set at the top of the old hill town, the stone-built 13thC building has a terrace garden giving long views (shared by many of the bedrooms) over the rooftops; there are tables here and also in an interior courtyard where they are shaded by mature wisteria. Inside, stone, beams and tiled floors give it a rustic ambience – furniture is generally simple, except in the plush sitting-room, where the baronial gets out of hand.

Nearby Rue Droite (14thC houses); Fôret de Grésigne (15 km).

Rue St-Michel 81170 Cordes
Tel 63.56.00.12
Location at top of town; with car parking nearby, and one garage
Meals breakfast, lunch, dinner
Prices rooms 230F-360F; menus 65F-180F
Rooms 21 double, 7 with bath, 13 with shower (5 twin); all rooms have central heating, phone; TV on request
Facilities dining-room with bar, sitting-room
Credit cards AE, DC, MC, V
Children accepted
Disabled no special facilities
Pets accepted
Closed mid-Jan to mid-Feb
Proprietor Yves Thuriès

La Metairie Neuve

Mazamet is not a notably appealing town except to students of sheepskin processing, but it is practically surrounded by the grand scenery of the Parc Régional du Haut Languedoc – and Pont de Larn lies just below the pretty Gorges du Banquet. The Metairie is a tastefully renovated old farm with its heritage properly respected – exposed beams, stone walls, polished tiled floors – and with a relaxed atmosphere. Mme Tournier is a charming hostess who keeps the antique-furnished public areas looking immaculate and inviting. Rooms are relatively plain.

Nearby Castres (15 km) – Goya museum; Carcassone (50 km).

81660 Pont-de-Larn
Tel 63.61.23.31
Location in countryside 2 km E of Mazamet on D65, 18 km SE of Castres; with private car parking
Meals breakfast, lunch, dinner
Prices rooms 220F-320F; menus 75F-230F
Rooms 9 double, (2 twin); 2 family rooms, all with bath; all rooms have central heating, phone; 7 have TV
Facilities 2 dining-rooms, sitting-room, conference room
Credit cards DC, MC, V
Children welcome; special menu available
Disabled ramp access on ground floor
Pets accepted
Closed mid-Dec to mid-Jan; restaurant only Sat
Proprietor Mme Tournier

Ardèche

Hôtel du Midi

This restaurant is named after the renowned Madame Barat-téro, a culinary heroine of British cookery writer Elizabeth David, from whom the Perriers took over in the 1950s. It remains the heart of the Hôtel du Midi, serving an ambitious (and expensive) blend of traditional and *nouvelle* dishes which earn modest awards from the gastronomic guides. The dining-room is rather plain but intimate, service helpful and friendly. Bedrooms are comfortably old-fashioned and spacious; those at the front can be somewhat noisy, those in the annexe across the road are quietest (they have a small garden in which to take breakfast).
Nearby Small steam train to Tournon (35 km); Valence (40 km).

Place Seignobos 07270 Lamastre
Tel 75.06.41.50
Location in middle of town, 40 km W of Valence; with garden, and garage
Meals breakfast, lunch, dinner
Prices rooms 150F–280F; meals 140F–320F
Rooms 15 double, 11 with bath, 4 with shower (8 twin); all rooms have central heating, phone
Facilities 3 dining-rooms; 2 sitting-rooms
Credit cards AE, DC, MC, V
Children welcome; special meals available **Disabled** one ground-floor bedroom **Pets** accepted
Closed 15 Dec to 1 Mar; Sun evening and Mon
Proprietor Bernard Perrier

Château d'Urbilhac

This fairytale château – 19thC but in Renaissance style, with round tower and steep slate roof – has a beautiful, peaceful, elevated setting in a very large park (much of the food comes fresh from the farms on the estate). The interior is rather ponderous in style, but it does not lack character or comfort. The bedrooms are exceptionally civilized, with plenty of space and some splendid old beds. A key feature is the smart swimming-pool, below the grand terrace. The Xomperos are a charming couple, much concerned for guests' happiness.
Nearby Tournon (35 km); Valence (40 km) – cathedral.

07270 Lamastre
Tel 75.06.42.11
Location in countryside on D2, 2 km S of village; in large grounds with ample car parking and garage
Meals breakfast, lunch, dinner
Prices rooms 350F–500F; menus 160F–250F; DB & B (obligatory in season) 420F–445F for one
Rooms 13 double, 10 with bath, 3 with shower (3 twin); all rooms have phone
Facilities sitting-room, 2 dining-rooms; swimming-pool, tennis
Credit cards AE, DC, MC, V
Children accepted
Disabled dining-room and one bedroom on ground floor
Pets accepted
Closed mid-Oct to 1 May
Proprietors M. and Mme Xompero

Ardèche

Manoir de Raveyron

When our inspectors arrived, this rustic village inn was bursting at the seams with Sunday lunchers. The atmosphere was genuinely entertaining: any minute one expected a fiddler to appear and the clientele to start dancing. The waiters were frantically overworked, but still ready to oblige, and there were no signs of impatience from the customers. Bedrooms are simple but not uncomfortable. Luxury, no; but atmosphere in plenty. The hotel is approached down an unprepossessing side street, and faces an ugly modern building; but the surroundings do not intrude, because the old stone building is set well back from the street, behind gates and a large and leafy courtyard-cum-garden.

Nearby Gorges de l'Ardèche; Pont d'Arc (5 km); Marzal (20 km) – cave.

Rue Henri Barbusse 07150 Vallon-Pont-d'Arc
Tel 75.88.03.59
Location in village on D579, 33 km S of Aubenas, 51 km NE of Alés; with garden and car parking
Meals breakfast, lunch, dinner
Prices rooms 110F-145F; menus 49F-165F, children's 25F
Rooms 13 double, 1 single, 11 with shower; all rooms have central heating
Facilities dining-room, sitting-room/bar
Credit cards MC, V
Children welcome
Disabled no special facilities
Pets accepted
Closed end Oct to end Mar
Proprietors M. Bourdat and M. Gauthier

Drôme

Les Hospitaliers

Le Poét-Laval perches on a hillside overlooking the valley of the Javron: an unspoilt medieval village dominated by the former Protestant stronghold that is now Les Hospitaliers. It is a remarkable spot. The somewhat precarious drive up a steep and narrow road will reward you with a stunning panorama, stretching to the hills on the horizon.

Formerly derelict and abandoned, Les Hospitaliers is now a hotel of various creature comforts, including a Michelin-starred restaurant and a pool and terrace from which there are splendid views. You can eat inside or out, weather permitting. The inside restaurant (where you can still appreciate the views) has an interesting collection of paintings, thanks to Yvon Morin, the owner, who was an art-dealer before becoming a hotelier. Tables are laid with fine china, white linen or lace, and candles; the service is hard to fault. The menu includes specialities of *carré d'agneau*, 'foie gras de canard' and Charollais beef in vintage wine.

The bedrooms come as something of a disappointment – by comparision with the rest of the hotel they are modern and sober – but the majority share the beautiful views.

Nearby Montélimar (20 km) – nougat; Viviers (30 km) – medieval town, cathedral; Valence (60 km) – cathedral, wines.

Le Poét-Laval, Dieulefit
26160 La Bégude-de-Mazenc
Tel 75.46.22.32
Location at top of old village, 5 km W of Dieulefit; with gardens and car parking nearby
Meals breakfast, lunch, dinner
Prices rooms 370F-640F; meals 170F-350F
Rooms 18 double, 16 with bath, one with shower (8 twin); 3 family rooms, all with bath; all rooms have central heating, phone
Facilities 2 dining-rooms, 2 sitting-rooms, bar; swimming-pool
Credit cards AE, DC, MC, V
Children accepted
Disabled no special facilities
Pets cats and dogs accepted
Closed 15 Nov to 1 Mar
Proprietors M. and Mme Yvon Morin

Hôtel Pic (see opposite)

170

Drôme

Auberge des Quatres Saisons

St-Restitut is one of the lesser known perched villages of Provence. The vine-clad *auberge* lies in the oldest part of the village – a fascinating conversion of ancient Roman houses, preserving many of the old stone walls. Bedrooms are quiet, comfortable and beautifully furnished thanks to Mme Viguet-Carrin, a one-time interior designer. Her husband is the chef of the adjoining restaurant (*36 Soupières*), where a medieval room with stone vaulting and period furniture provide the setting for regional fare. Jolly elevated breakfast terrace.

Nearby St-Paul-Trois-Châteaux (5 km); Grignan (20 km).

Place de l'Eglise, St-Restitut
26130 St-Paul-Trois-Châteaux
Tel 75.04.71.88
Location in middle of village, 9 km NE of Bollène, on D160; with small garden, and car parking nearby
Meals breakfast, lunch, dinner
Prices rooms 195F-460F; menus 70F-220F
Rooms 8 double (6 twin), 5 with bath, 3 with shower; 2 family rooms with bath; all rooms have phone
Facilities dining-room, sitting-room
Credit cards AE, DC, MC, V
Children accepted
Disabled no special facilities
Pets accepted
Closed mid-Nov to early Dec, mid- to end Jan
Proprietors M. and Mme Viguet-Carrin

Hôtel Pic

Most tourists give Valence a miss, but there is one good reason for making a detour – the Pic. Any meal here, whether an al fresco lunch, or dinner in the luxury of the dining-room, is a special event. The Pic is now regarded as one of the top restaurants in France – it has probably the most famous *menu dégustation* in the country, comprising nine exquisite courses – but is delightfully free of any snobby atmosphere. The four comfortable bedrooms are rarely vacant.

Nearby Cathedral; L'Hermitage (15 km); Montélimar (45 km).

285 Ave Victor-Hugo 26001 Valence
Tel 75.44.15.32
Location on S outskirts of town, east of A7 (exit Valence south); with garden and private parking
Meals breakfast, lunch, dinner
Prices rooms 400F-650F; menus 250F-480F
Rooms 3 double rooms (one twin) and one family room; all with bath; rooms reserved for restaurant clients only; all rooms have phone, TV, central heating
Facilities dining-room, sitting-room
Credit cards AE, DC, MC, V
Children welcome
Disabled access to restaurant
Pets accepted
Closed 3 weeks in Aug, 10 days in Feb; Wed, and Sun evening
Proprietors Jacques Pic

Gard

Country hotel, La Favède

A l'Auberge Cévenole

The usual approach is through the disagreeably industrialized valley which runs north from Alès; but don't be put off. The *auberge*, set in a little circle of hills, is as peaceful and alluring as any you could wish to find. The building is white, with a red-tiled roof and a shady, creeper-clad terrace. It is set in an exceptional garden: informal, full of flowers, with plenty of secluded corners in which to read, plus an (unheated) swimming-pool. Inside the pace is slow (though not the service, except on occasions when the waitresses are over-stretched), the atmosphere quietly old-fashioned. A rash of shepherds and shepherdesses covers many of the walls; bedrooms and bathrooms range from adequate to very comfortable without being luxurious (with the exception of the two apartments, which are). The place is run with professionalism and *politesse* by M. Chabaud and, in the background, his elderly mother. He is also the chef, and his cooking is above average, enjoyable and consistently interesting but without fireworks. Our exhausted inspectors spent five contented days here, stirring only to walk in the unspoilt hills of the Cévennes.

Nearby Château de Rousson (20 km); St-Jean-du-Gard and Corniche des Cévennes (25 km); Grotte de Trabuc (25 km).

La Favède 30110 La Grand-Combe
Tel 66.34.12.13
Location in hamlet on D283 off N106 14 km N of Alès; with large garden and ample car parking
Meals breakfast, lunch, dinner
Prices rooms 250F-550F; menus 150F-250F
Rooms 18 double (6 twin), 8 with bath, 10 with shower; all rooms have central heating, phone
Facilities dining-room, bar/sitting-room, TV room; swimming-pool
Credit cards AE, MC, V
Children accepted
Disabled 6 ground-floor rooms
Pets not accepted
Closed Dec to Mar
Proprietor M. Chabaud

Gard

L'Ermitage-Meissonnier

The experts say that since Paul-Louis Meissonnier's son Michel has taken over the reins in the kitchen, standards at L'Ermitage have slipped somewhat. Pay no heed: the menus are still mouth-watering, the execution of them still way above average and the prices still reasonable by the standards of Michelin-starred restaurants. It is a relaxing place to stay. Bedrooms lack coherent style but are comfortable and peaceful. The dining-room is pleasantly unpretentious, with solid furnishings on a tiled floor, but it is the delightful terrace that steals the show – shaded by mulberry trees, lit by oil lamps on the tables.

Nearby Avignon – Palais de Papes, cathedral; Nîmes (39 km).

Ave de Verdun 30133 Les Angles
Tel 90.25.41.02
Location on NW fringes of Avignon, 3 km from middle on RN900; with garden, terrace and private car parking
Meals breakfast, lunch, dinner
Prices rooms 180F-320F; menus 200F-350F,

children's 100F
Rooms 16 double (6 twin), most with bath; all rooms have central heating, phone
Facilities dining-room, sitting-area
Credit cards AE, DC, V
Children welcome
Disabled no special facilities
Pets accepted at extra charge
Closed Jan, Feb
Proprietor M. Meissonnier

Auberge du Pont Romain

This converted carpet factory – a massive and unconventional building for a hotel – has received some enthusiastic reports in the past. Certainly the scale of the place is amusing, and the management friendly and informal – and Sommières is a delightful little town. Perhaps our inspectors hit a bad night: dinner embarassingly late, trouble with the telephones, limited choice at the bar. Perhaps they had one of the least good rooms: it was uncomfortable and crudely converted. But the prices are high enough to make these failings difficult to excuse.

Nearby Roman road and aqueduct (directions from proprietress).

2 Rue Emile-Jamais 30250 Sommières
Tel 66.80.00.58
Location in town on RN110, equidistant from Nîmes and Montpellier; with large garden and ample car parking
Meals breakfast, lunch, dinner
Prices rooms 155F-320F; menus 135F-200F
Rooms 12 double (2 twin), 2

family rooms; central heating, phone
Facilities 3 dining-rooms, bar, conference room; swimming-pool
Credit cards AE, V
Children accepted
Disabled no special facilities
Pets accepted
Closed mid-Jan to mid-Mar; restaurant only, Wed
Proprietor Mme Monique Michel

Gard

Hotel de l'Atelier

In a quaint side street fairly near the main square, this old town house makes a complete contrast to our other recommendation in Villeneuve. It has nothing like the bustle of the Magnaneraie (there is no restaurant), but the welcome is sincere. The building has been sympathetically restored – original stone walls much in evidence – with careful attention to detail. Breakfast is served in a pleasant room, and you cannot fail to be charmed by the picturesque courtyard at the back – enclosed by a jumble of old buildings, and an ideal place in which to sit and drink muscat before dinner.

Nearby Avignon – Palais des Papes, cathedral, Pont St-Bénézet.

5 Rue de la Foire 30400
Villeneuve-lès-Avignon
Tel 90.25.01.84
Location in town, 2 km N of middle of Avignon; with garden and public parking only
Meals breakfast
Prices rooms 200F-350F
Rooms 19 double, 13 with bath, 6 with shower (8 twin); all rooms have central heating; 11 rooms have TV and phone
Facilities breakfast room, sitting-room
Credit cards AE, DC, V
Children welcome **Disabled** no special facilities **Pets** accepted
Closed never
Proprietors M. and Mme Garnier

Hôtel d'Entraigues

A cleverly converted 16thC townhouse – all cream stone walls, vaulted ceilings, bamboo furniture, Provençal fabrics. Up a flight of stairs you reach a sun-drenched terrace clinging to the side of the house, where both drinks and meals are served. Everything is small-scale, including the tiny dining-room; bedrooms are impeccable. If that sounds quaint, it should not: this is a chic, professional little place under the same management as the sumptuous château at nearby Arpaillargues. (In 1989 they are also opening a larger and very swish hotel-restaurant across the street.) Uzès is enchanting; Entraigues lives up to its surroundings.

Nearby Duché (castle), Tour Fenestrelle; St-Siffret (5 km).

8 Rue de Le Calade 30700
Uzès
Tel 66.22.32.68
Location in middle of town; with public car parking and private garage
Meals breakfast, lunch, dinner
Prices rooms 240F-340F; menus 70F-120F
Rooms 18 double, all with bath (4 twin); all rooms have central heating, phone
Facilities dining-room, sitting-room, bar
Credit cards AE, DC, V
Children accepted **Disabled** access difficult **Pets** dogs accepted in bedrooms at extra charge
Closed never
Proprietor Gérard Saury

Gard

Hostellerie La Magnaneraie

There are several hotels to choose from in Villeneuve-lès-Avignon – a pleasant and historically interesting base from which to explore nearby Avignon. The largest of them, the Prieuré, is also the best known; it is luxurious (and expensive), but it lacks the friendliness of the Magnaneraie – a solid, rectangular stone building which stands in a well-heeled residential corner of the town.

It has only recently been taken over by Eliane Prayal and her husband Gérard – a graduate of Vergé's kitchen and now making his own mark as a talented and committed chef. They are an energetic couple, determined to succeed, but not at the expense of an atmosphere which is 'genuinely easy-going', as one family commented. The garden has been ambitiously improved – statuary, a swimming-pool and immaculate flower beds. Inside, the decoration and furnishing is smart but a little heavy, successfully reassuring in the public rooms but slightly sombre in some of the bedrooms (though others are beautifully fresh).

Nearby Tour Phillipe-le-Bel, Chartreuse du Val-de-Bénédiction; Avignon – Palais des Papes, cathedral, Pont d'Avignon (Pont St-Bénézat); Nimes (40 km) – Roman amphitheatre, Maison Carrée.

Rue du Camp-de-Bataille
30400 Villeneuve-lès-
Avignon
Tel 90.25.11.11
Location in residential area
on fringe of village, across
the Rhône from Avignon;
with garden and car parking
Meals breakfast, lunch,
dinner
Prices rooms 450F-650F,
suites 650F-685F; menus
150F-220F
Rooms 20 double (13 twin),

2 suites, all with bath; all
rooms have central heating,
TV, phone, minibar
Facilities dining-room,
sitting-room, bar,
conference room;
swimming-pool, tennis
Credit cards AE, DE, MC, V
Children accepted
Disabled access easy
Pets not accepted
Closed never
Proprietors Gérard and
Eliane Prayal

Entraigues (see opposite)

Gard

Hostellerie du Seigneur

Surrounded by vineyards, Tavel is known for its rosé wines and for the *soigné* hotel on its outskirts, the Auberge de Tavel. Those seeking something plainer and more typically French, however, will head for this congenial spot in the middle. Perched above the main road, the Hostellerie is a safe, cosy place, with a pleasant little terrace overlooking a square. Inside, a bar-cum-reception area leads into the hotel's hub: a rambling, intimate dining-room where inexpensive *cuisine bourgeoise* is offered. Upstairs, bedrooms are plain, old-fashioned but adequate.

Nearby Avignon (15 km); Orange (15 km) – Roman theatre.

Place du Seigneur 30126 Tavel
Tel 66.50.04.26
Location in middle of village, 10 km NW of Avignon; with public car parking
Meals breakfast, lunch, dinner
Prices rooms 100F-180F; menus 72F-105F
Rooms 6 double (one twin); one family room; all rooms have central heating
Facilities dining-room, sitting-room, bar
Credit cards MC, V
Children accepted **Disabled** no special facilities **Pets** not accepted
Closed 15 Dec to 15 Jan
Proprietors Ange and Juliette Bodo

Auberge de Tavel

Tavel's old schoolhouse has been sympathetically converted into this smart and comfortable rustic-style hotel. One of the highlights has traditionally been the restaurant (star from Michelin, *toque* from Gault-Millau until recently), although the cooking is apparently in new hands so there must be some uncertainty about future standards. The other key attraction is the garden, with its shady gravelled terrace for outdoor eating and pretty swimming-pool with spacious surroundings.

Nearby Avignon – Palais des Papes, views over Rhône; Orange (20 km) – Roman theatre and other remains.

Voie Romaine 30126 Tavel
Tel 66.50.03.41
Location in middle of village, 14 km NW of Avignon; with garden and car parking
Meals breakfast, lunch, dinner
Prices rooms 250F-350F; menus 145F-310F
Rooms 11 double (3 twin), all with bath or shower; all rooms have central heating,
phone, minibar
Facilities dining-room, sitting-room, conference room; swimming-pool
Credit cards AE, DC, MC, V
Children welcome
Disabled no special facilities
Pets dogs accepted on leads
Closed closed long periods out of season
Proprietors M. and Mme Philippe Rozier

Vaucluse

Converted mill, Les Beaumettes

Le Moulin Blanc

This ancient mill, opened as a hotel in 1981, makes an attractive (though not cheap) base for an extended stay, equipped as it is with extensive lawns and a glamorous pool. Bedrooms are large, with restrained decoration and handsome antiques – some four-posters. The main dining-room is light and lofty. with rich colours in the furnishings and plenty of space, the sitting-room a rough-stone vault with rugs on a polished floor. There is a pretty courtyard for summer dining.

Nearby Village des Bories (5 km), Gordes (10 km).

Les Beaumettes 84220 Gordes
Tel 90.72.34.50
Location in countryside 40 km E of Avignon, off RN100; with garden and ample car parking
Meals breakfast, lunch, dinner
Prices rooms 380F-600F; menus 165F-265F
Rooms 12 double, with bath (6 twin); 5 family rooms, with bath; connecting rooms available; all rooms have TV, phone, minibar, radio alarm
Facilities 2 dining-rooms, sitting-room; swimming-pool, tennis
Credit cards AE, DC, MC, V
Children welcome; special meals available
Disabled no special facilities
Pets small dogs accepted
Closed never
Proprietors Serge Herail and Pierre Robert

Vaucluse

L'Aiguebrun

Away from the road, surrounded by woods and near the rushing river from which the hotel gets its name, this handsome pale stone house in the Lubéron national park is a calm and welcoming retreat. In front is a terrace shaded by an enormous fir tree – an ideal spot for enjoying an evening drink. The public rooms have a private-house feel, with paintings on the walls and comfy sofas in front of a grand fireplace in the sitting-room. Bedrooms are large, comfortable and tastefully furnished, with tiled floor and beamed ceilings. Food is ambitious and good, but not cheap.

Nearby Fort de Buoux (5 km); Lourmarin (10 km) – château.

84480 Bonnieux **Tel** 90.74.04.14 **Location** in countryside, 6 km E of Bonnieux on D943; with garden, private drive and car parking **Meals** breakfast, lunch, dinner **Prices** rooms 380F-400F; meals 200F, children's 80F **Rooms** 8 double (2 twin), all with bath; all rooms have central heating, phone	**Facilities** sitting-room, dining-room, bar **Credit cards** not accepted **Children** welcome **Disabled** no special facilities **Pets** dogs accepted, but not in dining-room **Closed** Nov to week before Easter **Proprietor** M. Chastel

Les Florets

Les Florets lies in the heart of the Gigondas wine region, at the foot of the Dentelles de Montmirail – spectacular jagged peaks which are a paradise for hikers and rock-climbers. The hotel is small, family-run and appropriately named: floral bedrooms, flowers on the tables, and (at the right time of year) a riot of blossom covering the nearby hills. Bedrooms are decorated in simple Provençal style; four are in an annexe on the hill behind the hotel. The greatest asset of Les Florets is surely the idyllic terrace, shaded by plane trees and with a view of the vineyards and mountains.

Nearby Vineyards; Vaison-la-Romaine (15 km) – Roman remains.

Route des Dentelles 84190 Gigondas **Tel** 90.65.85.01 **Location** in countryside 1.5 km E of Gigondas, 18 km E of Orange; with ample car parking **Meals** breakfast, lunch, dinner **Prices** rooms 200F-235F; meals 100F-155F **Rooms** 12 double, 9 with	bath, 3 with shower (5 twin); 2 single; one family room with bath; all rooms have central heating, phone **Facilities** dining-room, bar **Credit cards** AE, DC, V **Children** welcome **Disabled** no special facilities **Pets** accepted **Closed** Jan, Feb **Proprietors** Mme Germano and Mme Bernard

Vaucluse

La Chaumière

The village of Laurie lies overlooking the Durance valley. La Chaumière, in the upper part of the village, is a group of buildings clustered around a flowery terrace with broad views, where breakfast is served in summer. Each of the bedrooms is individually and simply furnished; three have private balconies and views of the valley. But pride of place at La Chaumière goes to the restaurant: the light, refined dishes, and excellent choice of wines, have earned it recognition in all the gastronomic guides.

Nearby Lubéron Nature Park (marked trails); Lourmarin Château (5 km); Aix-en-Provence (40 km); Avignon (55 km).

Place du Portail 84360 Lauris
Tel 90.08.20.25
Location in small village, 5 km NW of Cadanet; with ample car parking
Meals breakfast, lunch, dinner
Prices rooms 200F-275F; menus 145F-260F
Rooms 10 double, 4 with bath, 6 with shower (4 twin); all rooms have central heating, phone
Facilities 2 dining-rooms, sitting-room, meeting-room
Credit cards AE, DC, MC, V
Children accepted
Disabled access easy
Pets accepted in bedrooms only
Closed restaurant only, Tue and Wed lunch
Manager Mme A Diamant

Auberge de Cassagne

In a leafy suburb of Avignon, this Provençal-style *auberge* has ample room for relaxing – a swimming-pool, a shady terrace for meals, and attractive bedrooms with traditional furniture and fabrics – those in the annexe generally more spacious and airy. There is a cosy sitting-room with beams and open fireplace, and a more formal dining-room. The young chef was trained by two of France's best, and is now making his own mark.

Nearby Avignon – Palais des Papes, museum of the Petit Palais (Italian painting), Pont d'Avignon (Pont St-Bénèzet).

84130 Le Pontet
Tel 90.31.04.18
Location in rural suburb of Avignon, 4 km NW of middle, 3 km W of A7; with gardens and ample car parking
Meals breakfast, lunch, dinner
Prices rooms 450F-660F; menus 280F-380F, under-10's 100F
Rooms 12 double, 9 with bath, 3 with shower (6 twin); 4 family rooms, all with bath; all rooms have central heating, TV, phone, minibar, safe-box
Facilities dining-room, 2 sitting-rooms, bar; swimming-pool
Credit cards AE, MC, V
Children welcome
Disabled no special facilities
Pets accepted; 30F charge
Closed never
Proprietor Jean-Michel Gallon

Vaucluse

Table du Comtat

Séguret is a tiny medieval village, looking out over the rocky outcrops of the Dentelles de Montmirail. Built against the hillside, this hotel blends well into the surroundings. The much modernized interior is light, airy and spacious, with attractive fabrics and furniture, and masses of flowers in the restaurant, which has large windows to benefit from the view. Not all the bedrooms are so privileged, though they are thoroughly pleasant. The cooking is a source of pride here: Franck Gomez prepares light and original dishes. A delightful place, though not cheap.

Nearby Gigondas (15 km) – vinyards; Orange (25 km).

Le Village, Séguret 84110 Vaison-la-Romaine
Tel 90.46.91.49
Location above tiny village on D23, 8km SW of Vaison-la-Romaine; small garden, with car parking in front
Meals breakfast, lunch, dinner
Prices rooms 300F-500F; meals 230F-380F
Rooms 8 double, all with bath (3 twin); all rooms have central heating, phone
Facilities 2 dining-rooms, sitting-room;
Credit cards AE, DC, MC, V
Children accepted; special menu available
Disabled access difficult
Pets in bedrooms only
Closed Tue night and Wed, except Jul, Aug, Easter and Christmas
Proprietor M. Franck Gomez

Mas de Garrigon

This ochre-coloured building was purpose-built ten years ago in the traditional Provençal style (low colour-washed houses with pantiled roofs), in a peaceful rural position among pines and scrub. It faces a neat swimming-pool, and each of the few bedrooms (done out in restrained modern style) has a private terrace looking out over the countryside. The hotel is run slightly on house-party lines. Guests are encouraged to feel at home (that is to say a quiet home, without young children).

Nearby Gordes (7 km) – château; Village des Bories (5 km).

Rte de St-Saturnin d'Apt, Roussillon 84220 Gordes
Tel 90.05.63.22
Location in countryside, on D2 3 km N of Roussillon, 7 km E of Gordes; car parking
Meals breakfast, lunch, dinner
Prices rooms 550F-700F; meals 150F-300F
Rooms 7 double (2 twin), one family room, all with bath; all rooms have phone, TV, minibar
Facilities 3 dining-rooms, bar, library, sitting-room; pool, horse-riding
Credit cards AE, DC, V
Children older ones accepted if well behaved
Disabled ground-floor bedrooms
Pets if well behaved
Closed restaurant only 15 Nov to 27 Dec; Sun dinner and Mon
Manager Mme Christiane Rech-Druart

Vaucluse

Le Beffroi

In the heart of the medieval old town – and reached by a steep, narrow and cobbled road more suited to donkeys than cars – this fine hotel consists of several 16th and 17thC town houses, positively oozing charm. Beams, polished wood or ancient ceramic-tiled floors, stone fireplaces, antiques and paintings abound throughout the hotel; each bedroom is individually decorated and furnished. The atmosphere is that of a private house rather than a hotel, and so it is no hardship to find some bathrooms which are not entirely modern – they more than make up for this in charm. The drawing-room is formal, with heavy tables and chairs, and stern portraits looking down from vividly patterned walls – not at all suitable for boisterous children. But steam can be let off in the terraced, gravelled garden – with fine views over the town; and the restaurant, with its simple decoration, is relatively relaxed.

This has always been the family home of the owner, and is run with obvious pride and care. Despite its charms, the hotel does not suit those seeking conventional comfort (or the infirm).

Nearby Roman theatre and medieval quarter; Gigondas (15 km) – Côtes-du-Rhone wine and tasting.

Rue de l'Evêché, Haute Ville 84110 Vaison-la-Romaine
Tel 90.36.04.71
Location in middle of medieval town, 15 km S of Nyons; with garden, and parking for 11 cars
Meals breakfast, lunch, dinner
Prices rooms 200F-400F; DB&B (for one) 220F-320F; menus 90F-150F, children's 45F
Rooms 14 double, 5 with bath, 7 with shower (7 twin); 3 single, one with shower; 5 family rooms, 3 with bath, 2 with shower; all rooms have central heating, phone, minibar; 15 rooms have TV
Facilities 2 sitting-rooms, bar/tea room; mini-golf
Credit cards AE, DC, MC, V
Children welcome
Disabled no special facilities
Pets accepted in bedrooms; 25F charge
Closed Nov to mid-Mar; restaurant only Mon and Tue lunch out of season
Proprietors Catherine and Yann Christiansen

Mas de Garrigon (see opposite)

Alpes-de-Haute-Provence

Town inn, Château-Arnoux

La Bonne Etape

The setting of this 18thC coaching inn (on a busy road in an unremarkable town) is not auspicious, and the outside gives little hint of what lies within – one of the most satisfactory blends of refinement and hospitality to be found in France.

Where to start? Perhaps in the kitchen, where Pierre and Jany Gleize (father and son) make innovative and stylish use of largely home-grown ingredients, earning 2 stars from Michelin and 3 *toques* from Gault-Millau. Among their specialities is Sisteron lamb (raised on fragrant Provençal pastures). The light, warm dining-room is a supremely comfortable and relaxing place to savour their cooking, with well-spaced round tables.

But this is no restaurant-with-rooms. Bedrooms are more than comfortable – beautifully decorated and furnished with a tasteful mix of modern and antique pieces; some of the bathrooms, too, are delightfully individual. And even on the stairs and in the corridors there is attention to decorative detail. The swimming-pool is a superb sun-trap, with an attractive terrace surround.

To cap it all, the Gleize family are warmly welcoming hosts, happily committed to their work.

Nearby Les Mées (10 km) – rock formation; Sisteron – citadel; Ganagobie priory (20 km).

Chemin du Lac 04160
Château-Arnoux
Tel 92.64.00.09
Location in country town, on main RN 85 14 km SE of Sisteron; with car parking and garden
Meals breakfast, lunch, dinner
Prices rooms 400F-600F, suites 750F; menus 190F-400F
Rooms 11 double, 7 suites (9 twin) all with bath; all rooms have air-conditioning, phone, TV, radio, minibar
Facilities 2 dining-rooms, sitting-room, bar, conference room; swimming-pool
Credit cards DC, MC, V
Children accepted **Disabled** no special facilities **Pets** accepted
Closed 3 Jan to 15 Feb, last week Nov
Proprietors Gleize family

Alpes-de-Haute-Provence

Auberge de Reillanne

This country *auberge* excites much enthusiasm in visitors, and it is not difficult to see why. Converted from a magnificent old *bastide*, it is no ordinary hotel; here you really do feel like a guest in a private mansion.

Despite the grandeur of the building, it is not a place of four-star sophistication. There are seven very large rooms, where rows of books take the place of radios or TVs. In the dining-room, paintings, sculpture and flower bouquets seem in perfect harmony with the setting. Equally impressive is the cuisine. Madame Founes (journalist and goat-breeder by trade) uses only the freshest ingredients, either from the kitchen garden or from small local producers. She manages to produce wonderful dishes from simple ingredients.

The *auberge* is no newcomer to the public eye: it has featured extensively in guidebooks and the national press, inspiring journalists with its sober good taste and high standard of cooking. Added to this are the couple who run it – Florent and Anne-Marie Founès: elegant, warm-hearted hosts appreciated by countless guests for their flair and enthusiasm.

Nearby Lubéron Park – marked trails; St-Michel observatory (10 km); Aix-en-Provence (70 km); Avignon (80 km).

04110 Reillanne
Tel 92.76.45.95
Location in countryside, 1 km from village, 19 km SW of Forcalquier; in garden, with car parking
Meals breakfast, lunch, dinner
Prices rooms 380F; meals 200F-250F
Rooms 5 double, all with bath (2 twin); 2 family rooms, both with bath; all rooms have central heating, phone, minibar
Facilities sitting room, 2 dining-rooms
Credit cards AE, DC, V
Children welcome if well behaved
Disabled no special facilities
Pets welcome if well behaved
Closed Feb
Proprietors M. and Mme Founès

Alpes-Maritimes

La Gardiole

The views and beaches of the *exclusive* Cap d'Antibes are open to all, and there are modest hotels – of which the unassuming pink-washed Gardiole, right in the middle of the promontory, is the pick. It is furnished simply but effectively – dark-wood chairs and rugs on polished tiled floors, white walls hung with ornaments and paintings – and family-run in friendly fashion. The dining-room is light and airy but the terrace, surrounded by flowers and shaded by wisteria, is where everyone wants to sit. The sound regional cooking is good value.

Nearby Beach, pine forest, Thuret gardens; Antibes (5 km).

Chemin de la Garoupe 06600 Cap d'Antibes **Tel** 93.61.35.03 **Location** in woody residential area 500 m from beach, in middle of Cap; with car parking and large terrace **Meals** breakfast, lunch, dinner **Prices** rooms 190F-400F menus 110F-195F **Rooms** 14 double (7 twin), 4	single, 3 family rooms, all with bath or shower; all rooms have central heating, phone, safe; TV on request **Facilities** dining-room, sitting-room, TV room **Credit cards** AE, DC, V **Children** welcome **Disabled** no special facilities **Pets** accepted **Closed** Nov to Mar **Proprietor** Mme Anne-Marie Arama

Galerie des Arcades

One of the most charming establishments on the entire coast, this simple village café in a 15thC building is also about the best value. The bedrooms (some with four-poster beds) are refreshingly uncontrived. Pungent Provençal dishes are eaten under the arcades of the village square, or in the two dining-rooms crammed with modern paintings. But this is not all: as the proud possessor of a fine collection of modern works of art, including Vasarely, M. Brothier is only too pleased to give a private viewing. An excellent place for those who are happy to sit at a café table rather than in a proper sitting-room.

Nearby Potters, glass-blowers and Léger Museum; Nice (15 km).

16 Place des Arcades 06410 Biot **Tel** 93.65.01.04 **Location** in centre of village, 18 km NE of Cannes, near N7 **Meals** breakfast, lunch, dinner **Prices** rooms 160F-300F, 30%-50% reduction for children under 10; meals 150F-200F	**Rooms** 12 double, 7 with bath, 5 with shower (4 twin); all rooms have central heating, phone **Facilities** 2 dining-rooms **Credit cards** not accepted **Children** accepted **Disabled** no special facilities **Pets** accepted **Closed** Nov; restaurant only Sun dinner and Mon **Proprietor** André Brothier

Alpes-Maritimes

Town villa, Vence

La Roseraie

The gourmet guides have been quick to recognize the achievements of Maurice Ganier at La Roseraie, where he specializes in the cuisine of south-west France. But his charming *belle époque* villa has other attractions as well. It is set in shady gardens with palms, a huge magnolia and old cedars, with views over the old town of Vence and the surrounding hills. All the sunny bedrooms – simply furnished in Provençal style – look out over the garden or swimming-pool, where meals are served (in the evening by candle-light) and children can amuse themselves on swings. In the winter there is an open fire in the dining-room.

Nearby Place du Peyra; St-Paul-de-Vence (5 km).

Ave Henri Giraud 06140 Vence
Tel 93.58.02.20
Location on NW outskirts of town, on D2; with garden and private car parking
Meals breakfast, lunch, dinner
Prices rooms 240F-320F; menus 110F-260F
Rooms 11 double, 2 with bath, 9 with shower; 1 single, with bath; all rooms have central heating, phone
Facilities dining-room; swimming-pool, play area, solarium
Credit cards AE, MC
Children welcome; extra bed available
Disabled no special facilities
Pets accepted
Closed Jan
Proprietor Maurice Ganier

Alpes-Maritimes

Le Cagnard

Perched along the ramparts of old hill village, Le Cagnard has been smartly converted from a series of medieval houses. Thanks to expert restoration and period furnishings (with a few incongruous exceptions) the atmosphere is distinctly medieval. Food here is some of the best in the area, and the restaurant has regained its Michelin star; meals are eaten by candle-light in the dining-room (with its splendid vaulted ceiling), or on the terrace, where the wonderful view extends along the coast.

Nearby Château Grimaldi – modern art museum, with Renaissance courtyard; Nice (15 km); Grasse (30 km) – perfumes.

Rue Pontis-Long, Haut-de-Cagnes 06800 Cagnes-sur-Mer
Tel 93.20.73.21
Location in middle of hill village, 2 km above main town of Cagnes; with car parking beneath the hotel
Meals breakfast, lunch, dinner
Prices rooms 300F–1000F; meals 320F–410F
Rooms 16 double, all with bath (7 twin); 2 single, one with bath, one with shower; 2 family rooms, both with bath; all rooms have central heating, TV, phone, minibar
Facilities dining-room, bar
Credit cards AE, DC, MC, V
Children accepted
Disabled no special facilities
Pets accepted
Closed restaurant only, Thu lunch and 1 Nov to 20 Dec
Proprietor Felix Barel

Le Bosquet

Neither the modern building of this hotel, nor its furnishings, nor its garden (spacious but rough) can account for the special place Le Bosquet has in the affections of many British (and other foreign) visitors. Nor can the food, however wonderful the home-made jams served at the communal outdoor breakfast – there is no restaurant. The key is the exceptionally happy atmosphere engendered by the cheerful Simone Bernardi, coupled with the care she takes over the details of visitors' comfort and – last but not least – the very un-Provençal prices. The 7 studios have kitchenettes, and there is no shortage of good restaurants.

Nearby Mougins (5 km) – popular hill village.

Quartier du Château 06580 Pégomas
Tel 93.42.22.87
Location on NE outskirts of village, 10 km N of Cannes; with garden and covered parking
Meals breakfast
Prices rooms 175F–220F, studios 250F–300F
Rooms 15 double (4 twin), 2 single, all with bath or shower; 7 studios; all rooms have central heating, phone
Facilities breakfast room, sitting-room; swimming-pool, tennis
Credit cards not accepted
Children welcome
Disabled no special facilities
Pets not accepted
Closed Nov
Proprietor Jean-Pierre Bernard

Alpes-Maritimes

Village inn, Peillon

Auberge de la Madone

If you don't already know this hotel, you are likely to think that you have taken a wrong turning as you first spy the village of Peillon, perched impossibly above, with little sign of any road leading up. But access, though very steep, is possible; and once there you will be thankful that you have taken the trouble to venture into this rugged mountain landscape, just 18 km from Nice.

In Peillon, time stands still. This medieval village, as yet delightfully uncommercialized, consists of a few dark and dank cobbled alleys leading up to the church, and tall, grey stone houses with small windows, looking out over rocky crests and distant forests. The *auberge* is set just outside the walled village itself, although it shares the views. Behind, paths lead off into the hills, past the grazing sheep with their tinkling bells; in front, below the sunny terrace of the hotel, is the village car park and *boules* area. The *auberge* itself, while retaining a certain simplicity, provides attractive accommodation: bedrooms (with small balconies) are modernized and well decorated; there is a pretty terrace and awning, for outdoor eating, a TV lounge, and an attractive Provençal-style dining-room. Cooking is not particularly ambitious, but nonetheless above average, and the menus are fair value.

Nearby Monaco – Prince Rainier's Palace, oceanographic and doll museums, exotic gardens.

06440 Peillon-Village
Tel 93.79.91.17
Location on edge of perched village, 19 km NE of Nice; with ample car parking
Meals breakfast, lunch, dinner
Prices rooms 250F-420F; meals 90F-250F
Rooms 18 double, 13 with bath, 5 with shower (12 twin); 3 family rooms; all rooms have central heating, TV, phone
Facilities sitting-room, bar, 2 dining-rooms
Credit cards not accepted
Children very welcome
Disabled no special facilities
Pets accepted by arrangement
Closed 15 Oct to 15 Dec
Proprietors Millo family

Alpes-Maritimes

Auberge du Colombier

This is an old *mas*, low and white, whose chief attraction is its setting – amid large gardens with lawns and tall shady trees, and views over wooded hills towards the sea. There is also an especially attractive terrace for summer eating, a tennis court, and plenty of space around the swimming-pool for lounging. The bedrooms (some with balconies and views) are on the small side, but are light and comfortable. The cooking is excellent (the desserts sinful), and the Wolffs excellent hosts. A useful base for seeing the sights of the Côte d'Azur – though you may be tempted to stay put instead.

Nearby St-Paul (10 km); Grasse – perfumeries.

06330 Roquefort-les-Pins
Tel 93.77.10.27
Location in countryside off D2085, 15 km E of Grasse, 18 km N of Cannes; with large garden and ample car parking
Meals breakfast, lunch, dinner
Prices rooms 240F-600F; menus 135F-170F
Rooms 18 double (7 twin),

all with bath; all rooms have phone, TV
Facilities 2 dining-rooms, sitting-room, bar; swimming-pool, tennis court, night-club
Credit cards AE, DC, MC, V
Children accepted
Disabled no special facilities
Pets accepted
Closed Jan
Proprietor M. Wolff

Clair Logis

It is not easy to find a reasonable, cheap hotel in an area such as the exclusive and leafy Cap, near the pleasure port of St-Jean-Cap-Ferrat. It is even harder to find one like this, which has the charm of a turn-of-the-century private villa (it was turned into a hotel in 1950 by Pierre Melon's grandmother) and is set in lush, secluded gardens. Bedrooms are simple (those in the more recently built annexe are not particularly spacious) and four can accommodate families. Breakfast is taken in the cosy breakfast room/TV lounge in the main building – there is no restaurant, but that is no hardship in this area.

Nearby Villa-Museum Ile de France; Peillon (20 km) – one of many hilltop villages in this area; Monte Carlo (45 km).

12 Ave Centrale 06230 St-Jean-Cap-Ferrat
Tel 93.76.04.57
Location in middle of Cap Ferrat promontory, 5 km from Nice; in large garden with ample car parking
Meals breakfast
Prices rooms 200F-360F; extra bed 85F-95F
Rooms 16 double (8 twin), 4

family rooms; all with bath, 8 also with shower; all rooms have central heating, phone
Facilities sitting-room
Credit cards MC, V
Children welcome
Disabled access to annexe possible
Pets welcome
Closed 15 Nov to 15 Dec
Proprietor Pierre Melon

Alpes-Maritimes

Town Hotel, Vence

Auberge des Seigneurs

This fine, medieval *auberge* in the heart of the old town of Vence, just outside the walls and overlooking a little square, is the sort of place that should be found in every old town. The tall narrow building is beautifully maintained and everything inside polished and shining, simple and pretty, in an authentic Provençal style that makes many other less successful city inns seem contrived. Of course, Pierre Rodi's fine house lends itself to the rustic treatment, with its ornate old fireplaces, beams, quarry-tiled floors and old wooden doors. He has added massive wardrobes, copper bed warmers, period furniture and Provençal prints, and embellished it with plenty of flowers – charm is assured.

M. Rodi knows something about food, too – he has been cooking since 1920, and his repertoire, simple charcoal grills and Provençal specialities (fish soup, cheese tart), has changed little over the years, but is none the worse for that. The simple bedrooms. shuttered and quiet, have large, tiled, shower rooms and good solid beds. There is no sitting-room, but it hardly matters. The Auberge des Seigneurs is run by members of M. Rodi's family, and one can only hope that nothing will persuade them to change things in the future.

Nearby St-Paul-de-Vence (3.5 km); Grasse (20 km) – perfumes; Loup gorges (15 km).

Place du Frêne 06140 Vence
Tel 93.58.04.24
Location at edge of old walled town
Meals breakfast, lunch, dinner
Prices rooms 220F-230F; meals 140F-160F
Rooms 7 double, all with shower (3 twin); all rooms have central heating, phone
Facilities dining-room, bar
Credit cards V
Children accepted
Disabled no special facilities
Pets accepted
Closed 15 Oct to 1 Dec; Sun evening and Mon
Proprietor M. Rodi

Alpes-Maritimes

Village hotel, St-Paul-de-Vence

La Colombe d'Or

A famous, chic small hotel, distinguished by a considerable collection of modern art, but also a delightful place to stay. All is simple and in exquisite 'country' taste – white walls and bedspreads, vases of bright flowers, quarry-tiled floors, huge old stone fireplaces. Outside there is a creeper-surrounded terrace (huge white umbrellas). The dining-room has a wonderful carved fireplace, a lovely painted ceiling, and walls hung with the works of Matisse, Picasso, Utrillo and so on. The food wins no awards, but that hardly matters.

Nearby Maeght Foundation – modern art; Cagnes-sur-Mer (5 km) – château-museum; Nice; Grasse (25 km) – perfumes.

Place de Gaulle 06570
St-Paul-de-Vence
Tel 93.32.80.02
Location in village, 20 km
NW of Nice; with gardens
and ample car parking
Meals breakfast, lunch,
dinner
Prices rooms 820F-1,020F;
meals 140F
Rooms 24 double (12 twin) 3
family rooms, all with bath;

all rooms have air-conditioning, central
heating, phone, TV, radio
Facilities sitting-room,
dining-room; sauna,
swimming-pool
Credit cards AE, DC, MC, V
Children welcome **Disabled**
access difficult **Pets** accepted
Closed mid-Nov to mid-Dec,
10 days in mid-Jan
Proprietors Roux family

Village hotel, St-Paul-de-Vence

Les Orangers

The formula of Les Orangers is simple – an amiable, traditional Provençal house in a fine hillside setting, furnished with simple good taste and immaculately kept. In the the sitting-room there are exposed beams, solid antiques, fresh flowers, an open fire, colourful rugs on polished floors. The charming bedrooms are much the same, and most have balconies or terraces sharing the lovely view of St-Paul and the hills of the Alpilles. There is no restaurant, but a charming terrace for summer breakfasts (shady trees, white chairs and tables, plenty of flowers) and large gardens with olive and orange trees.

Nearby Maeght Foundation – modern art; Cagnes-sur-Mer (5 km) – château-museum; Nice; Grasse (25 km) – perfumes.

Chemin des Fumerates
06570 St-Paul-de-Vence
Tel 93.32.80.95
Location on edge of town,
20 km W of Nice; with
garden and car parking
Meals breakfast
Prices rooms 360F-520F
Rooms 8 double (5 twin),
one single, all with bath; all
rooms have central heating,

phone, minibar
Facilities sitting-room
Credit cards not accepted
Children accepted
Disabled no special facilities
Pets accepted
Closed never
Proprietor Mme Bianchéri

Alpes-Maritimes

Country villa, St-Paul-de-Vence

Le Hameau

St-Paul-de-Vence is among the best-preserved hill villages in France. Its ramparts, rising above green terraces of vineyards and bougainvillea, provide panoramic views of the hills and valleys of the Alpes-Maritimes; and its old streets, lined by galleries, workshops and chic boutiques, attract numerous day-trippers in season.

Of the few hotels in and around the village, Le Hameau is certainly one of the most desirable – an unusually stylish and notably relaxed place run by a friendly and eager-to-please young couple. It consists of a cluster of red-roofed Provençal villas, surrounded by orange, lemon and other fruit trees. Bedrooms are rustic in style, with beams, dark-wood furniture and rugs on red-tiled floors; they vary in size considerably – as do the prices (though even the most expensive can scarcely be considered expensive by local standards); many have their own terrace or balcony. There is a cool, neat breakfast room, but you will be hoping to have no need of it – one of Le Hameau's great delights is breakfast (with home-made jam) taken in the large terraced garden.

Nearby Maeght Foundation – contemporary arts; Cagnes-sur-Mer (5 km) – château-museum (Renaissance courtyard); Nice (15 km); Grasse (25 km) – perfumes.

528 Rte de la Colle 06570
St-Paul-de-Vence
Tel 93.32.80.24
Location one km outside village, 20 km from Nice; with gardens and ample car parking
Meals breakfast
Prices rooms 210F-375F, suites 470F
Rooms 13 double (5 twin), one single, 2 suites, all with bath or shower; one children's room; all rooms have central heating, phone, minibar
Facilities sitting-room, dining-room
Credit cards MC, V
Children accepted if well behaved
Disabled no special facilities
Pets accepted if well behaved
Closed 15 Nov to 24 Dec, mid-Jan to mid-Feb
Proprietors Simone and Xavier Huvelin

Bouches-du-Rhône

Mas d'Entremont

Just outside Aix stands this stylish old Provençal farmhouse – low red-roofed buildings clustered around a courtyard. Within are wooden beams and pillars, rustic furniture, tiled floors, open fireplaces and fresh flowers. Bedrooms (most in separate bungalows in the grounds) are more modern in style, but clean, comfortable and quite stylish. The gardens are a delight – a lovely swimming-pool shielded by cypresses, a covered dining-terrace looking over a pond and fountain, and plenty of secluded corners. Cuisine is classic and competent.

Nearby Aix-en-Provence; Abbaye de Silvacane (25 km).

Montée d'Avignon 13090
Aix-en-Provence
Tel 42.23.45.32
Location in countryside just
off N7, 2 km NW of Aix;
with large grounds and
ample car parking
Meals breakfast, lunch,
dinner
Prices rooms 400F-600F;
menus 160F-180F
Rooms 17 double (7 twin) all
with bath; all rooms have air-
conditioning, TV, phone,
private terrace
Facilities dining-room,
sitting-areas; swimming-
pool, tennis
Credit cards MC, V
Children accepted; some
rooms have side-rooms
Disabled lift/elevator **Pets**
accepted
Closed Nov to mid-Mar
Proprietors Mariguane
family

Relais de la Magdeleine

Despite elegant furnishings, this 18thC *bastide* is one of those rare hotels which caters equally well for grown-ups who want pampering and children who want nothing more than plenty of open space and a lovely swimming-pool. It is a tricky balancing act, which the charming Marignanes carry off with great flair and warmth. Sound Provençal meals cooked by the son of the household are served in refined dining-rooms or on a peaceful gravelled terrace. Bedrooms are spacious, decorated with restraint and furnished with antiques; fresh flowers abound.

Nearby Cassis (15 km) – coastal inlets; La Ste-Baume massif.

13420 Gémenos
Tel 42.82.20.05
Location on outskirts of
town, 23 km E of Marseilles;
with garden and ample car
parking
Meals breakfast, lunch,
dinner
Prices rooms 380F-550F;
menu 165F
Rooms 19 double, 15 with
bath, 4 with shower (12
twin); 4 family rooms, all
with bath; all rooms have
central heating, phone, TV
Facilities sitting-rooms,
dining-rooms; swimming-
pool
Credit cards MC, V
Children accepted
Disabled no special facilities
Pets accepted, except near
swimming-pool
Closed Nov to mid-Mar
Proprietors M. and Mme
Marignane

Bouches-du-Rhône

La Régalido

At the heart of Provence, the little town of Fontvieille is excellently situated for sightseeing, lying between the ancient cities of Avignon and Arles and close to many more fine sights. Down the road is the windmill about which the 19thC novelist Alphonse Daudet wrote in his *Lettre de Mon Moulin.*

At the edge of town, the Regalido is a former oil mill, built in the early 19thC, which has been converted into a fine *auberge.* It is extremely attractive, in a thoroughly Provençal style, decorated with great flair by Madame Michel. There is a charming sitting-room full of flowers, and a log fire lit on chilly days. Tables are beautifully set in the spacious dining-room, and there is an atmosphere of well-being which suits the excellent cooking of Jean-Pierre Michel. His style is classic, but he has a penchant for Provençal dishes (which make good use of seafood, olive oil, herbs and garlic). The bedrooms are all individually decorated, and very comfortable. Friendly staff and a pretty, flowery garden complete the pleasant picture, marred only by the steep prices.

Nearby Montmajour Abbey; Arles; the Camargue (10 km) – flamingoes, white horses; Tarascon (15 km) – château.

Rue Frederic-Mistral 13990 Fontvieille
Tel 90.97.60.22
Location in middle of village, 9 km NE of Arles; with gardens and ample car parking
Meals breakfast, lunch, dinner
Prices rooms 380F-1100F; menus 200F-350F
Rooms 14 double, 12 with bath, 2 with shower; all rooms have central heating, phone, minibar

Facilities dining-room, 2 sitting-rooms, bar
Credit cards AE, DC, MC, V
Children accepted in the summer
Disabled one specially equipped ground-floor bedroom
Pets accepted (at a charge)
Closed Dec and Jan; restaurant only Tue lunch, and Mon lunch (and dinner in low season)
Proprietor Jean-Pierre Michel

Bouches-du-Rhône

Auberge de la Benvengudo

The creeper-clad Benvengudo is a welcoming *auberge* with its own large garden and swimming-pool, much more affordable than most place in or near Les Baux. Rooms are furnished in the manner of a private country house: a cosy sitting-room with beams, fireplace and robust antiques, intimate dining-room and bedrooms with carefully chosen antiques and pretty patterned curtains. Weather permitting, breakfast and dinner are served on the terrace. Lunches are not available – an excuse to stretch your credit limit trying out some of the local gastronomy.

Nearby Montmajour abbey (15 km); Arles and the Camargue (15 km); Tarascon (20 km) – château; Avignon (40 km).

Vallon de l'Aicoule 13520 Les Baux-de-Provence **Tel** 90.54.32.54 **Location** in valley below village, towards Arles; in gardens, with garages **Meals** breakfast, lunch, dinner **Prices** rooms 340F-420F, suites 650F-980F **Rooms** 20 double (10 twin); 2 suites; all rooms have central heating, phone	**Facilities** dining-room, sitting-rooms; swimming-pool, tennis **Credit cards** not accepted **Children** accepted **Disabled** some ground-floor rooms **Pets** accepted in bedrooms; 40F charge **Closed** 10 Nov to 15 Feb **Proprietors** M. and Mme Daniel Beaupied

Mas d'Aigret

In a fine setting with views over the peaceful Provençal countryside, this old farmhouse is simpler than the more renowned (and pricey) hotels of the neighbourhood, but that is no bad thing. There is an extraordinary restaurant carved out of the rock, and all is fresh and pretty, decorated in rustic Provençal style. Bedrooms open out on to a terrace or balcony, and are well equipped. Pip Phillips (an Englishman) is new to the *mas*, and has plans for various improvements.

Nearby Ruined fortress-village; Arles (15 km) and the Camargue.

13520 Les Baux- de- Provence **Tel** 90.97.33.54 **Location** just below fortress, on D27A 500 m E of Les Baux; in large grounds with ample car parking **Meals** breakfast, lunch, dinner **Prices** rooms 290F-530F, suites 630F; menu 150F **Rooms** 12 double (6 twin), 3 family rooms, all with bath; all rooms have central heating, TV, phone, minibar	**Facilities** dining-room, sitting-room, bar; swimming-pool, boules, croquet, practice golf **Credit cards** AE, DC, MC, V **Children** welcome **Disabled** no special facilities **Pets** welcome, but not in restaurant **Closed** 4 Jan to 20 Feb; restaurant only, Thu out of season **Proprietors** Pip Phillips and family

Bouches-du-Rhône

Mas de la Fouque

Located near the main resort of the Camargue, the Mas de la Fouque is a small, ranch-like hotel with a herd of the region's famous white horses for hiring out to guests. Rooms throughout are smartly decorated – white walls, tiled floors, timbered ceilings – but the bedrooms are the epitome of comfort, with private balconies built over the lagoon and some their own jacuzzi. Despite the four-star luxuries, this is very much a family-run hotel with a friendly, relaxed atmosphere.

Nearby The Camargue; Aigues-Mortes (25 km); Arles (50 km).

Rte du Petit Rhône 13460 Les Stes-Maries-de-la-Mer **Tel** 90.47.81.02 **Location** in the Camargue, 4 km NW of Les Stes-Maries-de-la-Mer; with ample car parking **Meals** breakfast, lunch, dinner **Prices** rooms 500F-1500F; lunch 130F-220F, dinner 200F-280F **Rooms** 12 double, all with bath (6 twin); 3 family rooms, 2 with bath; all rooms have TV, phone, minibar **Facilities** 2 sitting-rooms, bar, dining-room; tennis, swimming-pool, putting **Credit cards** AE, DC, MC, V **Children** welcome if well supervised **Disabled** access easy; all on ground floor **Pets** dogs accepted **Closed** 15 Nov to 20 Dec; Jan and Feb **Proprietor** Jean-Paul Cochat

Bouches-du-Rhône

L'Oustaloun

The village of Maussane-les-Alpilles is close to the famous tourist sight of Les Baux, and makes a much cheaper base to stay. L'Oustaloun is to be found on the church square – a village *hostellerie* with masses of old-world charm and character. Stone walls, exposed beams and quarry tiles are all features of downstairs rooms. The restaurant is housed in three 16thC-rooms with stone-vaulted ceilings; tables are embellished with flowers and candelabra. The food is honest, regional fare: poultry and rabbit terrines are typical dishes. Bedrooms are simple in style but furnished with handsome antiques.

Nearby Montmajour Abbey (15 km); Arles (15 km) and the Camargue; Tarascon (20 km) – château; Avignon (40 km).

Place de l'Eglise 13520
Maussane-les-Alpilles
Tel 90.97.32.19
Location in middle of village, 2 km S of Les Baux; with street car parking and garage
Meals breakfast, lunch, dinner
Prices rooms 210F-320F; menu 125F

Rooms 9 double, 3 with bath, 6 with shower (4 twin)
Facilities 3 dining-rooms, sitting-room with TV
Credit cards AE, DC, V
Children accepted; smaller portions available
Disabled no special facilities
Pets not accepted
Closed Jan to mid-Mar
Proprietor Roberto Bartoli

Château des Alpilles

This is an elegant, upright early 19thC manor house just outside St-Rémy, set in large grounds with venerable trees, offering an atmosphere of gracious living combined with the facilities of a modern luxury hotel. The bedrooms are spacious and furnished with antiques, the bathrooms marble and modern, the salon and bar richly decorated. There is no proper restaurant, but snacks are available all day, and in summer there is a poolside grill.

Nearby Tarascon (15 km); Avignon (25 km); Arles (25 km).

Route Departmentale 31
13210 St-Rémy-de-Provence
Tel 90.92.03.33
Location in countryside 2 km W of village, on D31; in large grounds, with ample private car parking
Meals breakfast; light meals available by arrangement
Prices rooms 510F-690F, suite 880F, extra bed 75F, cot 45F; meals 100F-200F
Rooms 17 double (8 twin), 1 suite, all with bath; all rooms have central heating, TV,

phone, radio, minibar; air-conditioning in suite
Facilities sitting-room, bar, dining-room, conference room; swimming-pool, tennis, sauna
Credit cards AE, DC, MC, V
Children very welcome if well behaved
Disabled lift/elevator
Pets accepted on lead at extra charge
Closed Jan to Mar
Proprietors Françoise and Catherine Bon

Bouches-du-Rhône

Manor house hotel, Noves

Auberge de Noves

The name is a joke: this is no *auberge*, but a luxurious and pricey hotel (four red gables in Michelin) in a splendid house, isolated in the Provençal countryside. Of course, there are elegant antiques everywhere, and the bedrooms are splendid. Of course, the cooking is exquisite, and breakfast extraordinary. Of course, the service is polished to perfection. What comes as a bonus is the charming attention of the suave M. Lalleman, who manages to display a genuine interest in his guests despite the fact that they are paying him such outrageous sums.

Nearby Avignon – Palais des Papes, cathedral; Nîmes (40 km).

13550 Noves
Tel 90.94.19.21
Location in countryside off D28, 2 km NW of Noves, 11 km SE of Avignon; in grounds, with terrace and car parking
Meals breakfast, lunch, dinner
Prices rooms 860F-1,100F; menus 210F-390F, children's 140F
Rooms 23 double, all with bath; all rooms have central heating, TV, phone
Facilities dining-room, sitting-room/bar, conference room; swimming-pool, tennis
Credit cards V
Children welcome
Disabled 7 bedrooms accessible
Pets accepted
Closed Jan, Feb
Proprietor M. A Lalleman

Bouches-du-Rhône

Hôtel des Arts

For both locals and tourists, the shady pavement tables of this unpretentious place have long been a happy spot to sit and watch the Provençal world go by. Inside, the restaurant serves, at a reasonable price, well cooked, simple food (liberally laced with the region's herbs). Tables are crammed together, and loud greetings and gossipy exchanges fill the air at lunch and dinner; paintings cover the walls at random, floors are stone-flagged, chairs and tables simple wood – but there are vases of fresh flowers and crisp linen, too. Bedrooms seem secondary, but they are neatly done out in the local rustic style, and prices are modest.
Nearby Ruines de Glanum and Les Antiques – Roman remains.

30 Blvd Victor-Hugo 13210 St-Rèmy-de-Provence
Tel 90.92.08.50
Location on main street in middle of town, 18 km S of Avignon; with small car park
Meals breakfast, lunch, dinner
Prices rooms 120F-210F; menus 65F-130F
Rooms 12 double, all with bath (8 twin); 3 single, one with bath; 2 family rooms; all

rooms have central heating, phone
Facilities dining-room, TV room, bar
Credit cards AE, V
Children accepted
Disabled access to restaurant and one bedroom
Pets accepted
Closed Feb; restaurant Wed
Proprietor Mme Nicole Caritoux

Mas des Carassins

Of all the Provençal hotels that call themselves *mas*, this is one of the few authentic examples: a farmhouse built in 1854, which is both mellow and peaceful, set in large and rambling gardens where you can be sure of finding a secluded spot to sit. Almost all the bedrooms have views of the rocky Alpilles and there is a cosy sitting-room with books and plenty of local information. There is no restaurant, but in the evening you can order simple dishes – ham, *charcuterie*, eggs, cheese, yoghurts – and drinks. M. Ripert and his wife are attentive, friendly hosts.
Nearby Tarascon (15 km); Avignon (30 km); Arles (30 km).

1 Chemin Gaulois 13210 St-Rémy-de-Provence
Tel 90.92.15.48
Location 800m SW of middle of town; with gardens and ample car parking
Meals breakfast, simple evening meal on request
Prices rooms 280F-380F, family rooms 500F-700F
Rooms 14 double, all with bath (7 twin); 5 family

rooms, all with bath; all rooms have central heating, phone
Facilities 2 sitting-rooms
Credit cards not accepted
Children accepted if well behaved
Disabled no special facilities
Pets not accepted
Closed 15 Nov to 1 Mar
Proprietors M. and Mme Claude Ripert

Bouches-du-Rhône

Château bed and breakfast, St-Rémy-de-Provence

Château de Roussan

Staying in this beautiful 18thC château, on the outskirts of St Rémy and approached by an impressive avenue of trees, offers the chance to sample an aristocratic lifestyle: you are house-guests of the Roussels in their family home.

It is a gracious building – one part dates from 1440 and the other from 1720 – with a mellow exterior and fine rooms carefully and beautifully furnished with antiques. The bedrooms are large, also furnished in the appropriate style (though bathrooms are modern) and enormously atmospheric. There is a formal library/salon in the oldest part of the house, and a more cosy television room; breakfasts (and non-alcoholic drinks) are served in the bedrooms or outside on the gravel terrace. There is no restaurant, but St-Rémy is only a mile away (you can walk it more easily on a little by-road, rather than take the main road) and has sufficient restaurants to keep most people happy; more adventurous gourmets need not travel far either (Les Baux is a centre of culinary excellence). Some guests decide to take a lunchtime picnic into the grounds of the château, where there is plenty of room to sit in perfect solitude, overlooking a pool or fountain, or perhaps the 16thC farmhouse which belonged to Catherine de Medicis' famous astrologer, Nostradamus.

Nearby Tarascon (15 km) – château; Avignon (30 km); Arles (30 km) and the Camargue.

Rte de Tarascon 13210
St-Rémy-de-Provence
Tel 90.92.11.63
Location in countryside, 2 km W of town; in large park, with ample car parking
Meals breakfast
Prices rooms 350F-500F
Rooms 15 double (7 twin), 2 family rooms; 12 with bath, 5 with shower; all rooms have phone, central heating
Facilities TV room, library
Credit cards V
Children accepted
Disabled 2 ground-floor bedrooms
Pets accepted by arrangement
Closed 31 Oct to 15 Mar
Proprietor M. Roussel

Var

Moulin de la Camandoule

This lovingly restored olive-mill lies at the foot of the hilltop town of Fayence, in extensive private grounds. It has existed in one form or another since the 15thC, and the surviving aqueduct, which brought water to the mill, probably dates back to Roman times. The hotel was bought in 1986, by Wolf and Shirley Rilla, an English couple whose aim is to make visitors feel like guests in a private country house (and emphatically a French one, despite their origins).

What distinguishes the Moulin de la Camandoule from other converted mills is the fact that not only the mill building has been preserved: all the machinery that went with it has also been preserved in its proper place – the large wheel at the entrance to the restaurant, the wooden olive buckets and straw baskets, the long-handled pan used for heating and tasting the oil, and the fork for turning over the pulp. Bedrooms are named after some relevant piece of mill machinery or, in the case of the most expensive room, *'Ecurie'*, after the stables where the millers' mules were kept.

The hotel grounds are impressive, with a river and an inviting pool where meals are served in the summer months.

Nearby Grasse 30 km – perfumes; Cannes (30 km).

Chemin Notre-Dame-des-Cyprès 83440 Fayence
Tel 94.76.00.84
Location at foot of village, 30 km NW of Cannes; in large grounds with ample car parking
Meals breakfast, lunch, dinner
Prices DB&B (for one) 315F-357F
Rooms 9 double, all with bath and shower (4 twin); 2 single, both with bath and shower; all rooms have central heating, TV, phone
Facilities dining-room, sitting-room with bar; poolside restaurant, open-air bar; swimming-pool
Credit cards AE, DC, MC, V
Children welcome over 12
Disabled no special facilities
Pets cats and dogs accepted; 35F charge
Closed 2 to 20 Nov, 1 Jan to 15 Mar
Proprietors Wolf and Shirley Rilla

Var

Lou Calen

Almost all the hill villages behind the Côte d'Azur now boast a hotel or two in 'Provençal' style, even if they are often modern and purpose-built. Lou Calen is one of the more authentic examples – a fine townhouse on the village square, furnished in a home-like blend of antique and rustic styles, with plenty of flowers, plants, paintings and bric-a-brac. A bonus is the swimming-pool in a luxuriant shady garden. Bedrooms vary in size and style, but all feel welcoming. The cooking is simple.

Nearby Cascade de Bresque (5 km); Thoronet (20 km) – abbey; Tourtour (25 km) – Upper Var village; Gorges du Verdon.

1 Cours Gambetta 83850 Cotignac **Tel** 94.04.60.40 **Location** in middle of village, 20 km N of Brignoles; in garden, with public car parking nearby **Meals** breakfast, lunch, dinner **Prices** 200F-430F; meals 95F-220F **Rooms** 6 double, 5 with bath, one with shower; 10 family rooms, all with bath;	all rooms have central heating, phone; TV in 10 rooms **Facilities** sitting-room, meeting-room; pool **Credit cards** AE, DC, MC, V **Children** accepted **Disabled** no special facilities **Pets** accepted **Closed** Nov to end Mar; Wed except in Jul and Aug **Proprietor** Claudine Caren-Mendes

Auberge du Vieux Fox

The tiny village of Fox-Amphoux was once a staging post for the *Chevaliers Templiers*, and parts of this *auberge*, which was built as the priory to the adjoining church, date back to the 11th century. Many of the older features, such as beams and the old walls, have been preserved, and there are beautiful views over Aix and the Alps of Haute-Provence. The bedrooms – originally designed for the clergymen – are small and modest.

Jean-Charles Martha's English is good and his cooking is equally impressive. Prices are reasonable, and the *auberge* is ideally located for exploring the Gorges du Verdon.

Nearby Barjols (15 km); St-Maximin-la-Ste-Baume (40 km).

Place de l'Eglise 83670 Barjols **Tel** 94.80.71.69 **Location** in hill-top hamlet 7 km NW of Cotignac; with garden and car parking **Meals** breakfast, lunch, dinner **Prices** rooms 180F-280F, single room 90F **Rooms** 9 double, all with bath (one twin); one single	with shower; all rooms have central heating, TV, phone **Facilities** sitting-room, billiard room, TV room, music room, dining-room **Credit cards** AE, V **Children** welcome **Disabled** no special facilities **Pets** welcome **Closed** Christmas to 15 Feb **Proprietor** Jean-Charles Martha

Var

Village hotel, Grimaud

Coteau Fleuri

After several years of running a business in the Netherlands, and with no experience of the hotel industry, M. Goedkoop took over and renovated the Coteau Fleuri. He has done well.

The attractive stone house, built into the hillside at the edge of the perched village of Grimaud, is about a hundred years old and retains a simple Provençal style. There is a rambling garden, with olive trees and a small terrace. The spotless bedrooms have pretty furnishings and prints, and good bathrooms; most are rather small, though this matters little because many have a splendid view of vineyards and the Maures massif (others look out over the garden and the ruins of Grimaud castle and chapel). The public rooms are attractive and relaxing: there is a small bar, a dining-room in two parts (both of which benefit from the view), and a spacious sitting-room with tiled floor and grand piano. Throughout the hotel are masses of flowers. The cooking is fairly ambitious – dishes such as veal with langoustines as well as more traditional Provençal fare – and is well regarded. This is a peaceful place, only 10 km from St Tropez, yet as far removed from the bustle of the coast as can be.

Nearby St-Tropez (10 km) – smart resort and beaches; Pampelonne (15 km) – beach 5 km long.

Place des Pénitents, Grimaud 83310 Cogolin
Tel 94.43.20.17
Location in middle of village behind chapel; with car parking in front
Meals breakfast, lunch, dinner
Prices rooms 335F–370F; menus 115F–175F, children's half-price
Rooms 13 double, 8 with bath, 5 with shower (4 twin); one family room with bath; all rooms have phone

Facilities dining-room, sitting-room, bar
Credit cards AE, DC, MC, V
Children welcome; special meals available
Disabled no special facilities
Pets accepted if well behaved
Closed Nov and Feb; restaurant only mid-Oct to mid-May, and Wed except in summer
Proprietors Jacline and Jacques Minard

Var

Hôtel Belle-Vue

This provençal-style hotel lives up to its name, looking out from its slightly elevated setting to St-Clair beach and across the bay towards the yachts at Le Lavandou. The Belle-Vue (a *Relais du Silence*) offers unpretentious but comfortable accommodation. Simply decorated and furnished, with smart modern bathrooms, a few of the bedrooms have private balconies where you can take a drink in the evening sun – but there is also a pleasant gravelled garden dotted with shaded tables for the less privileged. The dining-room is bright and spacious, with large picture windows and plenty of plants; fish is of course a speciality, but the food is not a strong point.

Nearby Le Lavandou – harbour, boat trips to Iles d'Hyères.

Blvd du Four des Maures, St-Clair 83980 Le Lavandou **Tel** 94.71.01.06 **Location** a short distance from beach in small resort, 3 km from Le Lavandou, 35 km W of St Tropez **Meals** breakfast, lunch, dinner **Prices** rooms 270F-500F; meal 120F	**Rooms** 19 double, 12 with bath, 7 with shower (6 twin); all rooms have central heating, phone, TV **Facilities** dining-room, bar **Credit cards** MC, V **Children** accepted **Disabled** no special facilities **Pets** not accepted **Closed** Nov to Mar **Proprietors** Clare family

Le Logis du Guetteur

The Logis du Guetteur was originally the Château of Villeneuve – an 11thC fort, built to ward off invasions from the Saracens. It still looks more or less as it must have done nine centuries ago, with rough stone walls, plain rooms, and a tower from where the *guetteur* (watchman) surveyed the plain, all with appropriate period furnishings. The bedrooms, overlooking the rooftops of Les Arcs, are quiet, with lovely views. But the main emphasis here is on food. The medieval cellar restaurant offers a choice of reasonably priced menus or, if you prefer, gastronomic specialities – among them *foie gras frais*, truffle soufflé and quail *flambé* in Armagnac.

Nearby Other Var village – Lorgues (10 km); St-Tropez (45 km).

Place du Château 83460 Les Arcs **Tel** 94.73.30.82 **Location** 12 km S of Draguignan, not far from RN7; with car parking **Meals** breakfast, lunch, dinner **Prices** rooms 200F; meals 70F-200F **Rooms** 10 double, all with	shower (3 twin); one single with shower; all rooms have central heating **Facilities** dining-room, sitting-room **Credit cards** AE, DC, MC, V **Children** accepted **Disabled** no special facilities **Pets** accepted **Closed** mid-Nov to mid-Dec **Proprietor** Max Callegari

Var

Mas des Brugassières

This modern (1973) Provençal-style *mas* (the word means farm-house, although of course it has never been one) blends well into the surrounding countryside, achieving a happy mix of studied rusticity, modern comfort, and convenience. Bedrooms have tiled floors and traditional furniture; some open out directly on to the garden and swimming-pool. There is a friendly, rather cluttered sitting-room, but from Easter to October most sitting will be done outside. Charles and Huguette André's hotel has a sporty atmosphere – they organize tennis holidays (with instruction) during the winter.

Nearby Ste-Maxime – beach resort; Port-Grimaud (15 km).

Plan-de-la-Tour 83120 Ste-Maxime
Tel 94.43.72.42
Location in countryside 8 km NW of Ste-Maxime; with gardens and ample car parking
Meals breakfast
Prices rooms 390F (with breakfast for 2)
Rooms 10 double, all with bath and shower (5 twin); all rooms have phone (not direct dial), central heating
Facilities sitting-room; swimming-pool, tennis
Credit cards not accepted
Children older ones accepted
Disabled ground-floor bedrooms
Pets dogs not accepted
Closed Jan and Feb
Proprietors M. and Mme Charles André

Var

Ponte Romano

There is indeed a Roman bridge in the garden of this pleasing little Provençal-style hotel; there is also a stream and a swimming-pool with the odd stone column placed beside it – and it is the garden which is the chief attraction. Some of the bedrooms open out directly on to it, and some have individual terraces; they are prettily furnished in an antique style. Traditional furniture also embellishes the dining-room; the food is good but not particularly cheap; and piped music extends out to the terrace, where dinner is served during the summer.

Nearby Ste-Maxime; Port-Grimaud (15 km); St-Tropez (20 km).

Le Préconcil, Plan-de-la-Tour 83120 Ste-Maxime
Tel 94.43.70.56
Location in countryside 8 km NW of Ste-Maxime; with gardens and ample car parking
Meals breakfast, lunch, dinner
Prices rooms 460F-500F
Rooms 10 double, 8 with bath, 2 with shower; all rooms have central heating, phone
Facilities sitting-room/bar, dining-room, small conference room; swimming-pool
Credit cards AE, DC, MC, V
Children accepted, except babies
Disabled access difficult
Pets dogs accepted (at a charge)
Closed Nov to mid-Mar
Proprietor M. Boatto

Le Yaca

This smart little hotel has been cleverly converted from three 200-year-old buildings. There is a confusing mix of styles, but rustic-chic predominates. Bedrooms are furnished with antiques, simply decorated in a typical southern style, but with all the comforts including air-conditioning; some have private terraces and look over the sea – others over the garden, with its figs and palms, and splendid pool, around which tables are set for lunch and dinner when the weather permits. Josiane Aknine takes care to get to know her guests and to make sure they have everything they need.

Nearby Beaches – la Bouillabaisse (1 km), Tahiti (4 km).

1 Blvd d'Aumale 83990 St-Tropez
Tel 94.97.11.79
Location in middle of town; in pedestrian area, with car parking nearby
Meals breakfast, dinner
Prices rooms 650F-1250F; menus 200F-250F with wine
Rooms 23 double, all with bath (all convert to twin); all rooms have central heating, air conditioning, TV, phone, radio, minibar
Facilities dining-room, bar
Credit cards AE, DC, MC, V
Children accepted if well behaved
Disabled no special facilities
Pets accepted if well controlled
Closed 30 Oct to 20 Dec, 5 Jan to 25 Mar
Manager Josiane Aknine

Var

Village mansion, Seillans

Hôtel des Deux Rocs

This captivating hotel in a famously captivating hill village seems to have largely recovered from its exposure on British TV a few years back.

The hotel's setting (it is an 18thC mansion, just outside the medieval walls) remains its chief drawback as well as one of its main attractions: parking close to the hotel is impossible. But for most visitors that counts for little compared to the pleasure of breakfast or an evening drink beside the fountain on the shady little cobbled square in front, looking across the green valley.

Inside there are two inviting little *salons*, one serving as a bar, and a long wood-and-stone dining-room. The food is traditional and excellent – though what is offered to guests on *pension* terms may be unexciting. Bedrooms vary in size and standard. Those at the back of the house are rather cramped, while some of those at the front are marvellously spacious and light, with vigorous colour schemes designed by Mme Hirsch. She is ever-present, overseeing the scrupulous housekeeping – first-class linen and towels – taking the orders at dinner with chiffon scarf trailing, advising on excursions.

Nearby Cascade de Bresque (15 km); Tourtour (10 km); Thoronet Abbey (20 km); Gorges du Verdon (30 km).

Place Font d'Amont 83440 Seillans
Tel 94.76.87.32
Location at top of small village, 30 km W of Grasse; with terrace
Meals breakfast, lunch, dinner
Prices rooms 180F-380F; menus 118F-175F
Rooms 15 double (5 twin), all with bath or shower; all rooms have central heating, phone, minibar
Facilities dining-room, bar, sitting-room
Credit cards not accepted
Children accepted **Disabled** no special facilities **Pets** dogs accepted but not in dining-room
Closed Nov to mid-Mar
Proprietor Mme Hirsch

Var

Mas de Chastelas

Outside our normal size range, and outside many people's price range, but an irresistible combination of unpretentious luxury, simple good taste, informality and seclusion – despite proximity to frantic St-Trop.

The *mas* is an old three-storey farmhouse in extensive grounds, surrounded by vineyards. It is decorated and furnished in a relaxed modern private-house style – pastels, wicker, tiled floors, low sofas, pine. Residents can take lunch under white parasols in the lush surroundings of the heated swimming-pool, or join incomers on a pretty covered terrace surrounded by luxuriant vegetation and flower-filled beds.

The food here has traditionally been another attraction – essentially simple and with little choice, but of a high standard. In 1988 a new and even more highly regarded chef arrived – Michel Gaudin, all the way from Brittany – and to judge by his menus those lucky enough to eat here will be facing slightly more complex choices in future.

Nearby Beaches – la Bouillabaisse (1 km), Tahiti (4 km); Port Grimaud (5 km); Grimaud (10 km) – ruined château.

Rte de Gassin 83990
St-Tropez
Tel 94.56.09.11
Location in countryside
3 km SW of St-Tropez; with
large garden and ample
private car parking
Meals breakfast, light lunch,
dinner
Prices rooms 470F-1,050F,
suites 1,500F; menu 300F,
lunch 150F
Rooms 30 double, 28 with
bath, 2 with shower (21
twin); one family room; all

rooms have phone; 10
rooms have TV, minibar
Facilities dining-room,
sitting-room, bar;
swimming-pool, jacuzzi,
tennis
Credit cards AE, DC, MC, V
Children accepted but
numbers are limited
Disabled no special facilities
Pets accepted at extra
charge
Closed Oct to mid-Apr
Proprietor Dominique
Sulitzer

Var

Hôtel Marie Louise

Ste-Maxime is a lively resort appealing more to families and young impecunious people than to the smart set who head for St-Tropez across the bay. The family-run Marie Louise, a little way outside the resort at Guerrevieille, has much in common with it. It is up the wooded hillside from the sea (about 200 m from the beach), looking across to St-Tropez from a lush, pretty garden. Bedrooms both in the main, white-painted villa-style house and in the annexe across the garden are small, but neatly furnished in various simple styles. Mme Guerin's satisfying family meals are served by the *patron* in a jolly room roofed with bamboo and looking on to the garden.

Nearby Port Grimaud (10 km); St-Tropez (15 km).

Hameau de Guerrevieille 83120 Ste-Maxime **Tel** 94.96.06.05 **Location** 3 km SW of Ste-Maxime on side road off RN98; with garden and private car parking **Meals** breakfast, dinner **Prices** rooms 265F-270F; DB&B 260F **Rooms** 12 double (6 twin),	one single, all with bath and shower; central heating, phone **Facilities** dining-room, sitting-room, bar **Credit cards** DC, V **Children** welcome **Disabled** 2 ground-floor bedrooms **Pets** accepted **Closed** Oct **Proprietor** Jacques Guerin

La Grillade au Feu de Bois

An 18thC farmhouse set in large and wooded grounds, with swimming-pool and shady terrace for summer drinks and meals, La Grillade was purely a restaurant for many years before the Babb family added the bedrooms – which are large and exceedingly comfortable, some with private terraces. There are also rooms in small bungalows dotted around the grounds. The dining-room is vaulted and white-washed – a welcoming place in which good plain food (with the emphasis on charcoal grills, as the name implies) is served. All is peace, once the evening influx of diners is over.

Nearby Thoronet abbey (15 km); Massif des Maures (20 km).

Flassans-sur-Issole 83340 Le Luc **Tel** 94.69.71.20 **Location** surrounded by forest, 4 km W from Le Luc on the N7; with grounds and ample car parking **Meals** breakfast, lunch, dinner **Prices** rooms 280F-350F, extra bed 70F; meal 150F **Rooms** 9 double, 6 with	bath, 3 with shower; all rooms have central heating, phone, TV **Facilities** dining-room; swimming-pool **Credit cards** AE, DC, MC, V **Children** accepted if well behaved **Disabled** lift/ elevator **Pets** accepted if well behaved **Closed** never **Proprietor** Jacques Babb

Var

La Ponche

Tucked away in a tiny square in the old heart of St Tropez, just by the small fishing port and tiny beach of La Ponche, this cluster of 17thC houses is an oasis of quiet – yet is only a stone's throw from the action of the main port.

Simone Duckstein started her fishermen's bar in 1937, and has steadily changed it into the stylish little hotel that it is today; it is still a family enterprise (she has been joined by her daughter and son-in-law) and her enthusiasm has not lessened. The open-air restaurant on the square is comfortable and civilized, not merely a terrace café; there is a small but sophisticated dining-room, too. The food is memorable and there is an inexpensive lunch menu, and as everywhere in this people-watching resort, late hours are kept as diners linger over their final drink. (The bar area doubles as a sitting-room.) Bedrooms vary in style and size: some have air conditioning and a fridge, a few have a balcony, some are modern, others are furnished with antiques; the largest are suitable for families. In this artists' colony, it is entirely appropriate that paintings grace every wall; all is in good taste. This is a thoroughly atmospheric little hotel where you do not have to pay the over-inflated prices charged by the haunts of the stars.

Nearby Beaches – La Bouillabaisse (1 km), Tahiti (4 km); Port-Grimaud (5 km).

Place du Révelin 83990
St-Tropez
Tel 94.97.02.53
Location in middle of town, near Port des Pecheurs
Meals breakfast, lunch, dinner
Prices rooms 370F-800F, child sharing room 180F; meals 150F-250F
Rooms 19 double, all with bath (12 twin); 2 single, both with shower; 2 family rooms, both with bath; all rooms have central heating, phone
Facilities TV room, bar, 2 dining-rooms
Credit cards AE, V
Children accepted if well behaved
Disabled access difficult as hotel in pedestrian area
Pets accepted
Closed 15 Oct to 1 Apr
Proprietor Simone Duckstein

Grillade au Feu de Bois (see opposite)

Var

La Bastide de Tourtour

This country house was built by M. Laurent in the late 1960s in traditional style, with lovely honey-coloured stone but without much inspiration. What the hotel lacks in architectural elegance it makes up for in comfort and attentive service (it is in the Relais & Château group), and the food is excellent, if not in the first rank. But for many visitors the key attraction is the secluded setting, high up amid pine forests with a sun-trap swimming-pool and wonderfully long views.

Nearby Salernes (10 km); Cascade de Bresque (15 km).

Rte de Draguignan,
Tourtour 83690 Salernes
Tel 94.70.57.30
Location on outskirts of
village, 22 km NW of
Draguignan; with gardens
and ample car parking
Meals breakfast, lunch,
dinner
Prices rooms 300F-920F;
menus 200F-310F
Rooms 23 double, all with
bath (12 twin); 2 single, both
with bath; central heating,
TV, phone, minibar
Facilities sitting-room,
dining-room, bar, gym,
jacuzzi; tennis, swimming-
pool, table tennis, pétanque
Credit cards AE, DC, V
Children accepted; prices
on request **Disabled** no
special facilities **Pets**
accepted
Closed Nov to end Apr
Proprietor M. Laurent

Auberge St-Pierre

Just outside the hill-top village of Tourtour in its own rolling acres, the Auberge St-Pierre is a peaceful, unpretentious retreat – a 16thC manor-house run as a welcoming hotel by the helpful Marcellins. The public rooms preserve something of a medieval feel, with stone floors and a fountain in the dining-room, and great bay windows providing views over the terrace, where drinks are served. The bedrooms are more ordinary but none-theless comfortable. Most of the food – expertly cooked in classic and local styles by M. Marcellin – comes from the home farm.

Nearby Salernes (10 km); Cascade de Bresque (15 km).

St-Pierre-de-Tourtour
83690 Salernes
Tel 94.70.57.17
Location 3 km E of
Tourtour; in large grounds
with ample car parking
Meals breakfast, lunch,
dinner
Prices rooms 300F-350F;
menus 170F-200F
Rooms 15 double, 5 with
bath, 10 with shower (5
twin); all rooms have central
heating, phone
Facilities 2 dining-rooms,
sitting-room, TV room, bar;
swimming-pool, sauna,
fishing, archery
Credit cards not accepted
Children accepted **Disabled**
no special facilities **Pets**
accepted; food not provided
Closed mid-Oct to Apr
Proprietors Marcellin
family

Var

Château de Trigance

In the remote limestone hills that surround the dramatic Gorges du Verdon, there are few villages and even fewer hotels; if you are touring this region, it is a relief to know that you have a room booked at the Château de Trigance, for it is hard to imagine where else to stay. On arrival, you might be taken aback. Is this fortress perched high on a rocky hilltop really your hotel? And if it is, how are you going to penetrate its defences? Anyway, you will: up a steep flight of rocky stairs. (Your luggage will be carried up for you.)

Once inside, you are in the Middle Ages. Stone by stone, M. Thomas has painstakingly rebuilt his 11thC castle (it was largely destroyed in the Revolution, and for many years served as a quarry for the local villagers); he will be delighted to show you before and after photographs to prove it. The impressive stone-vaulted, candle-lit dining-room, and the sitting-room below, are windowless and highly atmospheric, furnished in appropriate medieval style. Most of the bedrooms (cut into the hill) are similar, with canopied beds, tiled floors, tapestries and banners – but they have fine views from their small windows. The cooking is surprisingly good, considering the remoteness of the place. A romantic and unusual hotel, though don't expect luxury.

Nearby Verdon gorge – Europe's 'Grand Canyon'.

83840 Trigance
Tel 94.76.91.18
Location overlooking tiny village, 10 km NW of Comps-sur-Artuby; with terrace, and private car parking
Meals breakfast, lunch, dinner
Prices rooms 240F-490F, suites 540F; DB&B (for one) 460F-640F; menus 145F-295F
Rooms 8 double, 7 with bath, one with shower (3 twin); all rooms have central heating, phone
Facilities dining-room, sitting-room
Credit cards AE, DC, V
Children welcome
Disabled access very difficult
Pets accepted
Closed 1 Nov to 20 Mar
Proprietor Jean Claude Thomas

Var/Hérault

Le Manoir

This large whitewashed, green-shuttered 19thC manor house stands on a lush, secluded island a few km off the south coast. The whole island used to belong to Pierre Buffet's family; today it is a state-owned nature reserve (the island appeals more to botanists than sun worshippers), and the charming M. and Mme Buffet run their home as a hotel – along house-party lines, with many regularly returning guests. White-walled bedrooms are furnished with 19thC pieces – simple but stylish and comfortable. Cooking is plain but good enough to win a GM *toque*, and meals are served in the peaceful garden full of palm and eucalyptus trees.

Nearby Marked trails to various points, scuba diving.

Ile de Port-Cros 83400 Hyères
Tel 94.05.90.52
Location in lush gardens close to port (boats from Le Lavandou or Port d'Hyéres)
Meals breakfast, lunch, dinner
Prices DB&B 460F-610F, FB 550F-700F
Rooms 22 double (14 twin), 10 with bath, 12 with shower; 6 family rooms with bath; all rooms have central heating, phone
Facilities 2 dining-rooms, 2 sitting-rooms, bar
Credit cards AE, DC, MC, V
Children children accepted if well behaved
Disabled no special facilities
Pets not accepted
Closed mid-Oct to Apr
Proprietor Pierre Buffet

Château de Ponderach

In 1963 Mme Counotte successfully transformed this solid country house – in the family since its construction over 200 years ago – into an intimate and relaxing hotel. It is completely secluded in extensive wooded grounds, and the spacious bedrooms have private terraces which look out over the forest. The family-home atmosphere is retained – the dining-room is full of family pieces and flowers, and Madame is a welcoming and gracious hostess who ensures that guests are kept happy. Good classic cusine, including a *menu régional Occitan*.

Nearby St-Pons – cathedral; Grotte de la Devèze (5 km).

Rte de Narbonne 34220 St-Pons-de-Thomières
Tel 67.97.02.57
Location in countryside 1 km S of St-Pons and 50 km NW of Narbonne; with large grounds, ample car parking and garage
Meals breakfast, lunch, dinner
Prices rooms 340F-395F; menus 150F-320F, children's 66F
Rooms 9 double (4 twin), all with bath and shower; all rooms have phone
Facilities sitting-room, dining-room, bar
Credit cards AE, DC, V
Children welcome
Disabled no special facilities
Pets accepted
Closed Oct to Apr
Proprietor Mme Pierre Counotte

Pyrénées-Orientales

La Châtaigneraie

Isolated among lush trees up the road to the peak of Fontrède, La Châtaigneraie – a substantial Catalan-style building with balconies and arcaded terraces – enjoys stunning views of the Pyrenees and the Mediterranean coast. Mme Decressac insists that her hotel is simple and she runs it more as a guest-house. But it is delightfully comfortable and serene: rooms are notably spacious, and decorated with taste in individual styles. The garden and pool area are beautifully kept. On chilly days, a fire is lit in the sitting-room. Barbecues and traditional puddings are dinner specialities.

Nearby Céret – museum of modern art; Fontrède – views.

Rte de Fontrède 66400 Céret **Tel** 68.87.03.19 **Location** in countryside, 2 km S of town; with garden and shaded car parking **Meals** breakfast, dinner **Prices** rooms 240F–420F; menus 110F–160F **Rooms** 8 double, 7 with shower (4 twin); all rooms have central heating, phone	**Facilities** dining-room, sitting-room; swimming-pool **Credit cards** not accepted **Children** accepted if well behaved **Disabled** access difficult; many steps **Pets** not accepted **Closed** 15 Oct to 30 Apr **Proprietor** Colette Decressac

La Terrasse au Soleil

This Catalan-style hotel has a lovely setting, with the splendid Canigou as backdrop on a fine day (320 days of sun per year are claimed, so you should be lucky). As you might expect, it has a terrace, where you can eat out or just observe the view (as Picasso is said to have done). Inside, a relaxed and casual atmosphere prevails. The food is good, but not wildly exciting; the bedrooms are not luxurious, but pleasant. A good base for the many excursions possible in the area.

Nearby Perpignan; beaches (30 km); Castelnou (30 km).

Rte de Fontrède 66400 Céret **Tel** 68.87.01.94 **Location** in Pyrenean foothills above town, 26 km SW of Perpignan; with gardens and car parking **Meals** breakfast, lunch, dinner **Prices** rooms 370F–430F, extra bed 90F; DB&B (for one) 550F–610F **Rooms** 17 double, 16 with bath, one with shower; one family room with bath; all	rooms have TV, phone, minibar **Facilities** dining-room, sitting-room, bar, ping-pong, swimming-pool **Credit cards** MC, V **Children** accepted **Disabled** no special facilities **Pets** accepted **Closed** end Oct to end Mar **Proprietor** Mme Leveille-Nizerolle

Pyrénées-Orientales

Le Cottage

Set in a peaceful position between the mountains and the sea on the fringes of the popular seaside resort of Argelès, this is a totally unpretentious *logis,* ideal for a cheerful family holiday. The plain but clean and peaceful bedrooms look out over the garden (which is not over-manicured). The dining-room too is plain, but Mme Paret cooks Mediterranean (Spanish and French) dishes excellently. Daughter Florence now runs the place; she speaks good English, and creates a happily relaxed atmosphere.

Nearby Collioure (5 km) – fortified city; Elne (10 km).

21 rue Arthur-Rimbaud
66700 Argelès-sur-Mer
Tel 68.81.07.33
Location in quiet part of resort, between village and sea; with garden and private car parking
Meals breakfast, lunch, dinner
Prices rooms 140F-260F, menus 55F-150F
Rooms 24 double (12 twin), 11 with bath, 5 with shower; 6 family rooms, 5 with bath,

1 with shower; all rooms have central heating, phone; TV on request
Facilities dining-room, bar/sitting-room; swimming-pool, pétanque, play area
Credit cards V
Children welcome; under 5s free
Disabled no special facilities
Pets accepted at extra charge
Closed 15 Nov to 15 Mar
Proprietor Florence Paret

Mouli del Riu

St-Pierre is a satellite of Font-Romeu, the major ski resort in this part of the Pyrenees, and has its own skiing on the massive Cambre d'Aze. This is a fast-developing area, and skiers' chalets have altered beyond recognition the area around the Mouli – itself a modern and undistinguished house, despite the traditional-sounding name. It is a simple and rather quirky place, run by a charming family who grow most of what appears (excellently prepared) on the table.

Nearby Mountain and forest walks.

St-Pierre-dels-Forcats 66210 Mont-Louis
Tel 68.04.20.36
Location in valley 3.5 km S of Mont-Louis by D32, near Spanish border; with gardens and ample car parking
Meals breakfast, lunch, dinner
Prices rooms 135F-195F; extra child's bed 40F; menus 55F-90F
Rooms 10 double, (4 twin), 5

family rooms, all with bath; all rooms have central heating
Facilities dining-room, sitting-room, TV room
Credit cards not accepted
Children accepted
Disabled access difficult
Pets accepted
Closed Oct to mid-Dec; Wed
Proprietor Josie Kirstetter-Saillarde

Pyrénées-Orientales

Village inn, Llo

Auberge Atalaya

Llo is an attractive pastoral village with château ruins and an old watchtower. It lies high up in the Pyrenees, at an altitude of 1,450m, close to the border, and is typical of the Cerdagne – a high sun-drenched plateau of pastures and pine forests, now popular for summer and winter sports. The Atalaya, which occupies a prime spot in the village, is a delightful small inn, expertly converted by the Toussaints from an old farmhouse almost 20 years ago. The bedrooms are quiet, comfortable and intimate, with romantic fabrics and soft lighting. Local specialities are served either in the rustic dining-room – gleaming antiques against stone walls – or, on warm days, on a charming flowery terrace.

Nearby Odeillo (10 km) – solar furnace; Font-Romeu (15 km)

Llo 66800 Saillagouse
Tel 68.04.70.04
Location in middle of village, 2 km E of Saillagouse and 10 km E of Bourg-Madame; ample car parking
Meals breakfast, lunch, dinner
Prices rooms 350F-450F; menus 125F-250F
Rooms 10 double, 7 with bath, 3 with shower (3 twin); all rooms have central heating, phone, minibar
Facilities sitting-room, bar, dining-room
Credit cards MC, V
Children welcome if well behaved
Disabled no special facilities
Pets accepted in bedrooms only
Closed 5 Nov to 20 Dec
Proprietors M. and Mme H. Toussaint

Corse

La Giraglia

The village of Barcaggio lies at the northern extremity of the Cap Corse peninsula, well off the tourist track. There is not much to see except the pretty cluster of fishermen's houses and the little port, but the beach is excellent and seldom crowded; and for anyone seeking a peaceful and simple base, the Giraglia is an excellent choice. From the terrace and garden you can practically dangle your feet in the water, and there are pretty views towards the centre of the village. The rooms are quiet and rustic, though not without modern conveniences. The hotel no longer has a restaurant, but several places in Barcaggio serve a variety of simply cooked fish and seafood.

Nearby Rogliano – stronghold (castles, churches, hamlets); Centuri-Port (15 km) – marina.

Barcaggio 20275 Essa
Tel 95.35.60.54
Location just outside village, 50 km N of Bastia; with garden and car parking
Meals breakfast
Prices rooms 250F–300F
Rooms 20 double, 8 with bath, 12 with shower (6 twin); 2 single, one with shower; one family room; central heating, phone
Facilities 3 sitting-rooms, bar, breakfast room
Credit cards not accepted
Children accepted
Disabled no special facilities
Pets accepted
Closed late Sep to mid-Apr
Proprietor M. Duhouse

Hôtel a Pasturella

Just inland from the resort of L'Ile Rousse, in a charming old hill village, A Pasturella sits on the village square at the very heart of local life. It is a traditional place, though much enlarged since the days when M Martini's parents ran a bar here in 1937; first a restaurant, then bedrooms were added (scattered in converted annexes, some of them are rather small). Now he sees to the running of the hotel while his wife does the cooking; children and grandfather help too. All is well-cared for, cheerful and friendly. Food is wholesome and generous. Some of the rooms have wonderful views – worth booking well ahead.

Nearby Ile Rousse (3 km); Calvi (25 km); Asco Valley (50 km).

Monticello 20220 l'Ile-Rousse
Tel 95.60.05.65
Location on main square of village 3 km S of L'Ile Rousse and the sea; with car parking
Meals breakfast, lunch, dinner
Prices rooms 200F; meals 100F
Rooms 15 double, all with shower (4 twin)
Facilities bar, dining-room, sitting-room
Credit cards accepted soon
Children accepted
Disabled no special facilities, access difficult
Pets accepted
Closed Nov; restaurant only Sun dinner and Mon, Dec to Mar
Proprietors M. and Mme Georges Martini

Corse

Le Maquis

In general, Corsican hotels are modest enterprises, with limited facilities; the Maquis, a hotel of comfort, style and sophistication, is one of the few clear exceptions. It is typically Mediterranean: a cluster of red-roofed villas stretching down to the sea, white-washed public areas with beams and arches, and rustic bedrooms with rugs on tiled floors. With a beautiful pool (heated and covered out of season), garden with tennis court and private beach facilities, it is one of the best-equipped hotels on the island.

The food does not impress every visitor, but you are guaranteed the freshest of fish and seafood, and a magnificent spread of hors-d'oeuvres. Ideally, meals are taken on the elegant restaurant terrace, with beautiful views of the Bay of Ajaccio. In cooler weather you eat in an attractive dining-room with timbered ceiling, arches and modern art hung on whitewashed walls. Bedrooms are similar in style but slightly simpler – unless you opt for one of the spacious sea-view suites. Some of the most coveted rooms are those on the ground floor with terraces right on the sandy beach.

Nearby Beaches; Ajaccio – Place Maréchal Foch, Bonaparte House, boats to Iles Sanguinaires; Filitosa (45 km) – prehistoric settlement, menhirs.

20166 Porticcio
Tel 95.25.05.55
Location above private beach, 20 km S of Ajaccio; in gardens, with ample car parking
Meals breakfast, lunch, dinner
Prices rooms 280F-500F; suites 750F-1,550F; DB&B (obligatory in season) 740F-1,450; menus 180F-220F, children's 80F-120F
Rooms 19 double, 16 with bath, 3 with shower (17 twin); 7 family rooms, all with bath; all rooms have TV, phone, air-conditioning, video, minibar
Facilities dining-room, bar, 2 sitting-rooms, conference room; swimming-pool, tennis, private beach, gym
Credit cards AE, DC, MC, V
Children accepted
Disabled no special facilities
Pets accepted but not in restaurant
Closed never
Proprietor Catherine Salini

Index of hotel names

The hotels are indexed by the *key* word in their names, though in every case the full name is given.

Index of hotel names

Index of hotel names

Index of hotel names / place names

An index of cities, towns and villages at which, or near which, hotels in the guide are located.

Index of place names

Index of place names

Index of place names

Acknowledgements

The editor is particularly grateful to:

Susie Boulton, Jo King, Eileen Broadbent and Fiona
Duncan for assistance with hotel inspection and writing
reports.

Design
Art director Mel Petersen
Design assistance Chris Foley, Beverley Stewart

Editorial
Research Pip Leahy, Deborah Flower
Proof reading Linda Hart
Editorial assistance Laura Harper